Repatriation, Insecurity, and Peace

Masako Yonekawa · Akiko Sugiki
Editors

Repatriation, Insecurity, and Peace

A Case Study of Rwandan Refugees

Springer

Editors
Masako Yonekawa
Department of Economics and Informatics
Tsukuba Gakuin University
Tsukuba, Ibaraki, Japan

Akiko Sugiki
Faculty of Law
Keio University
Tokyo, Japan

ISBN 978-981-15-2849-1 ISBN 978-981-15-2850-7 (eBook)
https://doi.org/10.1007/978-981-15-2850-7

This Springer imprint is published by the registered company Springer Nature Singapore Pte Ltd.
The registered company address is: 152 Beach Road, #21-01/04 Gateway East, Singapore 189721, Singapore

Contents

Introduction

Masako Yonekawa

Among the three durable solutions to the refugee problem—local integration in neighbouring countries, resettlement in the third countries of permanent asylum, and voluntary repatriation to the home country—, voluntary repatriation has been considered the most appropriate solution for refugees. During the Cold War, the settlement in a country of asylum and resettlement in a third country was preferred mainly because repatriation implied sending refugees back to communist countries.[1] However, the nature of the international response vis-à-vis durable solutions gradually changed especially since the 1980s when the nature and character of the flow of refugees have changed from the East–West to South–North refugee movement.[2] This growing number of refugees and changes implied increased financial, political, and environmental burden on donor and host countries.[3] Gradually, both donor and host countries became intolerant of supporting refugees.[4]

In 1980, the Executive Committee of the UNHCR examined voluntary repatriation for the first time, acknowledging it as the most appropriate solution.[5] Later in 1991, High Commissioner of the UNHCR Sadako Ogata declared that one of the organisation's primary goals was "to pursue every opportunity for voluntary repatriation. […] the right to return on one's homeland merited as much recognition

[1]L. Holborn, *Refugees: A Problem of Our Time- The Work of the United Nations High Commissioner for Refugees, 1951-1972,* with the assistance of P. and R. Chartrand. Metuchen, N.J., The Scarecrow Press, Inc., for the Radcliffe Institute, Cambridge, Massachusetts, 1975, 325–327.

[2]A Betts, G. Loescher and J. Milner, *UNHCR: The Politics and Practice of Refugee Protection*, Oxon, Routledge, 2008, 35.

[3]M. Barnett and M. Finnemore, *Rules for the World: International Organizations in Global Politics,* Itacha and London, Cornell University Press, 2004, 94–95.

[4]*Ibid.*

[5]UNHCR, Executive Committee of the High Commissioner's Programme, "Voluntary Repatriation, No. 18 (XXXI) – 1980", 16 Oct. 1980, (a) available at: https://www.refworld.org/docid/3ae68c6e8.html (last visited 1 June 2020).

as the right to seek asylum abroad".[6] Subsequently, she stated that the 1990s would be the decade of repatriation for refugees.[7]

Voluntary repatriation is considered the most appropriate solution only if the home country is peaceful and secure. However, voluntary repatriation often takes place during conflict situations, which can lead to security risks and potentially reignite conflicts and refugee movements. Such controversiality of repatriation particularly applies to post-genocide Rwandan refugees, among many others. Therefore, to avoid another potential conflict and forced movement of civilians, further study is required on the two major concerns regarding refugee repatriation, peace and security, using the case study of Rwandan refugees.

During and after the 1994 genocide in Rwanda, about two million people, in particular majority-group Hutu, fled for neighbouring countries. Since then, the United Nations High Commissioner for Refugees (UNHCR) has been facilitating and promoting repatriation for the past 25 years. This is because the UNHCR maintains that Rwanda has changed significantly since the 1994 genocide and today enjoys an essential level of peace and security. Yet, the vast majority of refugees have refused to return there. Even among those refugees who returned to Rwanda under the UNHCR-led voluntary repatriation, a certain percentage were then forced to flee again to host countries. Rwanda's current refugees include a number of high-profile political ones who have been subjected to imprisonment, kidnapping, threats, and assassination in and outside of Rwanda. Despite these incidents and the ongoing outflow of refugees, the governments of Rwanda and asylum countries, in addition to the UNHCR, are adamant that refugees should return to Rwanda—where returnees (former refugees who returned to their homeland) can end up facing death.

To make matters worse, Rwanda and asylum countries enforced the cessation clause of refugee status on 31 December 2017, recommended by the UNHCR. This suggests that Rwandan refugees can be refouled anytime by the host governments; this applies notably to the Republic of Congo that invoked cessation clause of Rwandan refugees' status. Despite the application of cessation clause of refugee status, once again, majority of refugees have not returned to Rwanda.

This attitude and movement of refugees lead to questions. Why do the refugees refuse to return? What is happening in Rwanda which prevents the refugees from returning? In what kind of environment have the refugees lived? Why have the governments of Rwanda and the host countries, as well as the UNHCR, promoted or rather "imposed" repatriation? Apart from these questions, it is also important to review how some legal principles, such as non-refoulement and the cessation clause of refugee

[6]UNHCR, "Statement of the High Commissioner to the 42nd session of the Executive Committee", 7 Oct. 1991, 4.

[7]UNHCR, "Statement by Mrs. Sadako Ogata, United Nations High Commissioner for Refugees, at the International Management Symposium", St. Gallen, Switzerland, 25 May 25, 1992, available at: https://www.unhcr.org/admin/hcspeeches/3ae68faec/statement-mrs-sadako-ogata-united-nations-high-commissioner-refugees-international.html (last visited 1 June 2020).

status, may affect the refugees. Moreover, some assumptions require re-examination, for instance, the assumption that refugees, in general wish to repatriate to their home countries and that repatriation is a part of the peace process. This review can help to develop and implement policies that consider the refugees' perspectives.

History of Rwandan Refugees (1959–2019)

In order to clarify the above-mentioned questions, we will attempt to review the history of Rwandan refugee, beginning with the "Social Revolution" in 1959, followed by the collapse of the traditional Tutsi-centred political system. Following the flight of 130,000 Tutsi as refugees by the end of 1963, land owned by these Tutsi was redistributed by the post-independence Grégoire Kayibanda regime, occupied by over 300 Hutu whose posts were previously monopolised by Tutsi.[8] In the early 1960s, in order to overthrow the government and restore monarchy, refugee leaders organised an armed attack from Burundi and Uganda, to no avail.[9] These raids resulted in unleashed reprisals against Tutsis, which led to massacre of more than 10,000 Tutsi and massive displacement in 1963–1964.[10] After having seized power through a coup d'état in 1973, President Juvénal Habyarimana founded the National Revolutionary Movement for Development (MRND) in 1974 as the single party.

Among the countries of asylum, Uganda was the most politically violent. In the 1970s and 1980s, Uganda experienced regime turnover from three coup d'états and civil wars by Milton Obote, Idi Amin, again Obote II, and Yoweri Museveni. Some Rwandan refugees, including the current Rwandan President Paul Kagame, joined in the anti-Amin war of 1978–1979, and later Museveni's National Resistance Movement (NRM) guerrilla war against Obote II from 1981 to 1986. In 1980, following the fall of Amin, refugees formed Rwandese Alliance for National Unity (RANU)[11] to discuss the question of an eventual return to Rwanda and to prepare for armed struggle.[12]

In October 1982, the Obote II authorities which were hostile to Rwandan refugees, expelled 40,000 of them, who were also not welcome by Rwanda.[13] 4000 people out of it were trapped at the border, remaining neither refugees nor returnees

[8]R. Lemarchand, *Rwanda and Burundi*, New York, Praeger Publishers, 1970, 171-173; C. Huggins, "The Presidential Land Commission; Undermining Land Reform," S. Straus and L. Waldorf (eds.), *Remaking Rwanda: State Building and Human Rights after Mass Violence Wisconsin,* University of Wisconsin Press, 2011, 255.

[9]Lemarchand, *Rwanda and Burundi*, 217.

[10]G. Prunier, *The Rwanda Crisis: History of a Genocide,* Kampala, Fountain Publisher, 1999, 56.

[11]Kagame was part of the RANU.

[12]P. Rutayisire et al, *RWANDA: la Renaissance d'une Nation*, Butare, Editions de l'université du Rwanda, 2012, 110, cited in J-P. Kimonyo, *Rwanda demain! Une Longue Marche vers la Transformation*, Paris, Karthala, 2017, 110.

[13]O. Otunnu, *Crisis of Legitimacy and Political Violence in Uganda 1979 to 2016,* Cham, Palgrave McMillan, 2016, 39.

for many years in dying circumstance.[14] This expulsion was a turning point for both the refugees and the Rwandan government. For the refugees, some of them joined the NRM in order to protect themselves, who did not believe in local integration and regarded Rwandan government as their new enemy.[15] Following the NRM's seizure of power in January 1986, the RPF was established in December 1987, which was dedicated to the return of exiles to Rwanda, "by force if necessary".[16] In August 1988, a World Congress of Rwandan Refugees was held in Washington D. C., supported by the United States Committee of Refugees and its Director, Roger Winter, which made a resolution to realise their right to return "by force if necessary".[17]

At the same time, this crisis of expulsion, along with international pressure, led the governments of Rwanda and Uganda to organise several meetings until 1990 to examine the possibility of repatriation of Rwandan refugees. The refugees' cross-border visit was to take place in October 1990, followed by a census in January 1991 to assess the refugees' intention on their return. This visit and the census eventually did not take place due to the RPF's invasion to Rwanda on 1 October 1990.

The RPF's invasion, which led to civil war until 1994, was carried out amid great political and economic upheaval.[18] Rwanda was facing three political tensions apart from that between the government and the RPF: Hutu-Tutsi and north-south dichotomy, and the MRND's conflict with opposition parties in the process of democratisation. Tutsi were discriminated against in education and access to government jobs.[19] Likewise, as Habyarimana concentrated political power to his native northern region, most Hutu from the south were discriminated against in terms of access to schools.[20] This concentration of power in the north sharpened competition for power and resources with southern Hutu, where Habyarimana's

[14]D. Newbury, "Returning Refugees: Four Historical Patterns of 'Coming Home' to Rwanda", *Society for Comparative Study of Society and History,* Vol. 47, Issue 2, 2005, 275.

[15]T. Rudasingwa, *Healing A Nation, A Testimony: Waging and Winning a Peaceful Revolution to Unite and Heal a Broken Rwanda,* South Carolina, CreateSpace Independent Publishing Platform, 2013, 38.

[16]Prunier, *The Rwanda Crisis,* 73.

[17]A. Des Forges, *Leave None to Tell the Story: Genocide in Rwanda*, March 1999, 42, available at: https://www.hrw.org/reports/1999/rwanda/ (last visited 1 June 2020); Kimonyo, *Rwanda demain!* 105.

[18]A. Guichaoua, *The Problem of the Rwandese Refugees and the Banyarwanda Populations in the Great Lakes Region,* UNHCR, May 1992, 11.

[19]C. Newbury, 'Ethnicity and Politics of History in Rwanda', *Africa Today* 45 (1996), 15; P. Uvin, *Aiding Violence: The Development Enterprise in Rwanda,* Connecticut, Kumarian Press, 1998, 35.

[20]Uvin, *Aiding Violence,* 35.

predecessor Kayibanda's supporters had been marginalised.[21] This resulted in the southern population's heightened grievance over land scarcities, structural famine, and 30% unemployment rate amongst rural adults at the end of the 1980s.[22] This land issue became the centre of conflict, continuing through the genocide and its aftermath.

Regarding economic crisis, apart from the above-mentioned famine and landless issue, there were three factors since the late 1980s: 50% drop of coffee price in 1989[23]; government's acceptance of the World Bank/International Monetary Fund-led Structural Adjustment Programme, which resulted in a 40 percent devaluation of the national currency few months prior to the invasion[24]; and increased military spending in 1992 following the RPF invasion.[25]

Worse, many civilians, in particular Hutus in the north, were displaced and killed. Upon the RPF's invasion, while the Armed Forces of Rwanda (FAR) under President Habyarimana committed various violations,[26] the scale of crimes by the RPF, such as massacre and forced displacement was much larger.[27] By February 1993, the number of internally displaced persons increased to one million, or one-seventh of the country's entire population.[28] The displacement of a mostly Hutu population, which was caused by the Tutsi-led RPF, and the tantamount suffering in IDP camps contributed to the rise in ethnicity, fuelling Hutu radicals.[29] These factors enabled Habyarimana to reclaim legitimacy and recruit people for the *Interahamwe,* youth wing of the MRND.[30]

Thus, when the Arusha (Tanzania) negotiations between the Rwandan government and the RPF began in July 1992, Habyarimana's team faced "the dual crises of war [with the RPF] and internal opposition [which] had merged into a single grave

[21]J. Gasana, "Natural Resource Scarcity and Violence in Rwanda", R. Matthew et al. eds., *Conserving the Peace: Resources, Livelihoods and Security*, Winnipeg, International Institute for Sustainable Development, 2002, 218.

[22]*Ibid*, 206, 210.

[23]I. Kamola, "The Global Coffee Economy and the Production of Genocide in Rwanda," *Third World Quarterly*, 28 (3), 2007, 578.

[24]Prunier, *The Rwanda Crisis*,160.

[25]M. Mamdani, *When Victims Become Killers,* 147–148.

[26]UN Economic and Social Council (ECOSOC), "Question of the Violation of Human Rights and Fundamental Freedoms in any part of the World, with Particular Reference to Colonial and other Dependent Countries and Territories", E/CN.4/1994/7/Add.1, 11 Aug. 1993, pp. 33–35.

[27]Human Rights Watch Arms Project, *Arming Rwanda: The Arms Trade and Human Rights Abuses in the Rwandan War*, 6 (1), Jan 1994. 4, available at: https://www.hrw.org/sites/default/files/reports/RWANDA941.PDF (last visited 1 June 2020); J. Gasana, *Rwanda: Du Parti-Etat a l'Etat-Garnison,* Paris, L'Harmattan, 2002, 185.

[28]UN ECOSOC, "Question of the Violation of Human Rights and Fundamental Freedoms," p. 23; Prunier, *The Rwanda Crisis*, 295.

[29]Gasana, "Natural Resource Scarcity", 223; R. Lemarchand, *The Dynamics of Violence in Central Africa,* Pennsylvania, University of Pennsylvania, 2009, 126.

[30]Lemarchand, *The Dynamics of Violence,* 126.

threat to their continued control".[31] Arusha Peace Agreement was signed in August 1993, which affirmed the rights of returning refugees, conditions for reclaiming their properties, and housing schemes in settlement sites.[32] Subsequently, the UN Assistance Mission to Rwanda (UNAMIR) was deployed in November 1993 to monitor the security and the ceasefire agreement.

The civil war eventually culminated in mass, targeted killings in April 1994, directly triggered by the shooting down of Habyarimana's presidential jet, and ended, at least publicly, on 19 July 1994 when the RPF established the new government. The phenomenon of this massacre is called genocide when a total of 9,37,000 persons were killed according to the Rwandan government.[33]

Most murders were blamed on the *Interahamwe* and Hutu peasants,[34] who participated in the killings because of fear. This fear includes that of punishment from other Hutus if they refused to participate in the violence, that of the advancing RPF that had come close to overthrowing the government, and that of Tutsi civilians suspected of secretly working with the RPF.[35] More importantly, killings were exacerbated to a large extent over access to, and control of, land.

While it has been widely reported and researched that the FAR/*Interahamwe* and Hutu peasants massacred Tutsi,[36] it is not well known that soon after the plane attack, all RPA forces quickly seized territory, cleared out FAR and *Interahamwe,* which was infiltrated by the RPF, and killed as many Hutus as possible.[37] The RPF also massacred Tutsis remainees—those who had not fled the country since 1959 and were considered by Kagame to be "collaborators" with the Hutu—fuelling the killing.[38] Adding to this dynamic were the RPF's indiscriminate killings of intellectuals, politicians of the Habyarimana regime, teachers, and business people, both Tutsi and Hutu, and the concerted wiping out of key members of political parties.[39]

[31]Human Rights Watch, Briefing Paper 1, *The Rwandan Genocide: How It Was Prepared*, April 2006, 4, available at: https://www.hrw.org/legacy/backgrounder/africa/rwanda0406/ (last visited 1 June 2020).

[32]Arusha Peace Agreement, "Protocol of Agreement between the Government of the Republic of Rwanda and the Rwandese Patriotic Front on the Repatriation of Rwandese Refugees and the Resettlement of Displaced Persons," 3 June 1993, Chapter 1, I.I.I.

[33]The source of this number is the Rwandan Government although this number has been contested. The New Humanitarian, "Census finds 937,000 died in genocide", 2 April 2004, available at: https://www.thenewhumanitarian.org/report/49384/rwanda-census-finds-937000-died-genocide (last visited 1 June 2020); S. Straus, *The Order of Genocide: Race, Power, and War in Rwanda,* New York, Cornell University Press, 2008, 51.

[34]Straus, *The Order of genocide*, 27, 96.

[35]J. Rever, *In Praise of Blood: The Crimes of the Rwandan Patriotic Front*, Random House Canada, 2018, 106.

[36]African Rights, *Rwanda: Death, Despair and Defiance,* African Rights, 1994, 1084–1086.

[37]Rever, *In Praise of Blood*, 182.

[38]A. Ruzibiza's statement to Judge Bruguière. C. Onana *Les secrets de la justice internationale: Enquêtes truquées sur le génocide rwandais,* Paris, Editions Duboiris, 2005, 118; Rever, *In Praise of Blood,* 70.

[39]Rever, *In Praise of Blood*, 108; ICTR's Special Investigations Unit summary document.

Amid the political vacuum, the RPF was able to fill these positions with its returnees from Uganda and elsewhere.[40] Although constant tension pertaining to property and land control was observed since the Habyarimana regime, this conflict intensified with an added ethnic dimension once the RPF regime gained control. Indeed, this land and property issue has discouraged a majority of refugees from returning to Rwanda.

During and after the genocide, two million people fled to neighbouring countries, mostly to Zaire,[41] together with the FAR and *Interahamwe*. In spite of the Rwandan government (RPF) and the UNHCR's repeated call, many refugees did not return. Rwanda claimed that ex-FAR and *Interahamwe* were holding refugees hostage to prevent their repatriation, and that the refugees in Zaire were used as a future military recruitment pool and as human shields by the ex-FAR and *Interahamwe*.[42] On the other hand, UNHCR consultant Robert Gersony, who assessed in August and September 1994 the prospects for the repatriation of refugees, reported that the overwhelming majority of refugees stated that "their main—in most cases their only—constraint to [returning] was the fear of being killed in their home areas, either upon their return or at a later time".[43] The report concluded that conditions were not yet conducive for their safe return.[44]

Rwanda's claim that refugees were controlled by the ex-FAR/*Interahamwe*, in part enabled it to justify the RPA's invasion in eastern Zaire in 1996 under the pretext of addressing its security concerns. While this attack led to massive forced repatriation of refugees from Zaire in 1996–1997, followed by Tanzania, other refugees opted to flee to western Zaire and other countries in and out of Africa. During this forced repatriation and movement, many refugees were massacred.

The UNHCR claimed that Rwanda "has changed significantly since the 1994 genocide, and today enjoys an essential level of peace and security".[45] This is why the UNHCR facilitated repatriation of Rwandan refugees from 1994 to 2002–2003, and promoted it actively from 2003 to 2013, followed by recommending the

[40]W. Madsen, *Genocide and covert operations in Africa, 1993–1999,* New York, Edwin Mellen Press, 1999, 132.

[41]The name of the country has changed four times since the country's independence in 1960. The post-independence name was Republic of Congo until 1 August 1964, when its name was changed to the DRC. On 27 October 1971, the then President Mobutu renamed the country Zaire. Following the First Congo War, the country was renamed the DRC on 17 May 1997. In this book, DRC, Congo or Zaire will be used interchangeably.

[42]Republic of Rwanda, Ministry of Foreign Affairs and Cooperation, "Rwanda's Comments on the Draft UN Mapping Report on the DRC", 30 Sep. 2010, p. 22, 25, available at: https://www.ohchr.org/Documents/Countries/CD/DRC_Report_Comments_Rwanda.pdf (last visited 1 June 2020).

[43]Gersony team did not have mandate to conduct an inquiry into the massacres by the ex-FAR and militias. UNHCR, "Prospects for Early Repatriation of Rwandan Refugees Currently in Burundi, Tanzania and DRC", Oct. 1994, 3, 14, available at: https://graphics8.nytimes.com/packages/pdf/world/gersony_report.PDF#page=17&zoom=auto (last visited 1 June 2020).

[44]*Ibid*, 1.

[45]UNHCR, "Implementation of the Comprehensive Strategy for the Rwandan Refugee Situation", Geneva, Dec. 2011, p. 28, available at: https://www.refworld.org/country,POLICY,,,RWA,,4f33a1642,0.html (last visited 1 June 2020).

cessation of their refugee status from 2013 to 2017. As of 2019, the Republic of Congo is the only country which invoked the cessation clause of refugee status under Article 1C [5] of the 1951 Refugee Convention. As a result, many Rwandan refugees there have lost refugee status since 1 January 2018.

The latest statistics on refugees worldwide stands at 279,071 at the end of 2019.[46]

Objective and Composition of This Book

Rwandan refugees endured the horror of the genocide, followed by another "genocide" and forced repatriation in eastern Zaire, or forced migration from eastern to western Zaire. Few of these refugees have published books since 2000. The first book was Marie Béatrice Umutesi's *Surviving the Slaughter: The Ordeal of a Rwandan Refugee in Zaire* (University of Wisconsin Press 2004), originally written in French in 2000. Since then, other books have been published, such as Maurice Niwese's *Le Peuple Rwandaise, Un Pied dans la Tombe: Récit d'un réfugié étudiant* (L' Harmattan 2001), and Pierre-Claver Ndacyayisenga's *Dying to Live: A Rwandan Family's Five-Year Flight Across the Congo* (Baraka Books 2013) which was originally written in French in 2012.

All these testimonies are very powerful; however, the refugee experience depicted in these testimonies stops around 1997 when the refugees fled outside Africa. It is not known what happened to other remaining refugees in eastern Zaire or those who were forced to continue their dreadful journeys to other countries. The refugees have been receiving political and physical threats from governments of Rwanda and the host countries, as well as the UNHCR; and the Rwandan Government is exploiting the second-generation Rwandan youth in exile. However, these facts are hardly researched and reported.

This book serves to partially fill in the research gaps regarding the current situation of Rwandan refugees, apart from those in Uganda where some research has been conducted by scholars and NGOs.[47] In particular, the refugees' refusal, for more than 25 years, to return to Rwanda in spite of the Rwandan Government and the UNHCR's continuous campaigns require investigation. Moreover, the impact of the cessation clause of Rwandan refugee status invoked in 2013 needs

[46]UNHCR, *Global Trends, Forced Displacement in 2019*, 18 June 2020, 80, available at: https://www.unhcr.org/5ee200e37.pdf (last visited 1 July 2020). This number includes refugees and asylum-seekers (pending case).

[47]International Refugee Rights Initiative and Refugee Law Project, *A Dangerous Impasse: Rwandan Refugees in Uganda*, June 2010, available at: https://www.refugee-rights.org/a-dangerous-impasse-rwandan-refugees-in-uganda/ (last visited 1 June 2020); C. Karooma, "Reluctant to return? The primacy of social networks in the repatriation of Rwandan refugees in Uganda", Refugee Studies Centre, University of Oxford, Working Paper Series No. 103, August 2014.

examination, because it has hardly been studied, and its legal and psychological impact on refugees has also been undermined and overlooked.

The highest number of Rwandan refugees have lived in eastern Democratic Republic of Congo (DRC) for more than 20 years without any protection from the "international community"—except for assistance for repatriation—since the massive forced return in 1996–1997. Since then, almost no research has been conducted there. This research gap is mainly due to the difficulties in accessing the refugees in the conflict zone, and the refugees' partial association with the Rwandan rebel group, Democratic Forces for the Liberation of Rwanda (FDLR). FDLR is partially composed of former FAR and *Interahamwe* militia, as well as young refugees recruited in refugee camps since 1994 and the survivors and orphans of 1996–1997 "genocide" in eastern DRC.[48] Unfortunately, despite their attempts, the editors of this book were not able to identify authors who could analyse the refugees' situation in eastern DRC.

In addition, the editors attempted to include more refugee authors living in other African countries, apart from Zambia which is the only country in Africa that discarded the plan to invoke the cessation clause of Rwandan refugees' status and enabled their local integration. It is important to share refugees' experiences, especially that of the hardly studied impact of the cessation clause of refugee status. However, this has not been feasible due to the ongoing discussions on and development of the cessation clause. We hope to cover these research gaps in the next project.

For this book, researchers including former United Nations (UN) staff members, a journalist, and most importantly, former Rwandan refugees from Zambia and Belgium have provided insight into both the theory and practice of repatriation as well as the security and peace issues. Emphasising refugees' perspectives is, in fact, the lesson retaught by the late Barbara Harrell-Bond, the founding director of the Refugee Studies Centre at Oxford University. She co-directed the Rights in Exile Programme, previously known as Fahamu Refugee Programme, which was the only organisation that has actively opposed the invocation of the cessation clause for Rwandan refugees.[49]

In chapter ""Voluntary" Repatriation of Rwandan Refugees in Uganda: An Analysis of Law and Practice", Frank Ahimbisibwe examines the gap between the legal principles and the practice of "voluntary" repatriation as a durable solution for Rwandan refugees in Uganda. Since the Tripartite Agreement was signed in 2003 to repatriate 25,000 Rwandan refugees, only 850 of them (0.03%) returned home; and most of them almost immediately went back to Uganda, claiming insecurity and

[48]Human Rights Watch, *Rwanda: Observing the Rules of War?* 13 (8) (A). Dec. 2001, 2, available at: https://www.hrw.org/reports/2001/rwanda2/Rwanda1201.pdf (last visited 1 June 2020); S. Hege, "Understanding the FDLR in the DR Congo: Key facts on the Disarmament & Repatriation of Rwandan Rebels", 2009, 1, available at: https://www.innercitypress.com/hege1underFDLR.pdf (last visited 1 June 2020).

[49]Fahamu Refugee Programme, *Rwanda: Cessation of Refugee Status is Unwarranted.* Memorandum of Fact and Law, 2011, available at: https://www.refugeelegalaidinformation.org/sites/srlan/files/fileuploads/Memo%20of%20Fact%20and%20Law.pdf (last visited 1 June 2020).

human rights violations in Rwanda. This chapter focuses on four legal principles: the right to return to one's home country, the principle of non-refoulement, returning in safety and dignity, and the cessation clause of refugee status. The author argues that current political and socioeconomic circumstances in Rwanda do not constitute a fundamental change that justifies repatriation and the cessation of refugee status for Rwandan refugees in Uganda.

Hajime Akiyama and Osamu Arakaki in chapter "Renouncing Nationality to Avoid Repatriation: A Perspective From the Convention on the Reduction of Statelessness" use the 1961 Convention on Reduction of Statelessness to analyse international law and the right to a nationality for Hutu refugees. The authors inquire whether the 1961 Convention which aims at the prevention (and not the complete elimination) of statelessness offers a new avenue to ensure that Rwandans in a host state are not illegitimately repatriated. Following a brief review of the increasing attention paid to the progress of international norms to prevent statelessness, the chapter highlights the fact that the 1961 Convention allows for someone to become stateless if being stateless prevents her or his illegitimate repatriation under circumstances incompatible with the principles in Articles 13 and 14 of the Universal Declaration of Human Rights, as expressed in Article 7(1)(b) of the 1961 Convention.

In chapter "The Legacy of RPF Violence and Why Rwandan Refugees Refuse to Return", Judi Rever argues that the reluctance of refugees to go home is linked to three decades of RPF violence against Rwandan civilians and the international community's overall failure to document and recognize this phenomenon. Rever describes the bidirectional nature of ethnic violence during the genocide—the Hutu-on-Tutsi and the Tutsi-on-Hutu killings—and highlights the role of the RPF's Directorate of Military Intelligence, the principal organ through which criminal ideas, deeds and propaganda are concocted. The lack of rigorous studies on RPF violence prior to, and during the genocide, led to a climate of indifference and near silence during the RPF's brutal counterinsurgency campaign against Hutus in northwestern Rwanda after the genocide, thus contributing to even more impunity and suffering for Rwandan refugees, Rever writes. The author castigates the UNHCR's controversial repatriation policy, which she sees as tantamount to sending refugees back to the people who killed their families. The UNHCR's longstanding policy and failure to protect Rwandan refugees have resulted in a breach of trust, in her opinion tantamount to sending refugees back to the people who killed their families. The UNHCR's longstanding policy and failure to protect Rwandan refugees have resulted in a breach of trust, in her opinion.

In chapter "Aggravated Trauma and Insecurity of Rwandan Hutu Refugees", Marceline Nduwamungu, a former refugee in eastern Zaire who is currently living in Belgium, describes several factors that have worsened Rwandan refugees' mental health conditions and fear. Apart from the experience of witnessing a genocide, leaving their home country, gaining asylum, looking for accommodation and a job, there are several aggravating factors. These include: attempts to prove their innocence in 1994 to the local authorities in countries of asylum, constant physical and political threats and assassination (attempts) against refugees by the Rwandan

Government, the official narrative of the Rwandan genocide against the Tutsi strongly supported by the superpower leaders, the RPF's ongoing demonisation and dehumanisation of the Hutu, and the Rwandan Government's exploitation of the second-generation Rwandan youth in exile in terms of the genocide narrative. Nduwamungu also explains that as the Hutu are denied victimhood and moral consideration, they cannot seek support from mental health experts, and Rwandan refugees do not even have the right to mourn and bury their loved ones in peace.

Masako Yonekawa, in chapter "Refugee Repatriation and Peace Process: Motive and Nature of Repatriation of Rwandan Refugees (1990–2017)", reviews the arguments of the two refugee scholars, Howard Adelman and B.S. Chimni. The former argues that the connection between peace and repatriation means that what must be addressed is not the repatriation of the refugees but the refugee problem itself; and the latter argues that the UNHCR aims to promote voluntary repatriation even in conflict situations although the same agency has been involved in peace-building activities since the 1990s. While Yonekawa agrees with the authors, she attempts to demonstrate that refugee repatriation is not necessarily part of the peace process due to the political motives that refugees, rebel groups, or governments of origin may have. Moreover, the nature of repatriation which can oppose the implementation of the peace process needs to be examined. In this chapter, Yonekawa first reviews the repatriation of old-caseload refugees, focusing on the motives of President Habyarimana's change of refugee policies and those of the rebel group, RPF. This is followed by an examination of the Rwandan Government (RPF)'s intent for repatriation of new-caseload refugees and the present-day refugees.

Ilyayo, another former refugee currently living in Zambia, also vividly describes his deadly refugee life in chapter "Where is Rwanda's Peace?" Since 1990, he has never found peace at home or in exile due to ongoing killing, harassment, kidnapping (attempts), and other security incidents committed by the Rwandan Government. He has lost some of his beloved family members and friends at home, during his journey from Rwanda to eastern Zaire, then to western Zaire, Republic of Congo, and Zambia. The RPF has also spread propaganda, stating that only the Hutus killed the Tutsis during the 1994 genocide, when in fact both ethnic groups were guilty of crimes, and most Rwandans are innocent. Worse, during this time, the UNHCR imposed repatriation and the cessation clause of refugee status, which may lead to the death of refugees. It is only at the end of 2017, when the Zambian government decided to locally integrate Rwandan refugees without the condition to apply for Rwandan passports, that Ilyayo and other Rwandan refugees finally felt at peace. He argues that apart from the generally known truth that the Hutu massacred the Tutsi, the other truth that the Tutsi massacred the Hutu also must be acknowledged, otherwise there will be neither forgiveness nor reconciliation among Rwandans. Without recognising what actually took place, there will be no genuine justice and everlasting peace.

In the Conclusion "Rethinking repatriation as a durable solution for refugees", Akiko Sugiki questions an enduring myth of repatriation. She also examines the conditions and types of governments in countries of origin where voluntary repatriation can take place with or without success. From the past experiences of repatriation of Rwandan and other refugees, she argues that it has become clear that in case premature or coercive repatriation takes place, secondary movement to other countries can be caused. Based on literature review and all chapters in this book, she concludes that this book has demonstrated that coercive repatriation to undemocratic or authoritarian regimes with excessive power is not successful, and that political conditions in post-genocide Rwandan were not an ideal environment for most refugees and returnees.

This book is a complementary with another book of Yonekawa, *Post-Genocide Rwandan Refugees, Why They Refuse to Return 'Home': Myths and Realities* (Springer 2019).

Research grant was provided by the Ministry of Education, Culture, Sports, Science and Technology in Japan under the JSPS KAKENHI Grant Number JP16H05699.

References

African Rights, *Rwanda: Death, Despair and Defiance* (African Rights, 1994), pp. 1084–1086

Arusha Peace Agreement, Protocol of Agreement Between the Government of the Republic of Rwanda and the Rwandese Patriotic Front on the Repatriation of Rwandese Refugees and the Resettlement of Displaced Persons (1993), Chapter 1, III

M. Barnett, M. Finnemore, *Rules for the World: International Organizations in Global Politics* (Cornell University Press, Ithaca and London, 2004), pp. 94–95

A. Betts, G. Loescher, J. Milner, *UNHCR: The Politics and Practice of Refugee Protection* (Oxon, Routledge, 2008), p. 35

A. Des Forges, *Leave None to Tell the Story: Genocide in Rwanda*, (1999), p. 42, available at: https://www.hrw.org/reports/1999/rwanda/ (last visited 1 June 2020)

Fahamu Refugee Programme, *Rwanda: Cessation of Refugee Status is Unwarranted. Memorandum of Fact and Law*, 2011, available at: https://www.refugeelegalaidinformation.org/sites/srlan/files/fileuploads/Memo%20of%20Fact%20and%20Law.pdf (last visited 1 June 2020)

J. Gasana, Natural Resource Scarcity and Violence in Rwanda, in: M. Halle, J. Mathew and J. Switzer (eds.), *Conserving the Peace: Resources, Livelihoods and Security* (Winnipeg, International Institute for Sustainable Development, 2002), p. 218

J. Gasana, *Rwanda: Du Parti-Etat a l'Etat-Garnison* (Paris, L'Harmattan, 2002), p. 185

A. Guichaoua, *The Problem of the Rwandese Refugees and the Banyarwanda Populations in the Great Lakes Region* (UNHCR, 1992), p. 11

S. Hege, Understanding the FDLR in the DR Congo: Key Facts on the Disarmament & Repatriation of Rwandan Rebels (2009), p. 1, available at: https://www.innercitypress.com/hege1underFDLR.pdf (last visited 1 June 2020)

L. Holborn, *Refugees: A Problem of Our Time- The Work of the United Nations High Commissioner for Refugees, 1951–1972*, with the assistance of P. and R. Chartrand, (Metuchen, N.J., Cambridge, Massachusetts, The Scarecrow Press, Inc., for the Radcliffe Institute, 1975), pp. 325–327

C. Huggins, The Presidential Land Commission; Undermining Land Reform, S. Straus, L. Waldorf (eds.), *Remaking Rwanda: State Building and Human Rights after Mass Violence* (Wisconsin, University of Wisconsin Press, 2011), p. 255

Human Rights Watch Arms Project, *Arming Rwanda: The Arms Trade and Human Rights Abuses in the Rwandan War*, **6**(1) (1994), available at: https://www.hrw.org/sites/default/files/reports/RWANDA941.PDF (last visited 1 June 2020)

Human Rights Watch, *Rwanda: Observing the Rules of War?* 13 (8) (A). Dec. 2001, 2, available at: https://www.hrw.org/reports/2001/rwanda2/Rwanda1201.pdf (last visited 1 June 2020)
Human Rights Watch, Briefing Paper 1, *The Rwandan Genocide: How It Was Prepared.* April 2006, 4, available at: https://www.hrw.org/legacy/backgrounder/africa/rwanda0406/ (last visited 1 June 2020)
International Refugee Rights Initiative and Refugee Law Project, *A Dangerous Impasse: Rwandan Refugees in Uganda* (2010), available at: https://www.refugee-rights.org/a-dangerous-impasse-rwandan-refugees-in-uganda/ (last visited 1 June 2020)
I. Kamola, The Global Coffee Economy and the Production of Genocide in Rwanda. *Third World Q.* **28**(3), 578 (2007)
C. Karooma, Reluctant to Return? The Primacy of Social Networks in the Repatriation of Rwandan Refugees in Uganda (Refugee Studies Centre, University of Oxford, 2014), Working Paper Series No. 103
J.-P. Kimonyo, *Rwanda demain! Une Longue Marche vers la Transformation* (Paris, Karthala, 2017), p. 110
R. Lemarchand, *Rwanda and Burundi* (New York, Praeger Publishers, 1970), pp. 171–173
R. Lemarchand, *The Dynamics of Violence in Central Africa* (Pennsylvania, University of Pennsylvania, 2009), p. 126
W. Madsen, *Genocide and Covert Operations in Africa*, 1993–1999 (New York, Edwin Mellen Press, 1999), p. 132
C. Newbury, Ethnicity and Politics of History in Rwanda. *Africa Today* **45**, 15 (1996)
D. Newbury, Returning Refugees: Four Historical Patterns of 'Coming Home' to Rwanda, *Comparative Studies in Society and History* **47**(2), 275 (2005)
C. Onana, *Les Secrets de la Justice Internationale: Enquêtes Truquées Sur Le Génocide Rwandais* (Paris, Editions Duboiris, 2005), p. 118
O. Otunnu, *Crisis of Legitimacy and Political Violence in Uganda 1979 to 2016* (Cham, Palgrave McMillan, 2016), p. 39
G. Prunier, *The Rwanda Crisis: History of a Genocide* (Kampala, Fountain Publisher, 1999), p. 56
Republic of Rwanda, Ministry of Foreign Affairs and Cooperation, "Rwanda's Comments on the Draft UN Mapping Report on the DRC", 30 Sep. 2010, para. 22, 25, available at: https://www.ohchr.org/Documents/Countries/CD/DRC_Report_Comments_Rwanda.pdf (last visited 1 June 2020)
J. Rever, *In Praise of Blood: The Crimes of the Rwandan Patriotic Front* (Random House Canada, 2018), p. 106
T. Rudasingwa, *Healing A Nation, A Testimony: Waging and Winning a Peaceful Revolution to Unite and Heal a Broken Rwanda* (South Carolina, CreateSpace Independent Publishing Platform, 2013), p. 38
P. Rutayisire et al., *RWANDA: la Renaissance d'une Nation* (Butare, Editions de l'université du Rwanda, 2012), p. 110
S. Straus, *The Order of Genocide: Race, Power, and War in Rwanda* (Cornell University Press, New York, 2008), p. 51
UN Economic and Social Council (ECOSOC), Question of the Violation of Human Rights and Fundamental Freedoms in any Part of the World, with Particular Reference to Colonial and other Dependent Countries and Territories, E/CN.4/1994/7/Add.1 (1993), pp. 33–35
UNHCR, Note on Non-Refoulement (Submitted by the High Commissioner), EC/SCP/2", 23 Aug. 1977, para. 1
UNHCR, Executive Committee of the High Commissioner's Programme, "Voluntary Repatriation, No. 18 (XXXI)–1980", 16 Oct. 1980, (a), available at: https://www.refworld.org/docid/3ae68c6e8.html (last visited 1 June 2020)
UNHCR, Statement of the High Commissioner to the 42nd session of the Executive Committee (1991), p. 4
UNHCR, Statement by Mrs. Sadako Ogata, United Nations High Commissioner for Refugees, at the International Management Symposium (St. Gallen, Switzerland, 1992), available at: https://www.unhcr.org/admin/hcspeeches/3ae68faec/statement-mrs-sadako-ogata-united-nations-high-commissioner-refugees-international.html (last visited 1 June 2020)

UNHCR, Prospects for Early Repatriation of Rwandan Refugees Currently in Burundi, Tanzania and DRC, Oct. 1994, 3, 14, available at: https://graphics8.nytimes.com/packages/pdf/world/gersony_report.PDF#page=17&zoom=auto (last visited 1 June 2020)

UNHCR, Guidelines on International Protection: Cessation of Refugee Status under Article 1C(5) and (6) of the 1951 Convention relating to the Status of Refugees (2003), p. 10, available at: https://www.unhcr.org/3e637a202.pdf (last visited 1 June 2020)

UNHCR, *Handbook for Repatriation and Reintegration Activities* (May 2004), One-2, One-4, available at: https://www.unhcr.org/411786694.pdf (last visited 1 June 2020)

UNHCR, *Convention and Protocol Relating to the Status of Refugees* (2010), 2

UNHCR, Implementation of the Comprehensive Strategy for the Rwandan Refugee Situation (Geneva, 2011), p. 28, available at: https://www.refworld.org/country,POLICY,,,RWA,,4f33a1642,0.html (last visited 1 June 2020)

UNHCR, *Global Trends, Forced Displacement in 2019* (2020), p.80, available at: https://www.unhcr.org/5ee200e37.pdf

P. Uvin, *Aiding Violence: The Development Enterprise in Rwanda* (Connecticut, Kumarian Press, 1998), p. 35

Terminology and Glossary

Refugee:

A refugee is "as a result of events occurring before 1 January 1951 and owing to well-founded fear of being persecuted for reasons of race, religion, nationality, membership of a particular social group or political opinion, is outside the country of his nationality and is unable or, owing to such fear, is unwilling to avail himself of the protection of that country; or who, not having a nationality and being outside the country of his former habitual residence as a result of such events, is unable or, owing to such fear, is unwilling to return to it" (Article 1A [2] of the 1951 Refugee Convention). "The 1951 Convention, as a post-Second World War instrument, was originally limited in scope to persons fleeing events occurring before 1 January 1951 and within Europe. The 1967 Protocol removed these limitations and thus gave the Convention universal coverage".[50]

The Organisation of African Union (OAU) in 1969 added the following definition of a refugee as: "every person who, owing to external aggression, occupation, foreign domination or events seriously disturbing public order in either part or the whole of his country of origin or nationality, is compelled to leave his place of habitual residence in order to seek refuge in another place outside his country of origin or nationality".

Voluntary Repatriation:

There are three durable solutions to the refugee problem: local integration in neighbouring countries, resettlement in the third countries of permanent asylum, and voluntary repatriation to the home country. Voluntary repatriation implies "the free and voluntary return to one's country of origin in safety and dignity". Core components of voluntary repatriation are physical safety, legal safety, material safety, and reconciliation.[51]

[50]UNHCR, *Convention and Protocol Relating to the Status of Refugees,* 2010, 2.

[51]UNHCR, *Handbook for Repatriation and Reintegration Activities*, May 2004, One-2, One-4, available at: https://www.unhcr.org/411786694.pdf (last visited 1 June 2020).

Principle of Non-Refoulement (Non-Expulsion):

According to the UNHCR, "the most essential component of refugee status and of asylum is protection against return to a country where a person has reason to fear of persecution".[52]

Cessation Clause of Refugee Status:

A refugee "can no longer, because the circumstances in connection with which he has been recognized as a refugee have ceased to exist, continue to refuse to avail himself of the protection of the country of his nationality" (Article 1C [5] of the 1951 Refugee Convention), and "because the circumstances in connection with which he has been recognized as a refugee have ceased to exist, *able to return to* the country of his former habitual residence" (1C [6]). For cessation to apply, the changes of circumstances in the country of origin must be fundamental and enduring, and "address the causes of displacement which led to the recognition of refugee status".[53]

Rwanda

- ***Interahamwe***:
  Although it is known as a Hutu radical militia organisation which committed genocide against Rwandan Tutsis in 1994, it was originally created in 1991 as a youth wing of the Habyarimana's political party to assemble grassroots party activists to spread the ideas of the party. They and the former Rwanda army fled to eastern DRC after the genocide, and established years later the rebel group **Democratic Forces for the Liberation of Rwanda (FDLR)**. Due to this background, *Interahamwe* is sometimes used to refer to the FDLR. The FDLR is currently composed of young refugees recruited in refugee camps since 1994 and survivors and orphans of 1996–1997 "genocide" in eastern DRC.[54]
- **International Criminal Tribunal for Rwanda (ICTR):**
  An international court established in November 1994 by the United Nations Security Council Resolution 955, prosecuting those considered most responsible for the gravest crimes committed in Rwanda.

[52]UNHCR, "Note on Non-Refoulement (Submitted by the High Commissioner), EC/SCP/2", 23 Aug. 1977, p. 1.

[53]UNHCR, "Guidelines on International Protection: Cessation of Refugee Status under Article 1C (5) and (6) of the 1951 Convention relating to the Status of Refugees," 10 Feb. 2003, p. 10, available at: https://www.unhcr.org/3e637a202.pdf (last visited 1 June 2020).

[54]Human Rights Watch, *Rwanda: Observing the Rules of War?* 13 (8) (A). Dec. 2001, 2; S. Hege, "Understanding the FDLR in the DR Congo: Key facts on the Disarmament & Repatriation of Rwandan Rebels", 2009, 1.

- **Rwandan Patriotic Front/Army (RPF/A)**:
  A political movement established in 1987 by the second generation of Rwandan refugees who fled to Uganda in 1959–early 1960s. Led by Tutsi, the RPF seized power during the Rwandan genocide in 1994.

- **Old-Caseload Refugee**:
  Mainly Tutsi who fled following the "Social Revolution" in 1959 and onwards.
- **New-Caseload Refugee**:
  Mainly Hutu, who fled during and in the aftermath of the 1994 genocide. *Rwandan ethnic or social group are divided into majority **Hutu**, minority **Tutsi**, and the remaining **Twa**.

DR Congo

- **Alliance of Democratic Forces for the Liberation of Congo (AFDL)**:
  A "Congolese" rebel group which assisted Rwandan troops' overthrow of the regime of Mobutu Sese Seko in 1996–1997.
- **March 23 Movement (M23)**:
  A Rwandan-backed "Congolese" rebel group which committed war crimes in eastern DRC in 2012–2013. It was said to be defeated by the Congolese army, but it is reported to remain active even after having fled to Rwanda and Uganda.

*Both AFDL and M23, as other Congolese rebel groups RCD and CNDP, were created by the Rwandan government army, often assisted by the Ugandan government army.

Uganda

National Resistance Movement/Army (NRM/A):
Former rebel group established by the current President Museveni in 1981, which seized power in 1986. One of NRM's deputy was Paul Kagame, the current Rwandan president.

History of Events Related to Rwandan Refugees and Their Policy

Regime	Month/Year	Events/Incidents
	Nov. 1959–1960s	Following the “Social Revolution” in Nov. 1959, 1,30,000 people, including the current President Paul Kagame, fled for neighbouring countries to seek refuge
President Grégoire Kayibanda (Hutu)	July 1962	Rwanda became independent
	1971	【Uganda】 Some Rwandan refugees in Uganda joined President Idi Amin’s army
President Juvénal Habyarimana (Hutu)	July 1973	Major General Habyarimana of the Minister of National Guards and Police staged a coup d’etat and seized power
	1981	【Uganda】 Some Rwandan refugees, including Kagame, joined the Yoweri Museveni-led National Resistance Movement (NRM)
	Jan. 1986	【Uganda】 The NRM, with more than a quarter of its members being Rwandan refugees, seized power, and Museveni became the Ugandan President
	Dec. 1987	【Uganda】 The Rwandan Patriotic Front (RPF) was formed by refugees with a view to returning home
	Oct. 1990–	The RPF invaded Rwanda from Uganda. Civil war with the government of Rwanda ensued until 1994. The number of internally displaced persons (IDPs, mainly majority-group Hutu) increased to one million by Feb. 1993, or one-seventh of the country’s entire population
	Aug. 1993	The Arusha Peace Accords were signed between the Rwandan government and the RPF
	Nov. 1993	United Nations Assistance Mission to Rwanda (UNAMIR) started deploying

(continued)

(continued)

Regime	Month/Year	Events/Incidents
Interim government	6 April 1994	Habyarimana's presidential jet was shot down
	7 April 1994–	Massive, targeted killing—whose phenomenon is called genocide—took place over 100 days. It is said that 8,00,000–1 million, mainly Tutsis, were murdered by Hutu forces. However, according to former RPF officers, RPF was responsible for shooting down the presidential plane and involved in targeted killing
	23 June–21 Aug. 1994	A "safe humanitarian zone" was established in southwestern Rwanda by the French troops (Operation Turquoise). France, a strong ally of the Rwandan government before 1994, was said to have facilitated the flight of the ex-Rwandan army soldiers and genocide leaders to eastern Zaire
President Pasteur Bizimungu (Hutu)/Vice President & Minister of Defense Paul Kagame (Tutsi)	19 July 1994	After the RPF gained control, a government of national unity was created. Refugees from 1959 started to repatriate to Rwanda. A total of 2 million refugees, mostly Hutu, fled Rwanda (1.2 million people fled for eastern DRC). Facilitation of repatriation started soon after refugees fled Rwanda
	May 1995	Rwandan troops massacred at least 2,000–4,000 Hutu IDPs at Kibeho IDP camp in Rwanda
	Aug. 1995	The government of national unity collapsed. The ex-Prime Minister and ex-Interior Minister went into exile
	Oct. 1996–Apr. 1997	【Zaire】 The RPA/AFDL attacked and destroyed refugee camps in eastern Zaire. On one hand many refugees returned home against their will, on other side, about 233,000 Rwandan refugees were assumed to have been killed in the DRC by Rwandan troop and AFDL allies. According to the UN, possible genocide took place. Many others fled from eastern to western DRC, then to neighbouring countries. UNHCR hunted and forcefully repatriated refugees 【Tanzania】 UNHCR and Government of Tanzania also forcefully repatriated refugees (Dec. 1996)
	May 1997	【DRC】 Fall of President Mobutu regime. L. D. Kabila self-declared as the President of the DRC
	Aug. 1998	【DRC】 Rwandan troops started to occupy eastern DRC

(continued)

(continued)

Regime	Month/Year	Events/Incidents
President Paul Kagame (Tutsi)	Jan. 2000	President Bizimungu was forced to resign, and Kagame took over the presidency
	Oct. 2002–2003	UNHCR started to promote voluntary repatriation
	Aug. 2003	At the presidential elections, Kagame obtained 95% of votes
	Oct. 2009	UNHCR announced the invocation of cessation clause of refugee status of Rwandan refugees
	Aug. 2010	Kagame was re-elected president with 93% of votes in election
	June 2013	Cessation clause of refugee status came into effect for refugees, which implies loss of refugee status
	Aug. 2017	Kagame was re-elected president with 99% of votes in election
	Dec. 2017	Invocation of cessation clause of Rwandan refugee status comes to an end

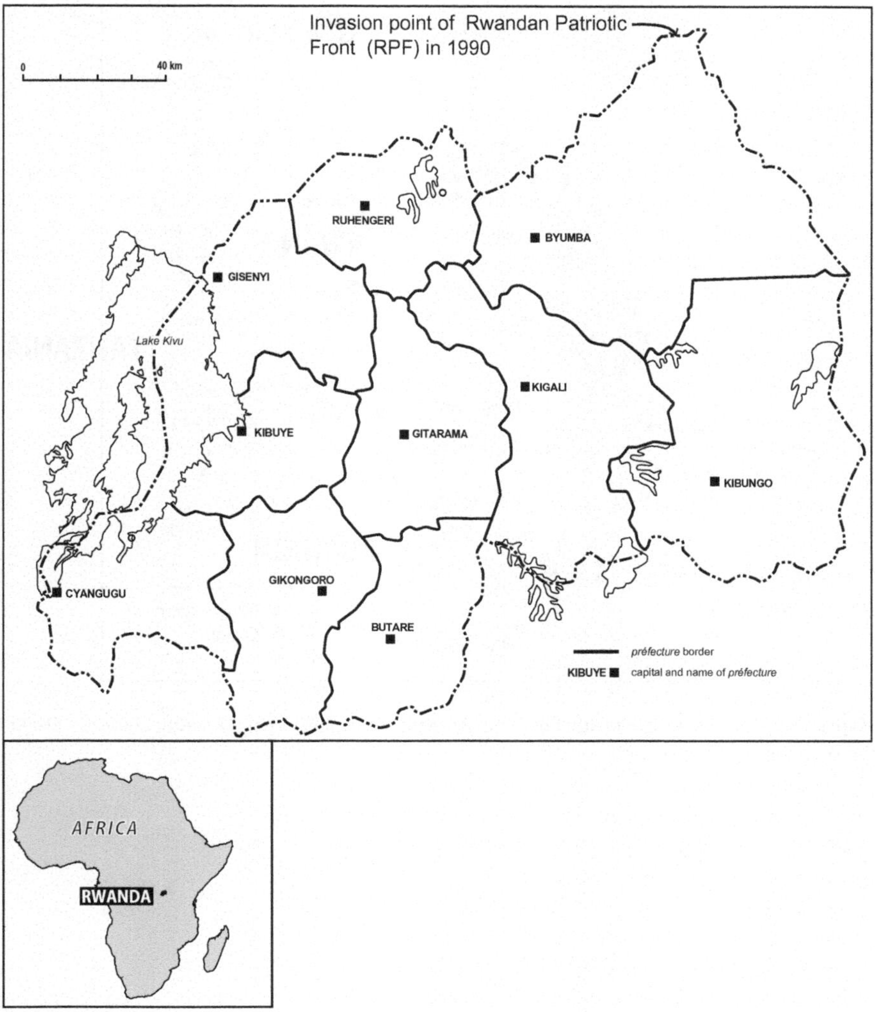

Map 1 Rwanda's administrative map until 2011

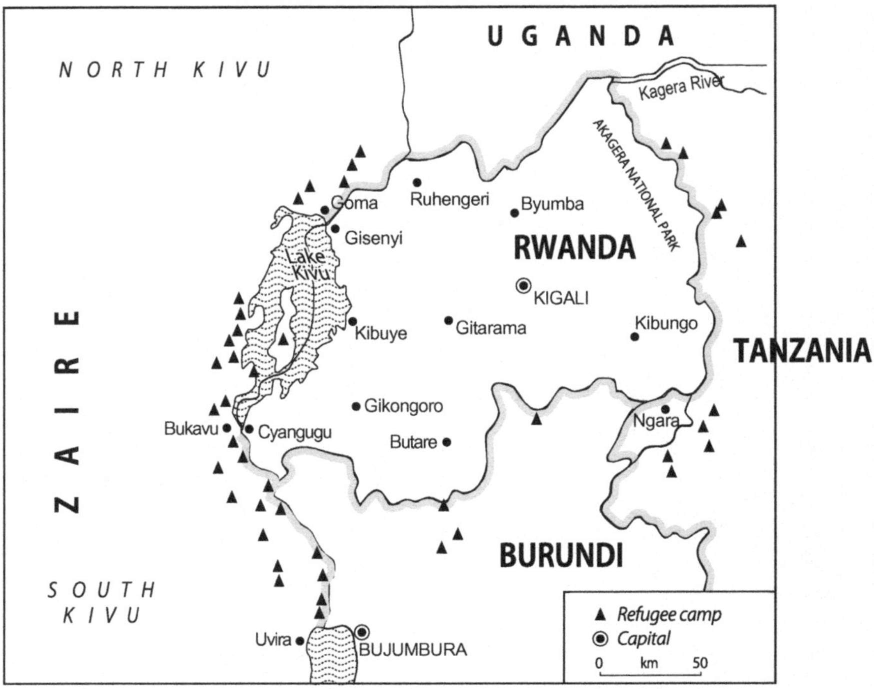

Map 2 Map indicating the location of Rwandan refugee camps in neighbouring countries (1994–1996)

Abbreviations

AFDL	Alliance of Democratic Forces for the Liberation of Congo-Zaire
CIJ	Commission Internationale des Juristes
DMI	Directorate of Military Intelligence (Rwanda)
DRC	Democratic Republic of Congo
DPKO	Department of Peacekeeping Operation
ECOSOC	Economic and Social Council (United Nations)
FAR	Armed Forces of Rwanda (before 1994)
FDLR	Forces démocratiques de libération du Rwanda
FGDs	Focus Group Discussions
ICCPR	International Covenant on Civil and Political Rights
ICTR	International Criminal Tribunal for Rwanda
IDP	Internally Displaced Person
IO	Intelligence Officer
IS	Intelligence Staff
JRS	Jesuit Refugee Service
MRND	National Revolutionary Movement for Development
MSF	Médecins Sans Frontières
NGO	Non-Governmental Organisation
NRM	National Resistance Movement
OAU	Organisation of African Unity
OPM	Office of the Prime Minister
PTSD	Post-Traumatic Stress Disorders
RANU	Rwandese Alliance for National Unity
RNC	Rwandan National Congress
RPA	Rwandan Patriotic Army
RPF	Rwandan Patriotic Front
UDHR	Universal Declaration of Human Rights
UK	United Kingdom
UN	United Nations
UNAMID	UN–African Union Hybrid Operation in Darfur

UNAMIR	UN Assistance Mission to Rwanda
UNHCR	United Nations High Commissioner for Refugees
UNSC	United Nations Security Council
WWII	World War II

"Voluntary" Repatriation of Rwandan Refugees in Uganda: An Analysis of Law and Practice

Frank Ahimbisibwe

1 Introduction

The UNHCR's Annual Global Trends report notes that by the end of 2017, Uganda was hosting 1.4 million refugees, the highest number in the country's history since the 1940s when it first hosted European refugees displaced by the Second World War. Uganda was the third largest refugee-hosting country in the world, and the largest in Africa.[1] The majority of these refugees come from neighbouring countries and the wider region, including South Sudan, the Democratic Republic of Congo (DRC), Burundi, Somalia, Rwanda, Kenya, Ethiopia, and Eritrea, among others. By June 2018, around 15,517 of these were Rwandans[2] who arrived during and after the 1994 Rwandan genocide.

Uganda is a party to international refugee and human rights law, which spells out the principles of voluntary repatriation as follows: the 1951 Convention[3] and its

[1]UNHCR, *Global Trends: Forced Displacement in 2017*, Geneva, UNHCR, 2018, 3, available at: http://www.unhcr.org/globaltrends2017/ (last visited 19 June 2018).

[2]OPM and UNHCR, *Uganda Comprehensive Refugee Response Portal*, 2018, available at: http://ugandarefugees.org/en/country/uga/ (last visited 28 Aug. 2018). This number reduced from 25,000 in 2003 when the tripartite agreement of voluntary repatriation was signed.

[3]Convention relating to the Status of Refugees, 189 UNTS 150, 28 July 1951 (entry into force: 22 Apr. 1954).

The original version of this chapter was revised: The title has been corrected. The correction to this chapter is available at https://doi.org/10.1007/978-981-15-2850-7_7

F. Ahimbisibwe
Mbarara, Uganda

M. Yonekawa and A. Sugiki (eds.), *Repatriation, Insecurity, and Peace*,
https://doi.org/10.1007/978-981-15-2850-7_1

1967 Protocol[4] (the principle of non-refoulement),[5] and the 1969 Organization of African Unity (OAU) Convention Governing the Specific Aspects of the Refugee Problem in Africa[6] (describing the voluntary character of repatriation, cooperation between countries of asylum and origin, the facilitation of returnees by the country of origin, and no penalty to returnees).[7] Other principles are provided in the UNHCR Executive Conclusions No. 40 (XXXVI) 1985 (the ceasing of causes for flight, and return in safety and dignity) and No. 18 (XXXI) 1980 (refugees' access to information about the country of origin, and monitoring returnees at home by the UNHCR). The above principles are emphasised by the 2003 Tripartite Agreement on the Voluntary Repatriation of Rwandan Refugees in Uganda (hereafter, "the 2003 Tripartite Agreement").[8]

Uganda has enacted domestic refugee and human rights laws that include the 2006 Refugees Act,[9] the 1995 Constitution, and the 1997 Children's Act, among others.

Although legal principles and norms exist on voluntary repatriation, in practice, they have been abused. This paper uses the case of Rwandan refugees to show the violations. I argue that the current political and socioeconomic circumstances in Rwanda do not constitute a fundamental change to justify repatriation and the cessation of refugee status for Rwandan refugees in Uganda. Rwandan refugees have been selected because of their long stay in Uganda (more than 20 years). Also, UNHCR has recommended the cessation clause for this caseload, which raises legal and protection concerns. This paper, based on theoretical texts and empirical research findings, analyses the violation of specific principles of repatriation: the right to return, the principle of non-refoulement, return in safety and dignity, and the ceasing of causes for flight.

---

[4]Protocol Relating to the Status of Refugees, UNTS, vol. 606, p. 267, 31 Jan. 1967 (entry into force: 4 Oct. 1967).

[5]Article 33(1) of the 1951 Convention calls upon States not to expel or return refugees to countries where their lives and rights would be threatened due to race, religion, nationality, or membership in a particular social group or political opinion.

[6]Convention Governing the Specific Aspects of Refugee Problems in Africa, 1001 UNTS 45, 10 Sept. 1969 (entry into force: 20 June 1974).

[7]See Article V of the 1969 OAU Convention.

[8]UN High Commissioner for Refugees (UNHCR), Tripartite Agreement between the Government of Uganda and the Government of the Republic of Rwanda and the United Nations High Commissioner for Refugees for the Voluntary Repatriation of Rwandan Refugees in Uganda to Rwanda, signed on 23rd July 2003, on file with the author.

[9]Section 42(1) provides for non-refoulement. It states that 'no person shall be refused entry into Uganda, expelled, extradited or returned from Uganda to any other country or subjected to any similar measures if, as a result of such refusal, expulsion, return or other measure, that person is compelled to return to or remain in a country where—(a) He/she may be subjected to persecution on account of race, religion, sex, nationality, membership of a particular social group or political opinion'.

Although there has been sufficient scholarly attention to the repatriation of Rwandan refugees in general,[10] there is little scholarly writing focused on the law and the practice of the principles of repatriation on Rwandan refugees in Uganda.

This study is based on three research visits carried out at different intervals in Nakivale and Oruchinga settlements in southwestern Uganda. The first visit was undertaken from June 2010 to December 2011. A second visit took place between June and August 2016. A third visit was carried out from 26th to 31st January 2018. The study focused on Rwandan new-caseload refugees[11] and used a qualitative research methodology. Semi-structured and key informant interviews, focus group discussions (FGDs), observation, and documentary evidence were the main research techniques. Purposive criterion sampling was used to select the study respondents, namely Rwandan refugees, Rwandan and Ugandan government officials, UNHCR and NGO officials, as well as local hosts around Nakivale settlement in Isingiro District.[12] In addition, "recyclers"[13] were identified through snowball sampling. Rwandan refugees and other categories of respondents answered questions on themes like

---

[10]See N.K. Lindsey, "Bringing Rwandan Refugees 'Home': The Cessation Clause, Statelessness, and Forced Repatriation", *International Journal of Refugee Law* 29(3), 2017, 417–437; F. Ahimbisibwe, *Repatriation as A Durable Solution to the Rwandese Refugee Problem in Uganda,* Saarbrucken, VDM Verlag Publishers, 2011; C. Karooma, "Preliminary Observations from the Field: Rwandan Refugees Perceptions of "Voluntary" Repatriation from Uganda", *Oxford Monitor of Forced Migration.* 3(2), 2013; C. Karooma, "Reluctant to Return? The Primacy of Social Networks in the Repatriation of Rwandan Refugees in Uganda", Refugee Studies Centre, University of Oxford, *Working Paper Series No.* 103, Aug. 2014; B.E. Whitaker, "Changing Priorities in Refugee Protection: The Rwandan Repatriation from Tanzania", in N. Steiner, M. Gibney, G. Loescher (eds.) *Problems of Protection: The UNHCR, Refugees and Human Rights;* and Amnesty International, *Great Lakes Region Still in Need of Protection: Repatriation, Refoulement and Safety of Refugees and the Internally Displaced,* London, International Secretariat, 24 Jan. 1997.

[11]Rwandan new caseload refugees refer to Hutu that came during and after the 1994 genocide. Before them, Uganda hosted old case load Rwandan Tutsi refugees who arrived in 1959 and the early 1960s. The majority returned to Rwanda after the genocide while a significant number stayed in Uganda.

[12]The first visit involved 162 respondents. One FGD, each with 12 Rwandans was organised in each of the three zones in Nakivale; Base Camp, Juru, and Rubondo. In each of the zones, I interviewed 10 refugee leaders. I also interviewed 10 recyclers, 10 Isingiro district officials, 11 officials from the Office of the Prime Minister (OPM), 16 NGO staff, 10 police officers, 36 local hosts (six locals from each of the six sub-counties bordering Nakivale), one expert on refugee studies, and two officials from the Rwandan High Commission in Kampala. In the second visit, a total of 182 respondents participated in the study. Four FGDs each with 10 Rwandan refugees were organised in four zones in Nakivale settlement; Base Camp, Juru, Rubondo, and Kabazana. The fifth FGD with 10 Rwandan refugees was organised in Oruchinga settlement. I interviewed 10 refugee leaders from each of the four zones in Nakivale. Ten refugee leaders were interviewed in Oruchinga settlement. Apart from the refugees, I interviewed 16 recyclers (10 in Nakivale and six in Oruchinga), 10 new asylum seekers (six in Nakivale and four in Oruchinga), six OPM officials (four in Nakivale and two in Oruchinga), four Isingiro district officials, 34 local hosts (24 in Nakivale and 10 in Oruchinga), 10 NGO staff (six in Nakivale and four in Oruchinga), and two officials from the Rwandan High Commission in Kampala. In the third visit, a total of 48 respondents participated. In Nakivale settlement, 24 Rwandan refugees, four recyclers, and two OPM officials were interviewed. In Oruchinga, I interviewed 14 refugees, two recyclers and two OPM officials.

[13]Recyclers are Rwandan refugees who have been repatriated to Rwanda but have returned to Uganda claiming human rights violations, insecurity, persecution, and the inability to recover land and property in Rwanda.

refugee physical security, refugee rights and obligations, voluntary and forced repatriation, local integration, resettlement, the so-called cessation clause, and, in general, avenues to find durable solutions.[14] The analysis further makes use of secondary data, both scholarly articles and grey literature.

This paper is structured as follows. The next section deals with the analysis of the international law. This is done by looking at the principles of repatriation as enshrined in the law. Then, the paper analyses the practice of Rwandan refugee repatriation. The paper finally concludes with policy and methodological implications.

2 Rwandan Refugee Repatriation: Analysis of Law

2.1 Right to Return to One's Country

International human rights law provides for the right to return to one's country. Article 13(2) of the Universal Declaration of Human Rights provides that "Everyone has the right to leave any country, including his own, and to return to his country". The right to return has been enshrined in various binding international human rights instruments, including the International Covenant on Civil and Political Rights,[15] the International Convention on the Elimination of all Forms of Racial Discrimination,[16] and the African Charter on Human and Peoples' Rights.[17] The 2003 Tripartite Agreement also provides for the right to return.[18]

The UNHCR Handbook on Voluntary Repatriation (hereafter "the UNHCR Handbook") explains that the right to return entails that a State is duty-bound to its nationals and cannot compel other States to keep them through measures like denationalization.[19]

According to Chetail, the United Nations Human Rights Committee recalled in its General Comment 27 on Freedom of Movement that "the right to return is of the utmost importance for refugees seeking voluntary repatriation".[20] "Even

[14]The study observed ethical principles in research. The study was cleared by the Office of the Prime Minister and Isingiro District in Uganda. During the data collection exercise, the respondents were briefed on the purpose of the study, which was purely academic. Their confidentiality, informed consent, and voluntary participation were observed and respected.

[15]Article 12(4).

[16]Article 5(d)(ii).

[17]Article 12.

[18]Article 1 provides that 'Any Rwandan national who is a refugee in Uganda and who wishes to return to the Republic of Rwanda has the right to do so without having to satisfy any pre-condition'.

[19]UNHCR, *Handbook on Voluntary Repatriation: International Protection*, Geneva, UNHCR, 1996, 7.

[20]United Nations Office of the High Commissioner for Human Rights, CCPR General Comment No. 27: Article 12 (Freedom of Movement) Adopted at the Sixty-seventh session of the Human Rights Committee, on 2 Nov. 1999, CCPR/C/21/Rev.1/Add.9, General Comment No. 27. (General

more precisely, the right to return constitutes the legal precondition to realize repatriation".[21] Chetail further argues that "voluntary repatriation presupposes that the refugees are entitled to exercise the human right to return to their country of origin. As a corollary of this right, the State of origin is bound to admit its nationals".[22]

The UN resolution 194 stresses the importance of the international legal principles on the right to return established in different international human rights instruments. It imposes obligations on States to allow refugees to return to their country of origin without any discrimination.[23]

According to Human Rights Watch, "Refugees retain the fundamental human right to return to the country of origin regardless of the conditions of repatriation or conditions in their country. However, this right becomes meaningless where conditions exist that impair its free exercise".[24]

In the same vein, Gervais Coles argues that "It cannot be said that a right to return exists where conditions in the country of origin, in particular the grave violations of human rights, are such that no reasonable person would wish to return".[25] Yasmin Naqvi has argued that "while there is no doubt that this right is guaranteed under international law, it is less obvious how refugees can make use of such a right, given the fact that they are in exile precisely because they cannot enter their country of nationality because of the risk of human rights violations".[26]

Therefore, given the connection between massive human rights violations and refugee status, return should only take place after the UNHCR and the host country have made an objective assessment of the human rights situation in the country of origin. In this way, it can be ascertained that the returnees' rights will be protected if they choose or are required to return.[27]

Comments) quoted by V. Chetail, 'Voluntary Repatriation in Public International: Concepts and Contents', *Refugee Survey Quarterly*, 2004, 23 (3), 26.

[21] See Chetail, Voluntary Repatriation in Public International Law.

[22] *Ibid.*

[23] See Y. Kathirgamathamby, "Voluntary Repatriation as a Durable Solution to Sri Lankan Refugees in India: A Critical Analysis with Legal Perspective", in *Proceedings of 8th International Research Conference*, KDU, Nov. 2015, 191.

[24] Human Rights Watch, "Uncertain Refuge: International Failures to Protect Refugees", New York, Human Rights Watch, Apr. 1997 available at: https://www.hrw.org/report/1997/04/01/uncertain-refuge/international-failures-protect-refugees, (last visited 12 June 2017) quoted by Y. Kathirgamathamby, 'Voluntary Repatriation as a Durable Solution'.

[25] See G.J.L. Coles, Voluntary Repatriation: A Background Study, Geneva, UNHCR, 1985, 94 quoted by N. Yasmin, "Between a Rock and Hard Place? A Legal Analysis of the Voluntary Repatriation of Guatemalan Refugees", *Refugee Survey Quarterly* 23(3), 2004, 83.

[26] Yasmin, Between a Rock and Hard Place, 82–83.

[27] *Ibid*, 83.

2.2 Principle of Non-refoulement

According to Guy Goodwin-Gill and Jane McAdam, "The international legal status of the refugees necessarily imports certain legal consequences, the most important of which is the obligation of States to respect the principle of non-refoulement through time".[28] Refugee and human rights law provides for the right of non-refoulement for refugees who have a well-founded fear of being persecuted in their countries of origin.

Furthermore, the right of non-refoulement is provided for in the 1951 Convention and its 1967 Protocol, and ostensibly protects recognized refugees from being expelled from countries that are signatories. Article 33(1) of the 1951 Convention calls upon States not to expel or return refugees to countries where their lives and rights would be threatened due to race, religion, nationality, or membership in a particular social group or political opinion.[29] The Convention Against Torture and Other Cruel, Inhuman, or Degrading Treatment or Punishment (CAT) provides that no State shall expel, return (refouler), or extradite a person to another State where there are substantial grounds for believing that he or she would be in danger of being subjected to torture.[30]

The African Charter on Human and Peoples' Rights prohibits the mass expulsion of non-nationals.[31] The 1969 OAU Convention makes reference to the right of non-refoulement.[32] By putting the emphasis on voluntary repatriation, the convention outlaws any attempts at forcing refugees to return home where they have a well-founded fear of being persecuted. Voluntary repatriation essentially emphasizes the principle of non-refoulement.[33]

The UNHCR Handbook makes a connection between voluntariness and non-refoulement as follows:

---

[28] See G.S. Goodwin-Gill, J. McAdam, *The Refugee in International Law*, 3rd edn., Oxford, Oxford University Press, 2007, 1.

[29] The principle of non-refoulement is international customary law and it applies to all states regardless of whether or not they have ratified the 1951 UN Convention.

[30] Article 3.

[31] Article 12(5) provides that "the mass expulsion of non-nationals shall be prohibited. Mass expulsion shall be that which is aimed at national, racial, ethnic, or religious groups".

[32] Article V(1) states that "the essentially voluntary character of repatriation shall be respected in all cases and no refugee shall be repatriated against his will".

[33] At the domestic level, Uganda's 2006 Refugees Act provides for non-refoulement. Section 42(1) states that "no person shall be refused entry into Uganda, expelled, extradited or returned from Uganda to any other country or subjected to any similar measures if, as a result of such refusal, expulsion, return or other measure, that person is compelled to return to or remain in a country where—(a) He/she may be subjected to persecution on account of race, religion, sex, nationality, membership of a particular social group or political opinion". Also, the 2003 Tripartite Agreement provides for the voluntary character of repatriation. Article 2 states that "The contracting states fully recognize the essentially voluntary character of the solution of voluntary repatriation and reaffirm that no Rwandan refugee will be compelled to return against his or her will".

> The principle of voluntariness is the cornerstone of international protection with respect to the return of refugees. While the issue of voluntary repatriation as such is not addressed in the 1951 Refugee Convention, it follows directly from the principle of non-refoulement: the involuntary return of refugees would in practice amount to refoulement. A person retaining a well-founded fear of persecution is a refugee, and cannot be compelled to repatriate.[34]

The UNHCR Handbook further explains that the principle of voluntariness must be viewed in relation to the conditions in the country of origin (calling for an informed decision) as well as the situation in the country of asylum (permitting a free choice).[35] The Handbook states, "Voluntariness means not only the absence of measures which push the refugee to repatriate, but also means that he or she should not be prevented from returning, for example by dissemination of wrong information or false promises of continued assistance. In certain situations economic interests in the country of asylum may lead to interest groups trying to prevent refugees from repatriating".[36]

According to UNHCR, ensuring the voluntary nature of repatriation includes the following[37]:

- The decision to repatriate is made freely.
- The refugees are making an informed decision based on an accurate country profile.
- The decision is made expressly.

In other words, voluntariness means that there should be no pressure on the refugees to repatriate. They should also be able to make an informed decision based on accurate information about the country of origin.

Domestic and regional courts have noted that refoulement of refugees is a violation of fundamental human rights. For example, in the Organisation Mondiale Contre la Torture and Association Internationale des Juristes Democrates, the Commission Internationale des Juristes (CIJ), and the Union Interafricaine des Droits de l'Homme v. Rwanda, October 1996, the African Commission on Human and Peoples' Rights in paragraph 33 stated that "There is ample evidence in this communication that groups of Burundian refugees have been expelled from Rwanda on the basis of their nationality. This constitutes a clear violation of Article 12(5) of the African Charter".[38] The African Commission on Human and Peoples' Rights found that Guinea violated Article 12(5), which prohibits the mass expulsion of non-nationals

[34] UNHCR, *Handbook on Voluntary Repatriation*, 10.

[35] *Ibid.*

[36] *Ibid.*

[37] See UNHCR, *Handbook for Emergencies*, 2nd Ed, Geneva, UNHCR, 2000, 453–454.

[38] Organisation mondiale contre la torture, Association Internationale des juristes démocrates, Commission Internationale des juristes, Union interafricaine des droits de l'Homme v. Rwanda, 27/89-46/90-49/91-99/93, African Commission on Human and Peoples' Rights, October 1996, available at: http://www.refworld.org/docid/51b6f4374.html (last visited 8 May 2014); Article 12(5) of the African Charter states that "The mass expulsion of non-nationals shall be prohibited. Mass expulsion shall be that which is aimed at national, racial, ethnic or religious groups".

and the right of non-refoulement in the 2004 case of Institute for Human Rights and Development in Africa (on behalf of Sierra Leonean refugees in Guinea) v. Guinea.[39]

In the March 1997 case of Haitian Centre for Human Rights et al. v. United States, the Inter-American Commission on Human Rights ruled that "The United States has breached the 'right to liberty' contained in Article 1 of the American Declaration with regard to Jeannette Gedeon, Dukens Luma, Fito Jean, the four interviewees at Guantanamo and unnamed Haitian Interdictees".[40] This was after the United States forcefully repatriated Haitian asylum seekers back to Haiti.

2.3 Return in Safety and Dignity

Return in safety and dignity is another principle of repatriation. It is provided for by the UNHCR Executive Conclusion No. 40 (XXXVI) 1985.[41] The 1969 OAU Convention makes reference to the notion of safe return.[42]

Furthermore, the 1992 UNHCR Discussion Note on Protection Aspects of Voluntary Repatriation provides that the return of refugees to their country of origin "must be carried out under conditions of safety and dignity".[43] The 2003 Tripartite Agreement also provides for voluntary repatriation in safety and dignity.[44]
According to the UNHCR Handbook, "return in safety" is defined as:

> Return which takes place under conditions of legal safety (such as amnesties or public assurances of personal safety, integrity, non-discrimination and freedom from fear of persecution or punishment upon return), physical security (including protection from armed attacks, and mine-free routes and if not mine-free then at least demarcated settlement sites), and material security (access to land or means of livelihood).[45]

---

[39]Institute for Human Rights and Development in Africa (on behalf of Sierra Leonean refugees in Guinea) v. Guinea, 249/02, African Commission on Human and Peoples' Rights, Dec. 2004, available at: http://www.refworld.org/docid/51b6fc794.html (last visited 8 May 2014).

[40]The Haitian Centre for Human Rights et al. v. United States, Case 10.675, 10.675, Inter-American Commission on Human Rights (IACHR), 13 Mar. 1997, available at: http://www.refworld.org/docid/3ae6b71b8.html (last visited 8 May 2014).

[41]"(a) The basic rights of persons to return voluntarily to the country of origin is reaffirmed and it is urged that international cooperation be aimed at achieving this solution and should be further developed; (b) The repatriation of refugees should only take place at their freely expressed wish; the voluntary and individual character of repatriation of refugees and the need for it to be carried out under conditions of absolute safety, preferably to the place of residence of the refugee in his country of origin, should always be respected".

[42]Article V(2) states that "the country of asylum, in collaboration with the country of origin, shall make adequate arrangements for the safe return of refugees who request repatriation".

[43]UNHCR, Discussion Note on Protection Aspects of Voluntary Repatriation, EC/1992/SCP/CRP.3, 1992, available at: http://www.refworld.org/docid/3ae68cd314.html (last visited 1 Jun 2014).

[44]Article 4, Clause 1 states that "The Republic of Rwanda shall take all measures necessary to ensure that the refugees" voluntary repatriation takes place in safety and dignity and to enhance conditions conducive to their reintegration'.

[45]UNHCR, *Handbook on Voluntary Repatriation*, 11.

"Return with dignity" is explained as:

> The concept of dignity is less self-evident than that of safety. The dictionary definition of 'dignity' contains elements of 'serious, composed, worthy of honour and respect'. In practice, elements must include that refugees are not manhandled; that they can return unconditionally and that if they are returning spontaneously they can do so at their own pace; that they are not arbitrarily separated from family members; and that they are treated with respect and full acceptance by their national authorities, including the full restoration of their rights.[46]

According to Goodwin-Gill and McAdam,

> The right of safe and free return is important in refugee protection. The countries of origin have responsibility of ensuring that refugees are able to return safely and freely. In Security Council Resolution 1203 (1998), the Security Council reaffirmed the right of refugees return and the right of humanitarian organizations to access. The right of 'safe and free' return has also been emphatically repeated in later resolutions, such as resolutions 1239 and 1244 (1999), and in those adopted in respect of East Timor.[47]

2.4 Cessation Clause of Refugee Status

The UNHCR Executive Conclusion No. 40 (XXXVI) 1985 provides for the principle of ceasing of causes for flight.[48] According to this, voluntary repatriation should take place after the United Nations and States directly concerned have assessed that the causes of flight for refugees have ceased to exist. The UNHCR Handbook points out the role of the country of origin in addressing the root causes of flight.[49]

Refugee law provides grounds for ending refugee status because the causes for flight have ceased to exist. This is referred to as the cessation clause. The cessation clause in the 1951 Convention defines the situations in which the refugee status

[46] *Ibid.*

[47] See Goodwin-Gill and McAdam, The Refugee in International Law, 6.

[48] "(c) The aspect of causes is critical to the issue of solution and international efforts should also be directed to the removal of the causes of refugee movements. Further attention should be given to the causes and prevention of such movements, including the co-ordination of efforts currently being pursued by the international community and in particular within the United Nations. An essential condition for the prevention of refugee flows is sufficient political will by the States directly concerned to address the causes which are at the origin of refugee movements".

[49] "(e) The country of origin should seek lasting solutions to refugee problems, inter alia by assuming responsibility for the elimination of root causes of refugee flows and the creation of conditions conducive to voluntary return and reintegration. It should provide full support to the efforts of UNHCR and other actors to the same end".

ends.[50] The 1969 OAU Convention also provides for a cessation clause.[51] Domestically, the 2006 Uganda Refugees Act similarly makes reference to the cessation clause. Section 6 is titled "Cessation of Refugee Status". It provides that the person shall cease to be a refugee if the circumstances in connection with which that person was recognized as a refugee have ceased to exist. The Act also provides other circumstances under which a person may cease to be a refugee.

In 2011, the UNHCR established the Comprehensive Strategy for the Rwandan Refugee Situation to bring the Rwandan refugee situation to a proper closure.[52] According to the UNHCR strategy, the strategy comprised four components: (i) enhancing the promotion of voluntary repatriation and the reintegration of refugees in Rwanda; (ii) pursuing opportunities for local integration or alternative legal status in countries of asylum; (iii) continuing to meet the needs of those individuals unable to return to their country of origin for protection-related reasons; and (iv) elaborating a common schedule leading to the cessation of refugee status, foreseen to commence as of 3I December 2011.[53] However, this recommendation did not apply to Rwandan refugees who fled after 1998.

The cessation clause, when invoked, puts an end to the international protection provided to a specific group of refugees. This provision strips the targeted individuals of their refugee status and forces them to return to their country of origin. The comprehensive strategy targets refugees who fled between 1959 and 1998. Unlike refugee flows from Rwanda after 1998, the abovementioned period shares the character of group or large-scale forced population movements as a result of armed conflict, events seriously disturbing the public order, and/or the presence of a consistent pattern of mass violations of human rights, including genocide.[54] In 1959 and the early 1960s, Rwandans fled because of the mass killings and violence that targeted the Tutsi. The majority of these refugees returned to Rwanda in and after 1994. The other caseload of refugees includes the Hutu who fled the civil war in the early 1990s, the genocide in 1994, and the insecurity that followed up to 1998. It is asserted that all these conditions have since stopped and now "Rwanda enjoys an essential level of peace, security, reconciliation, democracy and human rights".[55]

---

[50] Article 1(C)(5) states: "He can no longer, because the circumstances in connection with which he has been recognized as a refugee have ceased to exist, continue to refuse to avail himself of the protection of the country of his nationality".

[51] Article 1(4)(e) states: "He can no longer, because the circumstances in connection with which he was recognized as a refugee have ceased to exist, continue to refuse to avail himself of the protection of the country of his nationality".

[52] UNHCR, Implementation of the Comprehensive Strategy for the Rwandan Refugee Situation, Including UNHCR'sRecommendation on the Applicability of the 'Ceased Circumstances' Cessation Clauses, 31 Dec. 2011, 1.

[53] *Ibid.*

[54] *Ibid*, 6.

[55] *Ibid.*

3 The Practice of Rwandan Refugee Repatriation

3.1 Right to Return to One's Country

The repatriation of Rwandan refugees in Uganda since 2003 is an attempt to fulfil and respect their fundamental right to return. Although refugee and human rights law provides for return that is voluntary and made out of free will, Rwandan refugees are forced to return.[56] The majority of Rwandans continue to resist return.[57] In fact, a majority have questioned why they were forced to exercise their right to return[58] and argue that exercising one's right should be voluntary.[59] The right to return is meaningless in a situation where Rwandans are forced to return against their will.

Furthermore, as Coles has argued above, the right to return does not exist in circumstances where there are grave human rights violations.[60] Human rights organizations have reported that Rwanda continues to undermine freedom of speech and expression by silencing those critical of the regime. There are cases of arbitrary detention, ill treatment, and torture.[61] Amnesty International has reported cases of enforced disappearances, unlawful killings, harassment of opposition parties, unfair trials, and violations of freedoms of association, expression, and assembly.[62]

3.2 Principle of Non-refoulement

A close assessment of the Rwandan refugee repatriation reveals that the principle of non-refoulement has been undermined, as shown below. Since 2009, Rwandan

[56]See Amnesty International, *Memorandum to the Government of Uganda about the Cessation of Refugee Protection for Rwandans, Index: AFR 59/021/2011*, London, Amnesty International Publications, 2011; F. Ahimbisibwe, "The Host State and Refugee Security in Uganda: The Case of Rwandan Refugees in Nakivale Settlement", doctoral dissertation, Unpublished, Mbarara, Mbarara University of Science and Technology, 2015; C. Karooma, "Rwandan Refugees and their Attitudes to Repatriation, 1994–2012", doctoral dissertation, unpublished, Mbarara, Mbarara University of Science and Technology, 2013; and International Refugee Rights Initiative, Refugee Law Project and Social Science Research Council, *A Dangerous Impasse: Rwandan Refugees in Uganda*, 9 June 2010, 8, available at: https://refugeelawproject.org/files/briefing_papers/10_06_28_A_Dangerous_Impasse,Rwandan_Refugees_in_Uganda.pdf (last visited 15 Nov 2016).

[57]*Ibid.*

[58]Interviews and FGDs with Rwandan refugees in Uganda, June–Aug. 2010, June–Aug. 2016, and Jan. 2018.

[59]*Ibid.*

[60]Coles, *Voluntary Repatriation.*

[61]Human Rights Watch, *World Report 2019: Rwandan Events of 2018*, 2019, available at https://www.hrw.org/world-report/2019/country-chapters/rwanda (last visited 15 Feb. 2019).

[62]Amnesty International, *Rwanda 2017/2018*, 2018, available at https://www.amnesty.org/en/countries/africa/rwanda/report-rwanda/ (last visited 15 Feb. 2019).

refugees have been banned from cultivation, and their food rations were reduced.[63] They have been issued with several deadlines to return in 2009, 2011, and 2013.[64] The issuing of deadlines against refugees is tantamount to refoulement because refugees are put in a situation where they have to make a decision to return for fear of being arrested and imprisoned. The refugees are forced to make a decision to return even when they are not willing to return or have well-founded of persecution. Although Uganda has not been strict with these deadlines, a number of Rwandan refugees chose to return out of fear of the consequences arising from not returning. Also, in October 2007 and July 2010, Uganda forcefully returned Rwandan refugees and asylum seekers, contrary to the principle of non-refoulement.[65]

Furthermore, Rwandan refugees also faced the possibility of invocation of the cessation of refugee status, as recommended by UNHCR in December 2011.[66] It is very clear that the threats of declaration and implementation of the cessation clause violate refugee rights and undermine the voluntary nature of repatriation. In circumstances where refugees are not given optional durable solutions like local integration or resettlement, the invocation of cessation of refugee status means forced repatriation to Rwanda.[67]

Despite the legal provisions and case law on non-refoulement, Uganda has violated this principle.[68] It has forcefully returned Rwandan refugees and asylum seekers to their country of origin where they have a well-founded fear of being persecuted.

[63]F. Ahimbisibwe, The Host State; C. Karooma, Rwandan Refugees; B. Harrell-Bond, Cessation clause Uganda style, keynote speech delivered at the Northwestern University Conference on Human Rights, 23 January, Working Paper 11-001, 2011; Amnesty International, Memorandum to the Government of Uganda; Human Rights Overlooked in Mass Repatriation Report,Amnesty International, 14 Jan. 1997, available at: https://www.essex.ac.uk/armedcon/story_id/Human%20Rights%20Overlooked%20in%20Mass%20Repatriation.pdf (last visited 12 Nov 2012); International Refugee Rights Initiative Refugee Law Project, and Social Science Research Council, A Dangerous Impasse, 8.

[64]*Ibid.*

[65]*Ibid.*

[66]The cessation of refugee status originally set for implementation by 30 June 2013 was suspended by the Uganda government till further notice. After the 2016 UNHCR executive committee meeting in Geneva, the implementation of the cessation clause was scheduled for 31 Dec. 2017 and later postponed indefinitely.

[67]F. Ahimbisibwe, *The Host State*; Amnesty International, *Memorandum to the Government of Uganda*; interview with a protection officer, Centre for Refugee Rights, Mbarara on 1 July 2016.

[68]See Amnesty International, Memorandum to the Government of Uganda; Amnesty International, Rwanda Protecting Their Rights; and Human Rights First, A Decade of Unrest: Unrecognized Rwandan Refugees in Uganda and the Future of Refugee Protection in the Great Lakes (2004), available at: https://www.humanrightsfirst.org/wpcontent/uploads/pdf/Decade-of-Unrest.pdf (last visited 30 June 2013).

3.3 Return in Safety and Dignity

The principle of return in safety and dignity may have been violated in the Rwandan refugee repatriation. I shall make an assessment of the present-day Rwanda and show that the legal, physical, and material security of returnees may not be guaranteed. I will focus on two elements: human rights and reconciliation. In this section, I argue that although bureaucratic/technocratic governance in Rwanda is good, with obvious achievements in socioeconomic indicators, there is scholarly consensus on the fact that its political governance is deeply flawed. This is consistently mentioned by refugees and recyclers, and this is the main reason why they refuse to return to Rwanda, despite progress in socioeconomic development.

The UNHCR in its Comprehensive Strategy for the Rwandan Refugee Situation[69] argued that the level of human rights protection has improved greatly. They point to the adoption of the 2003 Constitution, the accession to international human rights treaties, the establishment of the National Human Rights Commission, free and fair elections, the abolition of the death penalty, and the promotion of women's rights.

However, observers have argued that Rwanda continues to violate human rights both at home and abroad. Filip Reyntjens has focused on the violations of the right to life by Rwanda for the periods, 1994–1996 (in Rwanda), 1996–1997 (in Zaire/DRC), 1997–1998, and later (in Rwanda). He further makes an assessment of systematic human rights violations, including torture, murder, forced displacement, arrests and detentions, and restrictions on the freedoms of the press, expression, assembly, and association.[70]

These views are also shared by human rights organizations and the United Nations. For example, the 2009 United Nations Human Rights Committee Report[71] on Rwanda reported:

> cases of enforced disappearances and summary or arbitrary executions in Rwanda and [...] the impunity apparently enjoyed by the police forces responsible for such violations, the large number of persons, including women and children, reported to have been killed from 1994 onwards in the course of operations of the Rwandan Patriotic Front.[72]

---

[69]UNHCR, "Implementation of the Comprehensive Strategy for the Rwandan Refugee Situation".

[70]See F. Reyntjens, *Political Governance in Post-genocide Rwanda*, New York, Cambridge University Press, 2013, 98–123.

[71]F. Reyntjens notes that the United Nations Human Rights Committee lauds Rwanda for the abolition of the death penalty and for the representation of women in its parliament. These are the issues that UNHCR mentions in its Comprehensive Strategy for the Rwandan Refugee Situation as fundamental changes in Rwanda to justify the cessation of refugee status.

[72]United Nations General Assembly, Official Records, Report of the Human Rights Committee, Volume 1, A/64/40, 2009 quoted from F. Reyntjens, *Political Governance*, 121.

Leading human rights organizations like Amnesty International and Human Rights Watch have continuously released reports accusing Rwanda of torture, unresolved disappearances, illegal detentions, the harassment of opposition parties, restrictions on the media and civil society, and unlawful killings.[73]

The other element in assessing the durability and stability of changes in Rwanda is reconciliation. Rwanda has been credited for moving very well on the road towards reconciliation. The Rwandan government enacted a law that criminalizes ethnicity ("There are no longer Tutsi and Hutu, we are all Rwandans now") with the aim of promoting unity and patriotism. However, a close look at the Rwandan society reveals very serious flaws in the reconciliation process. Susan Thomson shares her findings on one aspect of reconciliation and looks at "re-education through 'Ingando'".[74] She argues and this was her main finding among ordinary Rwandans that:

> Ingando does little to reeducate confessed genocidaires on how to reconcile with family, friends and neighbors. Instead of promoting a sense of national unity and reconciliation, it teaches these men, the majority of whom are ethnic Hutu, to remain silent and not question the RPF's vision for creating peace and security for all Rwandans. For us, Ingando was an alienating, oppressive, and sometimes humiliating experience that worked hard to silence all forms of dissent—something that may, paradoxically, crystallize and create stronger dissent in the future.[75]

The Ingando re-education program has been hailed by the Rwandan government as a useful tool that has helped the Hutu learn to tell the truth, learn the "objective history" of Rwanda and be "good citizens". In the process of re-education, history was changed to suit the Tutsi and genocide survivors, and make Hutu collectively guilty. In the end, most participants saw Ingando not as a means for reconciliation and unity but as "efforts to exercise social control over adult Hutu men".[76]

The other aspect of reconciliation includes the Gacaca courts[77] meant for promoting justice and reconciliation. Instead, Gacaca promoted injustice and hatred, and became a tool for settling personal grievances.[78] This view was echoed in a research

---

[73]See Amnesty International's and Human Rights Watch's Annual Reports (2003–2019) on the status of human rights, justice, and democracy in Rwanda.

[74]Ingando camps are Rwandan political and civic re-education and indoctrination camps. These camps were created by the ruling party of Rwanda, the Rwandan Patriotic Front (RPF). Ingando camp participants are required to wear military uniforms, live together, and participate in shared activities. The aims are to reduce fear and suspicion and encourage reconciliation between genocide survivors and those whose family members perpetrated the genocide. Also, the Ingando trainings serve to reduce the distance between some segments of the Rwandan population and the government.

[75]See S. Thomson, Reeducation for Reconciliation: Participant Observations on Ingando, in S. Scott, Waldorf (eds.), Remaking Rwanda: State Building and Human Rights after Mass Violence, Madison and London, The University of Wisconsin Press, 2011, 332.

[76]*Ibid*, 338.

[77]Gacaca is a neo-traditional approach of transitional justice established in 2002 to try cases in post-genocide Rwanda. The Gacaca courts closed on 18 June 2012. However, their legacy continues to haunt Rwandan refugees.

[78]See B. Ingelaere, *Inside Rwanda's Gacaca Courts: Searching Justice After Genocide*, Madison, University of Wisconsin Press, 2016; F. Reyntjens, *Political Governance in Post Genocide Rwanda*;

report titled "A Dangerous Impasse: Rwandan Refugees in Uganda" by International Refugee Rights Initiative, Refugee Law Project and Social Science Research Council. The Report states that "Rather than being a tool for promoting justice, the Gacaca courts were seen…to target only Hutus; to be a tool for people who want to take revenge or gain access to property; and as an arm of a repressive government".[79] Human Rights Watch agrees with this view and argues that "despite the contribution of Gacaca in reconciling people, the situation is far from one of non-discrimination and freedom from fear of persecution".[80]

3.4 *Cessation Clause of Refugee Status*

As explained earlier, the principle of the ceasing of causes for flight exists under refugee law. However, this principle has been neglected and has not been given serious consideration and attention in the Rwandan repatriation. One fundamental question is whether the changes in Rwanda address the causes for flight. The majority of refugees that fled from 1959 to 1963, in 1973, and from 1994 to 1998 were recognized as refugees due to the violence, war, genocide, and massive human rights violations. In fact, the majority of refugees that fled these events were granted refugee status under Article 1(2) of the 1969 OAU Convention on a *prima facie* basis.

According to the UNHCR 2011 Comprehensive Strategy for the Rwandan Refugee Situation:

> Since the events of war, armed conflicts and generalized violence described above, Rwanda has undergone rapid, fundamental and crucially positive changes. The country has changed significantly since the 1994 genocide, and today enjoys an essential level of peace, security, reconciliation, democracy and human rights While various concerns continue to be raised by different actors, such as restricted space for political opposition in the country, the above positive developments are noteworthy.[81]

The UNHCR claims that:

> Reflecting these positive developments, and as noted earlier, the greatest part of the Rwandan refugee population had returned home as of the end of 1998.[82] From August 1994 to October 2002, some 3.1 million Rwandan refugees returned to their home country. Between October 2002, when UNHCR started promoting returns, and the end of November 2011, 150,519

Human Rights Watch, *Rwanda Justice Compromised: The Legacy of Rwanda's Community Based Courts*, New York, Human Rights Watch, 2011.

[79]International Refugee Rights Initiative, Refugee Law Project, and Social Science Research Council, *A Dangerous Impasse*, 25.

[80]See Human Rights Watch, *Law and Reality: Progress in Judicial Reform in Rwanda*, 2008, available at http://www.hrw.org/en/reports/2008/07/24/law-and-reality-0 (last visited 15 Oct. 2018).

[81]UNHCR, Implementation of the Comprehensive Strategy for the Rwandan Refugee Situation, 6, para. 28.

[82]The UNHCR does not admit that most of the returned refugees came by force from DRC and Tanzania. Their return was involuntary contrary to refugee and human rights law. Source? See F. Ahimbisibwe, *The Host State*.

refugees repatriated with the assistance of the Office including 6,855 assisted returns in 2011.[83]

However, observers challenge the position that Rwanda is democratizing, protects human rights, and has achieved reconciliation. They argue that although Rwanda has achieved bureaucratic governance, it has taken steps backward in the democratization process. Reyntjens has argued that:

> Ten years after the 1994 genocide, Rwanda is experiencing not democracy and reconciliation but dictatorship and exclusion. Although the government led by the Rwanda Patriotic Front has achieved rapid institutional reconstruction and relatively good bureaucratic governance, it has also concentrated power and wealth in the hands of a very small minority, practiced ethnic discrimination, eliminated every form of dissent, destroyed civil society, conducted a fundamentally flawed 'democratization' process, and massively violated human rights at home and abroad.[84]

He argues that these dynamics have led to structural violence which may lead to future acute violence.[85] Rwandans had previously fled the genocide and its aftermath but they now face structural violence[86] as evidenced by the flight of asylum seekers that continue to leave Rwanda on a daily basis. The majority of Rwandan refugees are reluctant to return home.

Timothy Longman points out the undemocratic nature of Rwanda's transition. He argues that

> In the post-genocide era, Rwanda has made a transition from one type of authoritarian regime to another. The RPF regime has systematically intimidated, co-opted and suppressed civil society, so that Rwanda today lacks independent social organizations capable of articulating most public interests. The regime tolerates very little public criticism, strictly limiting freedoms of speech, press and association.[87]

He further notes that "Political parties are restricted by arresting their leaders, banning their activities and intimidated, while constraints and manipulation of the electoral process have prevented elections from being truly free and fair".[88] For example, during the 2017 presidential elections, Frank Habineza (Democratic Green Party of Rwanda, DGPR), and an independent candidate, Philippe Mpayimana, experienced harassment, threats, and intimidation ahead of the election.[89] The other potential candidates, Diana Rwigara and Gilbert Mwenedata, were not registered by the National

[83] *Ibid*, 6, para. 29.

[84] See F. Reyntjens, "Rwanda Ten Years on: From Genocide to Dictatorship", *African Affairs* 103, 177, 2004.

[85] *Ibid*.

[86] By looking at the history of violence in Rwanda, structural violence can easily turn into war and erupt any time in future.

[87] T. Longman, "Limitations to Political Reform: The Undemocratic Nature of Transition in Rwanda" in S. Scott, L. Waldorf (eds.), *Remaking Rwanda: State Building and Human Rights After Mass Violence*, Wisconsin, University of Wisconsin Press, 2011, 26–27.

[88] *Ibid*, 27.

[89] Human Rights Watch, World Report 2018: Rwandan Events of 2017, 2018, available at https://www.hrw.org/world-report/2018/country-chapters/rwanda (last visited 16 Feb. 2019).

Electoral Commission, claiming that many of the signatures supporting their candidacy were invalid. Another potential candidate, Thomas Nahimana, was denied access to Rwanda in January, when he tried to enter the country from France.[90]

It is interesting to note that all the refugee respondents in Nakivale shared these views on Rwanda. They noted that dictatorship, human rights violations, and other reasons continue to be impediments to repatriation and generate new asylum seekers.[91]

The same view is shared by the International Refugee Rights Initiative, Refugee Law Project, and Social Science Research Council, who argue that "while the genocide and its immediate aftermath might have been the original cause of flight for many, ongoing political repression in Rwanda is not only preventing many refugees from returning, but is generating new refugees".[92] Similar views are shared by other sources.[93]

It can be argued that the end of war and genocide in Rwanda has created structural violence (in the form of human rights violations, dictatorship, and political repression) that pose a threat to individual refugees. The above observations suggest that there is no fundamental change in Rwanda to justify repatriation.

4 Conclusion

This article has argued that although legal principles and norms exist on voluntary repatriation, they have been undermined and violated in the case of the repatriation of Rwandan refugees living in Uganda. Our finding is that there exists a gap between the legal principles and the practice of repatriation. The current political, socioeconomic circumstances in Rwanda do not constitute a fundamental change to justify repatriation and the cessation of refugee status for Rwandan refugees.

The insights in this article have methodological and policy implications. From a methodological perspective, more work needs to be done to identify and explore the gap between the official narrative of the governments of Uganda and Rwanda and the UNHCR and what actually takes place in actual practice with regard to refugee protection. Most times, the official UNHCR narrative supports the view that

---

[90] *Ibid.*

[91] Focus Group Discussion, Sangano Base Camp, Nakivale on 24 June 2010; Focus Group Discussion, Rubondo zone, Nakivale settlement on 12 July 2016; Interviews with Rwandan refugees, Nakivale and Oruchinga settlements, Jan. 2018.

[92] See International Refugee Rights Initiative, Refugee Law Project, and Social Science Research Council, *A Dangerous Impasse*, 2.

[93] See Fahamu Refugee Programme, *Rwanda: Cessation of Refugee Status is Unwarranted—Memo of Fact and Law*, Sept. 2011, available at: http://www.refugeelegalaidinformation.org/sites/srlan/files/fileuploads/Memo%20of%20Fact%20and%20Law.pdf (last visited 27 Jan. 2014); J. G. Cooke, Center for Strategic and International Studies, *Rwanda: Assessing Risks to Security*, June 2011, available at: https://csis-prod.s3.amazonaws.com/s3fs-public/legacy_files/files/publication/110623_Cooke_Rwanda_Web.pdf (last visited 13 June 2017).

repatriation is voluntary and done in accordance with the law. This narrative claims that States, the UNHCR, and NGOs fulfil their legal and moral obligations in the repatriation process, and more generally provide refugee protection. The findings in this article do not correspond with the view that repatriation was done legally. It is important to analyse the theory-practice gap and find ways to bridge this gap. This would help improve refugee protection by States.

From a policy point of view, the insights in this article call for an understanding of how and why policies and decisions are made by States with regard to (in-) voluntary repatriation and refugee protection. States' decisions and policies on refugee status definition and determination are influenced by political, security, and diplomatic interests.[94] The decision to forcefully repatriate Rwandan refugees was influenced by, among others, regional security interests, diplomatic relations between the two countries, and the view that the refugees no longer have any reasons for being refugees because their country is now "stable and peaceful". In the end, the interests of States prevailed at the expense of refugee protection. This example of Rwandan involuntary repatriation calls for the need to understand States' interests and how best to engage them. This approach of engaging States will help in designing and implementing policies and decisions that cater to their interests while at the same time ensuring that refugees are protected.

References

F. Ahimbisibwe, *Repatriation as A Durable Solution to the Rwandese Refugee Problem in Uganda* (Saarbrucken, VDM Verlag Publishers, 2011)

F. Ahimbisibwe, The Host State and Refugee Security in Uganda: The Case of Rwandan Refugees in Nakivale Settlement, Doctoral Dissertation, Unpublished (Mbarara, Mbarara University of Science and Technology, 2015)

F. Ahimbisibwe, Rwandan Refugee Rights in Uganda: Analysis of Law and Practice. *US–China Law Rev.* **13**(12), 879 (2016)

Amnesty International, *Memorandum to the Government of Uganda*; *Human Rights Overlooked in Mass Repatriation Report* (Amnesty International, 14 Jan. 1997). http://www.essex.ac.uk/armedcon/story_id/Human%20Rights%20Overlooked%20in%20Mass%20Repatriation.pdf (last visited 12 Nov 2012)

Amnesty International, *Great Lakes Region Still in Need of Protection: Repatriation, Refoulement and Safety of Refugees and the Internally Displaced*, London, International Secretariat, 24 Jan. 1997

Amnesty International, *Rwanda Protecting Their Rights: Rwandese Refugees in the Great Lakes Region* (2004). http://www.amnesty.org/en/library/asset/AFR47/016/2004/en/f22d9445-d556-11dd-bb241fb85fe8fa05/afr470162004en.pdf (last visited 4 Apr. 2012)

Amnesty International, *Memorandum to the Government of Uganda about the Cessation of Refugee Protection for Rwandans, Index: AFR 59/021/2011* (London, Amnesty International Publications, 2011)

V. Chetail, Voluntary Repatriation in Public International: Concepts and Contents. *Refug. Surv. Q.* **23**(3), 26 (2004)

[94]See F. Ahimbisibwe, "Rwandan Refugee Rights in Uganda: Analysis of Law and Practice", *US-China Law Review*, 13(12), 2016, 879.

G.J.L. Coles, Voluntary Repatriation: A Background Study, Geneva, UNHCR, 1985, 94 quoted by N. Yasmin, Between a Rock and Hard Place? A Legal Analysis of the Voluntary Repatriation of Guatemalan Refugees. *Refug. Surv. Q.* **23**(3), 83 (2004)

J.G. Cooke, *Rwanda: Assessing Risks to Security*, Center for Strategic and International Studies, June 2011, available at: https://csis-prod.s3.amazonaws.com/s3fs-public/legacy_files/files/publication/110623_Cooke_Rwanda_Web.pdf (last visited 13 June 2017)

Fahamu Refugee Programme, Rwanda: Cessation of Refugee Status is Unwarranted—Memo of Fact and Law, Sept. 2011, available at: https://www.refugeelegalaidinformation.org/sites/srlan/files/fileuploads/Memo%20of%20Fact%20and%20Law.pdf (last visited 27 Jan. 2014)

G.S. Goodwin-Gill, J. McAdam, *The Refugee in International Law*, 3rd edn. (Oxford, Oxford University Press, 2007)

B. Harrell-Bond, *Cessation clause Uganda style*, keynote speech delivered at the Northwestern University Conference on Human Rights, 23 January, Working Paper 11-001, 2011

Human Rights First, *A Decade of Unrest: Unrecognized Rwandan Refugees in Uganda and the Future of Refugee Protection in the Great Lakes* (2004). http://www.humanrightsfirst.org/wp-content/uploads/pdf/Decade-of-Unrest.pdf (last visited 30 June 2013)

Human Rights Watch, "Uncertain Refuge: International Failures to Protect Refugees", New York, Human Rights Watch, Apr. 1997, available at: https://www.hrw.org/report/1997/04/01/uncertain-refuge/international-failures-protect-refugees, (last visited 12 June 2017) quoted by Y. Kathirgamathamby, "Voluntary Repatriation as a Durable Solution"

Human Rights Watch, *Law and Reality: Progress in Judicial Reform in Rwanda*, 2008, available at: https://www.hrw.org/en/reports/2008/07/24/law-and-reality-0 (last visited 15 Oct. 2018)

Human Rights Watch, Rwanda Justice Compromised: The Legacy of Rwanda's Community Based Courts (New York, Human Rights Watch, 2011)

Human Rights Watch, *World Report 2019: Rwandan Events of 2018, 2019,* available at https://www.hrw.org/world-report/2019/country-chapters/rwanda (last visited 15 Feb. 2019)

B. Ingelaere, *Inside Rwanda's Gacaca Courts: Searching Justice After Genocide* (Madison, University of Wisconsin Press, 2016)

International Refugee Rights Initiative, Refugee law project and social science research council, a dangerous impasse: Rwandan refugees in Uganda, 9 June 2010, p. 8. https://refugeelawproject.org/files/briefing_papers/10_06_28_A_Dangerous_Impasse,Rwandan_Refugees_in_Uganda.pdf (last visited 15 Nov 2016)

C. Karooma, Preliminary Observations from the Field: Rwandan Refugees Perceptions of "Voluntary" Repatriation from Uganda.*Oxf. Monit. Forced Migr.* **3**(2) (2013a)

C. Karooma, Rwandan Refugees and their Attitudes to Repatriation, 1994–2012, doctoral dissertation, unpublished (Mbarara, Mbarara University of Science and Technology, 2013b)

C. Karooma, Reluctant to Return? The Primacy of Social Networks in the Repatriation of Rwandan Refugees in Uganda, *Working Paper Series No. 103,* Refugee Studies Centre, University of Oxford, Aug. 2014

Y. Kathirgamathamby, Voluntary Repatriation as a Durable Solution to Sri Lankan Refugees in India: A Critical Analysis with Legal Perspective, in *Proceedings of 8th International Research Conference*, KDU, Nov. 2015, p. 191

N.K. Lindsey, Bringing Rwandan Refugees "Home": The Cessation Clause, Statelessness, and Forced Repatriation. *Int. J. Refug. Law* **29**(3), 417–437 (2017)

T. Longman, 'Limitations to Political Reform: The Undemocratic Nature of Transition in Rwanda' in S. Scott and L. Waldorf (eds.), *Remaking Rwanda: State Building and Human Rights After Mass Violence* (Wisconsin, University of Wisconsin Press, 2011), pp. 26–27

Office of Prime Minister (OPM) and UNHCR, Uganda Comprehensive Refugee Response Portal, 2018, available at: https://ugandarefugees.org/en/country/uga/ (last visited 28 Aug 2018)

F. Reyntjens, Rwanda Ten Years on: From Genocide to Dictatorship. *African Affairs* **103**, 177 (2004)

F. Reyntjens, *Political Governance in Post-genocide Rwanda* (New York, Cambridge University Press, 2013), pp. 98–123

S. Thomson, Reeducation for Reconciliation: Participant Observations on Ingando, in *Remaking Rwanda: State Building and Human Rights after Mass Violence*, S. Scott and Waldorf (eds.) (Madison and London, The University of Wisconsin Press, 2011), p. 332
UNHCR, Discussion Note on Protection Aspects of Voluntary Repatriation, EC/1992/SCP/CRP.3, 1992, available at: https://www.refworld.org/docid/3ae68cd314.html (last visited 1 Jun 2014)
UNHCR, *Handbook on Voluntary Repatriation: International Protection*, Geneva, UNHCR, 1996
UNHCR, *Handbook for Emergencies*, 2nd edn., Geneva, UNHCR, 2000, 453–454
UNHCR, Implementation of the Comprehensive Strategy for the Rwandan Refugee Situation, Including UNHCR's Recommendation on the Applicability of the "Ceased Circumstances" Cessation Clauses, 1, 31 Dec. 2011
UNHCR, *Global Trends: Forced Displacement in 2017*, Geneva, UNHCR, 2018, 3, available at: https://www.unhcr.org/globaltrends2017/ (last visited 19 June 2018)
B.E. Whitaker, Changing Priorities in Refugee Protection: The Rwandan Repatriation from Tanzania, in *Problems of Protection: The UNHCR, Refugees and Human Rights*, N. Steiner, M. Gibney, G. Loesher (eds.) (New York and London, Routledge, 2013), pp. 141–154
N. Yasmin, Between a Rock and Hard Place? A Legal Analysis of the Voluntary Repatriation of Guatemalan Refugees. *Refug. Surv. Q.* 23(3), 83, 2004

Renouncing Nationality to Avoid Repatriation: A Perspective from the Convention on the Reduction of Statelessness

Hajime Akiyama and Osamu Arakaki

1 Introduction

A variety of writings about fears of the forced repatriation of Rwandan "refugees"[1] in host states refer to the 1951 Convention related to the Status of Refugees (1951 Convention), in particular, the cessation clause.[2] In contrast, few of them deal with the 1954 Convention on the Status of Stateless Persons (1954 Convention) and the 1961 Convention on Reduction of Statelessness (1961 Convention)[3] when the topic is examined.[4]

Recently, it has often been stressed that nationality is a means to protect human rights and that statelessness should be avoided. For instance, Weissbrodt and Collins

[1]In this chapter, the term "refugees" refers to individuals of the following two categories. The first category is refugees under the terms of Article 1(A) (2) of the 1951 Convention related to the Status of Refugees (the 1951 Convention). The second category is former refugees whose refugee status has ceased in accordance with Article 1(C)(5) of the 1951 Convention but who are refusing return to their state of nationality.

[2]See for instance, K. O'Connor, "Repatriation: The Politics of (Re)-Constructing and Contesting Rwandan Citizenship", Working Paper Series No. 92, Refugee Studies Centre, University of Oxford, 2013; F. Ahimbisibwe, "The Politics of Repatriation: Rwandan Refugees in Uganda, 2003–2017", Working Paper/2017.09, ISSN 2294-8643, IOB, University of Antwerp, 2017, available at: https://www.uantwerpen.be/images/uantwerpen/container2673/files/Publications/WP/2017/wp-201709.pdf (last visited 9 June 2019).

[3]This chapter refers to the 1954 and 1961 Conventions as "statelessness conventions".

[4]The following is one of few pieces of literature that analyses the Rwandan refugees from the perspectives of statelessness and the statelessness convention. L. N. Kingston, "Bringing Rwandan Refugees 'Home': The Cessation Clause, Statelessness, and Forced Repatriation", *International Journal of Refugee Law*, 29(3), 2017, 417–437.

H. Akiyama
Tsukuba, Ibaraki, Japan

O. Arakaki
Tokyo, Japan

M. Yonekawa and A. Sugiki (eds.), *Repatriation, Insecurity, and Peace*,
https://doi.org/10.1007/978-981-15-2850-7_2

state that "[t]he human right not to be stateless, or the right to a nationality, is important because many states only allow their own nationals to exercise full civil, political, economic, and social rights within their territories".[5] In practice, states have promoted international norms to prevent statelessness. Essential norms are represented in the 1961 Convention, which aims to prevent statelessness by conferring a nationality by birth and by preventing the loss of nationality for those who already possess one. Although the value of norms to prevent statelessness has been promoted as a source of human rights, excessive deference to this claim could obscure the presence of a device found in the 1961 Convention which permits the renunciation of a nationality even if a person becomes stateless to avoid the perils of human rights violations caused by the state of nationality.

By shedding light on a number of normative and interpretative perspectives, this chapter enquires if the 1961 Convention offers a new avenue to ensure that Rwandans in a host state are not illegitimately repatriated.[6] Part Two of this chapter articulates the Rwandan situation in which nationality could operate as an instrument to help re-construct the state, causing a risk of repatriation, and consequently, human rights violations upon return. Part Three offers an overview of increasing concerns about the norms to prevent statelessness in international law. Part Four illuminates a provision for renouncing nationality under the 1961 Convention which allows statelessness for some persons in exceptional cases. Part Five elaborates on the challenges of applying the provision to allow for renunciation of nationality to the Rwandan case.

2 Rwandan Case: Repatriation and Nationality

The government of Rwanda has actively encouraged the repatriation of refugees in neighbouring states. In 2002 and 2003, the government of Rwanda and the United Nations High Commissioner for Refugees (UNHCR) concluded the Tripartite Agreement with some governments including Uganda for the voluntary

---

[5]D. Weissbrodt & C. Collins, "The Human Rights of Stateless Persons", *Human Rights Quarterly*, 28, 2006, 245–276, 248.

[6]In this chapter, illegitimate repatriation implies repatriation to Rwanda after an application of the cessation clause (Article 1(C)(5) and (6) of the 1951 Convention) which does not fully consider the following factors for cessation of refugee status. Firstly, for application of the cessation clause, there must be evidence which shows not only a substantial political transformation of Rwanda in a durable sense but also the re-establishment of a relationship with the state to resume protection. Secondly, it is necessary to confirm the presence of a system and procedure to examine the circumstances of each refugee, not the Rwandan national group as a whole, since a risk of being persecuted must be specific to the individual. See the relevant argument in J. Hathaway & M. Foster, *The Law of Refugee Status*, 2nd ed., Cambridge, Cambridge University Press, 2014, 476–494.

repatriation of refugees to Rwanda.[7] In 2009, UNHCR promoted voluntary repatriation of refugees through the Comprehensive Strategy for the Rwandan Situation.[8] UNHCR has claimed that Rwanda has experienced significant positive changes and that there is peace and security there,[9] and it recommended the ending of refugee status by 2017.[10] However, the vast majority of refugees has remained in host states, refusing return.[11]

The immediate and direct evidence that host states use to determine to which state a refugee should be repatriated is nationality. In principle, the destination of repatriation for a refugee is the state of nationality which the refugee possesses. Among the functions of nationality which have been revealed through various research projects,[12] this part of the chapter illustrates that for sovereign states, nationality, as an instrument to achieve specific political goals in the context of repatriation, has been an instrument to exclude as well as to include certain individuals or groups of the population. As a recent example, nationality laws have been amended in the UK, the Netherlands, Turkey and so on as an instrument to disenfranchise a targeted portion of population

---

[7]UNHCR, "Uganda: Tripartite Agreement Signed on Return of Rwandans", 25 July 2003, available at: https://www.unhcr.org/news/briefing/2003/7/3f20fbe2c/uganda-tripartite-agreement-signed-return-rwandans.html (last visited 18 May 2019). For the Tripartite Agreement with other states, see the followings. UNHCR, "Rwanda: Voluntary Repatriation Campaign Begins", 7 Nov. 2003, available at: https://www.unhcr.org/news/briefing/2003/11/3fab7c95b/rwanda-voluntary-repatriation-campaign-begins.html (last visited 13 November 2019). The New Humanitarian, "Namibia-Rwanda: Kigali, Windhoek and UN Agency Sign Refugee Pact", 7 Nov. 2003, available at: https://reliefweb.int/report/rwanda/namibia-rwanda-kigali-windhoek-and-un-agency-sign-refugee-pact (last visited 13 Nov. 2019). The New Humanitarian, "Rwanda-Zimbabwe: Harare, Kigali and UNHCR Sign Tripartite Agreement", 10 Dec. 2003, available at: https://reliefweb.int/report/rwanda/rwanda-zimbabwe-harare-kigali-and-unhcr-sign-tripartite-agreement (last visited 13 Nov. 2019). U.S. Committee for Refugees and Immigrants, "U.S. Committee for Refugees World Refugee Survey 2004—Mozambique", 25 May 2004, available at: https://www.refworld.org/docid/40b459418.html (last visited 13 Nov. 2019).

[8]O'Connor, "Repatriation: The Politics of (Re)-Constructing and Contesting Rwandan Citizenship", 18; UNHCR, "Implementation of the Comprehensive Strategy for the Rwandan Refugee Situation, including UNHCR's Recommendations on the Applicability of the 'Ceased Circumstances' Cessation Clauses", 31 Dec. 2011, para. 28, available at: https://www.refworld.org/docid/4f33a1642.html (last visited 13 May 2019).

[9]UNHCR, "Implementation of the Comprehensive Strategy for the Rwandan Refugee Situation, including UNHCR's Recommendations on the Applicability of the 'Ceased Circumstances' Cessation Clauses", para. 28.

[10]UNHCR Rwanda, "Homepage", available at: https://www.unhcr.org/rw/ (last visited 13 May 2019). Caution must be exercised that asylum states such as Uganda evaluate the UNHCR's recommendation as evidence to justify cessation of refugee status and repatriation, given that decision-making is not mandated to UNHCR but to state authorities. Hathaway & Foster, *The Law of Refugee Status*, 485–486.

[11]O'Connor, "Repatriation: The Politics of (Re)-Constructing and Contesting Rwandan Citizenship", 19.

[12]For an overview of various functions of nationality, see A. Edwards, "The Meaning of Nationality in International Law in an Era of Human Rights: Procedural and Substantive Aspects", in A. Edwards and L. van Waas (eds.), *Nationality and Statelessness under International Law*. Cambridge, Cambridge University Press, 2014, 11–43. For the role of nationality in controlling individuals, see

in these states.[13] The African region is not an exception, and this type of function of nationality has been a common political phenomenon there. There are cases in which the nationality of political opponents has been withdrawn by nationality laws, excluding them from the category of "nationals". For example, the Citizenship Act of Zimbabwe was enacted in preparation for the presidential election of 2002.[14] This Act excluded specific ethnic groups and farmworkers with "non-Zimbabwean" surnames from Zimbabwean nationality, and it also threatened them.[15]

At the same time, the function of nationality to achieve specific governmental purposes by including certain groups of the population as nationals has also been confirmed in the Rwandan case. Following the Rwandan genocide in 1994, the government of Rwanda, led by the Rwandan Patriotic Front (RPF), engaged in an inclusion project. Considering the previous work on the repatriation of Rwandan refugees, which has revealed the motivations of the government of Rwanda in the project, this part of the chapter looks at two relevant factors. Firstly, as an attempt to remove the divisionism existing between Tutsi and Hutu, the government has promoted an idea of the unity of the state by creating a new ethnicity which shares 'Rwandanness'.[16] As the presence of refugees abroad contradicts this idea in essence, refugees are included in the plan as being part of the "nationals" which will constitute a new Rwanda.[17]

Secondly, there is the matter of a security concern which is rooted in the experience of Africa, including Rwanda itself. In recent history, the region has witnessed that refugees can transform themselves into military forces during the course of armed conflicts.[18] The government of Rwanda fears, in particular, that refugees outside the state may be intent on fomenting dissidence against the Rwandan government.[19] This

---

H. Akiyama, "Enforcement of Nationality and Human Insecurity: A Case Study on the Securitised Japanese Nationality of Koreans during the Colonial Era", *Journal of Human Security Studies*, 7(2), 2018, 79–94.

[13]O. Arakaki, "*Mukokuseki toha Nanika?: Mukokuseki Sakugen Johyaku no Gendaiteki Kadain-iokeru Sayo* [What is Statelessness?: Function of the 1961 Convention in Modern Issues]", in K. Koizumi (ed.), Nanmin wo Do Toraeruka? [How do We Conceive of "Refugees"?], Tokyo: Keio University Press, 2019, 200–203.

[14]Open Society Initiative, "The Africa Citizenship & Discrimination Audit Preparatory Meeting: Report of a Conference held in Dakar, Senegal on July 19–20, 2004", 2004, 5, available at: https://www.opensocietyfoundations.org/sites/default/files/audit_20040727.pdf (last visited 10 May 2019).

[15]*Ibid*, 5.

[16]S. Buckley-Zistel, "Dividing and Uniting: The Use of Citizenship Discourses in Conflict and Reconciliation in Rwanda", *Global Society*, 20(1), 2006, 101–113, 108.

[17]O'Connor, "Repatriation: The Politics of (Re)-Constructing and Contesting Rwandan Citizenship", 11; Kingston, "Bringing Rwandan Refugees 'Home': The Cessation Clause, Statelessness, and Forced Repatriation", 429–432. See also H. Hintjens, "Post-genocide identity politics in Rwanda", *Ethnicities*, 8(1), HAL Id: hal-00571890, 2008, 5–41.

[18]Human Rights First, "A Decade of Unrest: Unrecognized Rwandan Refugees in Uganda and the Future of Refugee Protection in the Great Lakes", 2004, 26, available at: https://www.humanrightsfirst.org/wp-content/uploads/pdf/Decade-of-Unrest.pdf (last visited 10 May 2019).

[19]*Ibid*, 26.

can be interpreted as a national security strategy for Rwanda to take back refugees who are considered to be potential rebels and to re-absorb them internally so that they may be under the control of and monitored by the authorities.

Under both cases, the government of Rwanda views refugees as an essential subject for the inclusion project. To achieve the purposes of this project, nationality plays a role as a critical instrument for the inclusion of refugees in Rwanda. Externally, the government of Rwanda advocates that host states repatriate individuals who hold its nationality, claiming that the safety of the state no longer justifies refugee status. For instance, President Kagame of Rwanda stated that "no *Rwandan* should be called a refugee since there is no longer any reason for this" (*sic*).[20] Internally, the government of Rwanda may compel returnees to act as part of the unified and inclusive nationals of Rwanda in accordance with its laws and norms which the government can shape.[21]

Possessing Rwandan nationality furthermore serves as an instrument to enhance the fears of refugees while they are in host states. When someone is recognised as a refugee, she or he acquires an identity document. However, when the refugee status ceases, the person does not possess the document anymore. Then, the government of Rwanda encourages persons whose refugee status has ceased to apply for Rwandan passports. In Zambia, Rwandan refugees believe that a Rwandan passport will be used to repatriate them.[22] When refugees apply for a Rwandan passport, they must reveal the names of their parents and relatives to the Rwandan embassy. Such information could jeopardise not only their families but also the refugees themselves if a threat to the families would also operate as a way to gain the agreement of the refugees on repatriation. Another significance of the practice is that the issuance of a passport provides host states with solid proof that there is a formal tie of nationality between a refugee and Rwanda.

The next parts of this chapter divert course and seek out a point of contact in the theory between the Rwandan case and the 1961 Convention, and it explores if any possible basis exists in the Convention through which Rwandans might avoid illegitimate repatriation.

---

[20]Cited in O'Connor, "Repatriation: The Politics of (Re)-Constructing and Contesting Rwandan Citizenship", 22.

[21]*Ibid.*, 23.

[22]M. Yonekawa, Ayatsurareru Nanmin: Seifu, Kokuren, NGO no Hazama de [*Manipulated Refugees: In between Governments, UN and NGOs*]. Tokyo: Chikuma Shobo, 2017, 249–50. Kingston, "Bringing Rwandan Refugees 'Home': The Cessation Clause, Statelessness, and Forced Repatriation", 433.

3 Prevention of Statelessness

The prevention of statelessness was addressed in international instruments in earnest after the end of World War II (WWII).[23] States have traditionally regarded nationality as a matter which falls within the authority of each state to decide for itself.[24] Thus, the presence of statelessness was an inevitable consequence. However, mass denationalisation became a serious problem before and during WWII,[25] and Europe witnessed a multitude of refugees and stateless persons after the end of WWII.[26] In this context, the prevention of statelessness was considered as a solution to the problem of displacement.[27] Article 15 of the Universal Declaration of Human Rights (UDHR), which was drafted and adopted not as a legally-binding instrument,[28] states that "[e]veryone has the right to a nationality". It continues that "[n]o one shall be arbitrarily deprived of his nationality". It is notable that the drafters of the UDHR paid greater attention to the inclusion of a prohibition of arbitrary deprivations of nationality than to a conceptualisation of the "right to a nationality", an expression which was inserted at the very last phase of the drafting process of the UDHR without substantial discussion as to what "the right to a nationality" meant.[29] This indicates that during the drafting process of the UDHR, one of the primary concerns of the discussion on nationality matters was the prohibition of arbitrary deprivations of nationality to prevent statelessness.[30]

---

[23] It must be noted that Articles 7, 8, 9, 13, 14, 15 and 16 of the 1930 Convention on Certain Questions Relating to the Conflict of Nationality Laws (1930 Convention) contained provisions to prevent statelessness. However, the convention attempted to prevent both dual nationality and statelessness, so prevention of statelessness was not the particular focus of the 1930 Convention.

[24] See Article 1 of the 1930 Convention.

[25] Regarding the denationalisation during WWII and concerns related to this issue after the end of WWII, see the following. G. G. Schram, "Article 15", in A. Eide, G. Alfredsson, G. Melander, L. A. Rehof & A. Rosas (eds.), *The Universal Declaration of Human Rights: A Commentary*, Drammen: Scandinavian University Press, 1992, 231.

[26] At the time, refugees and stateless persons were not separated, but they were regarded as the same category of people. O. Arakaki, "*Mukokusekisha no Nanminsei: Nyujirando no Jissen no Kentou wo Chuushinni* [Stateless Refugees: Practice of New Zealand as a Case Study of the Refugee Status Determination]", Sekaihougakkai, Sekaihounenpou[Yearbook of World Law], 31, 2012, 66–68.

[27] See UN, *A Study of Statelessness*, UN Doc. E/1112, E/1112/Add. 1, 1949, 12.

[28] However, some argue that Article 15 of the UDHR is recognised as a part of customary international law. J. P. Humphrey, "The Universal Declaration of Human Rights: Its History, Impact and Juridical Character", in B.G. Ramcharan (ed.), *Human Rights: Thirty Years after the Universal Declaration*, The Hague, Boston and London: MartinusNijhoff, 1979, 21.

[29] See UN General Assembly, "Draft International Declaration of Human Rights: Recapitulation of Amendments to Article 13 of the Draft Declaration (E/800)", UN Doc. A/C.3/286/Rev.1, 30 Oct. 1948. See also Commission on Human Rights, "Summary Record of the Fifty-Ninth Meeting, Held at Lake Success, New York, Friday, 4 June 1948, at 10.45 a.m.", UN Doc. E/CN.4/SR.59, 7, 10 June 1948.

[30] It must be noted that human rights perspectives were not the only contexts in which statelessness was concerned. In the orthodox conception of the international order, the presence of stateless persons contradicts the assumption that everyone should belong to a state as its member. A single nationality principle is one example. The Preamble to the 1930 Convention notes that "every person

At a later stage, several treaties began to focus on and provide for the prevention of statelessness. The 1961 Convention is the central pillar among them to prevent statelessness. It aims to reduce statelessness by ensuring that children acquire a nationality by birth and by preventing losses of nationality to those who already possess it.[31] Given the magnitude of risk that children can be stateless if they do not acquire a nationality in the first place, a right of a child to acquire a nationality has been articulated in Articles 24(3) of the International Covenant on Civil and Political Rights (ICCPR) and Article 9(1) of the Convention on the Rights of the Child. Although the provisions of these conventions do not explicitly mention the norm of preventing statelessness, this intention can be seen from the drafting process of these articles.[32] Furthermore, Article 7 of the Convention on the Elimination of All Forms of Discrimination Against Women provides for women's equal rights with men concerning the nationality of their children. Where a nationality is conferred by the *jus sanguinis* principle, women's equal right with men to transmit a nationality was covered by this article; so it functions to prevent statelessness in some cases. The development of international human rights law boosted the growth of norms relevant to the prevention of statelessness and activated discourse on the "right to a nationality".

4 Renuncitation of Nationality

The previous part of this chapter has explained the increasing concerns about the norm of preventing statelessness in international law. Despite growth of the norm, there is an international treaty that provides an exemption to allow a person to be stateless under the specific environment. This part focuses on a provision in the 1961 Convention relevant to the renunciation of nationality. Renunciation of nationality means severing the link of nationality between an individual and a state by her or his will.[33] In the process of developing norm for avoiding statelessness, Article 7(1)(a)

---

should have a nationality and should have one nationality only". See also R. Donner, *The Regulation of Nationality in International Law*, 2nd ed., New York: Transnational Publishers, 1994, 18. In this context, statelessness was viewed as an "anomaly". P. Weis, "The United Nations Convention on the Reduction of Statelessness, 1961", *International & Comparative Law Quarterly*, 11(4), 1962, 1073; UN, *A Study of Statelessness*, E/1112; E/1112/Add.1, V.1.1.

[31] For acquisition of a nationality by birth, see Articles 1 to 4 of the 1961 Convention. For prevention of the loss of a nationality, see Articles 5 to 10 of the convention.

[32] UN General Assembly, "Draft International Covenants on Human Rights, Report of the Third Committee", UN Doc. A/5365, para. 25 (17 Dec. 1962). Commission on Human Rights, "Report of the Working Group on a Draft Convention on the Rights of the Child", UN Doc. E/CN.4/L.1575, para. 14 (17 Feb. 1981).

[33] At the level of domestic law and practice in some states, renunciation has been allowed even if she or he becomes a stateless person. For example, Thomas Jolley renounced US citizenship at the US consulate in Toronto to avoid the draft to serve in the Vietnam War, and he made himself stateless though his action. In the early 1990s, a few hundreds Romanians filled for political asylum in

of the 1961 Convention was provided to prohibit a renunciation of nationality if it would cause statelessness as follows.

> If the law of a Contracting State permits renunciation of nationality, such renunciation shall not result in loss of nationality unless the person concerned possesses or acquires another nationality.

Definitely, this provision aims to avoid statelessness. However, the 1961 Convention also contains exemptions which make a person stateless.[34] One of them is Article 7(1)(b):

> The provisions of sub-paragraph (a) of this paragraph shall not apply where their application would be inconsistent with the principles stated in Articles 13 and 14 of the Universal Declaration of Human Rights approved on 10 December 1948 by the General Assembly of the United Nations.

Articles 13 and 14 of the UDHR provide for the right to freedom of movement and "the right to seek and to enjoy in other countries asylum from persecution". The plain reading of this exemption, in sense of its ordinary meaning, is that renunciation of nationality may be permitted even if it results in statelessness when possession of a nationality conflicts with principles concerning the right to freedom of movement and the right to seek and enjoy asylum.[35] The drafting history of the convention and what became Article 7(1)(b) underpins the understanding that respect for the principles of Articles 13 and 14 of the UDHR takes priority over the consequence that statelessness will occur. The idea for Article 7(1)(b) was motivated by an assertion from the delegate of the Holy See that for some individuals, statelessness could be more beneficial than possessing a particular nationality.[36] Through discussion with

---

Germany and renounced their Romanian citizenship, thereby instantly making themselves stateless. D. Weissbrodt, *The Human Rights of Non-citizens*, Oxford, Oxford University Press, 2008, 92.

[34]Concerning other exceptions for which the 1961 Convention allows a state party to render a person stateless, see, for instance, Article 7(4) (loss of nationality of a naturalised person spending an extended period abroad), Article 8(2)(b) (deprivation of nationality acquired by misrepresentation or fraud) and Article 8(3) (deprivation of nationality of a person acting in a manner seriously prejudicial to the vital interests of a state party that is inconsistently with her or his duty of loyalty to the state).

[35]Article 31 of the Vienna Convention on the Law of Treaties, which provides the general method to interpret treaties, states that "A treaty shall be interpreted in good faith in accordance with the ordinary meaning to be given to the terms of the treaty in their context and in the light of its object and purpose".

[36]UN General Assembly, "United Nations Conference on the Elimination or Reduction of Future Statelessness, Committee of the Whole, Summary Record of the Seventh Meeting Held at the Palais des Nations, Geneva, on Monday, 6 April 1959, at 3 p.m.", UN Doc. A/CONF.9/C.1/SR.7, 4, 24 Apr. 1961. The delegate submitted the proposal to insert the following prototype of Article 7(1)(b):

> The provisions of the preceding sub-paragraph [the present Article 7(1)(a)] may not be invoked against the exercise by a person of the rights defined in articles 13 and 14 of the Universal Declaration of Human Rights.

UN General Assembly, "United Nations Conference on the Elimination or Reduction of Future Statelessness, HOLY SEE: Amendments to article 7 adopted by the Committee of the Whole", UN Doc. A/CONF.9/L.65, 1, 16 Apr. 1959.

other delegates, the delegate of the Holy See argued that the idea contained in the present Article 7(1)(b) could prevent violations of fundamental human rights, and he requested states to adopt the convention with a humanitarian intention.[37] The delegate then proposed the provision which refers to articles 13 and 14 of the UDHR because "[t]hat seemed to him to be the only way of protecting individuals against infringement of their basic liberties".[38]

Some states opposed the inclusion of references to the UDHR in the 1961 Convention. However, they did so not because of the aim of the proposal which became Article 7(1)(b), but because it involved the insertion of a reference to the UDHR, a non-binding instrument, into a treaty.[39] Nevertheless, the proposal was ultimately adopted by 14 votes over 5 in opposition and 12 abstentions.[40] This implies that the priority of the right to freedom of movement and the right to asylum over the prevention of statelessness was formally recognised in the 1961 Convention.

It is intriguing that, despite various writings about the 1961 Convention in recent years, few mention Article 7(1)(b), as if it has been forgotten. To the knowledge of the authors of this chapter, this provision has never been invoked. The 2013 expert meeting on statelessness explains why Article 7(1)(b) has not received attention. In the meeting there was a conclusion that the exceptions in Article 7(1)(b) "which refer to UDHR Articles 13 and 14 are of limited relevance and that they have largely been superseded by subsequent developments in international law, in particular the right to leave any country including one's own, as set out in ICCPR Article 12".[41]

Indeed, the development of international human rights law has challenged the perception that states hold free discretional power over individuals' exit from a state. Nonetheless, the significance of Article 7(1)(b) should not be overlooked given the circumstance that possession of a nationality can play a role in creating a path to causing a serious threat to human rights. In such cases, its renunciation can be an option for some nationals to evade that risk. Importantly, the scope of Article 7(1)(b) may not be fully covered by the focus on the right in international human rights law to leave any state. Like the Rwandan case, a state may exercise its power to influence the regional environment so that its nationals, who have been outside of the state, may be pressed to return. During the discussion of Article 7(1)(b), the drafters of the 1961 Convention were aware of this peril. In advance of his submission of the proposal for Article 7(1)(b), the delegate of the Holy See had already cautioned that Article 7(1)(a) "might permit forced repatriation" of individuals possessing a

---

[37] UN General Assembly, "United Nations Conference on the Elimination or Reduction of Future Statelessness, Summary Record of the Tenth Plenary Meeting Held at the Palais des Nations, Geneva, on Tuesday, 16 April 1959, at 10.15 a.m.", UN Doc. A/CONF.9/SR.10, 8, 24 Apr. 1961.

[38] *Ibid*, 8.

[39] *Ibid*, 9–10.

[40] UN General Assembly, "United Nations Conference on the Elimination or Reduction of Future Statelessness, Summary Record of the Eleventh Plenary Meeting Held at the Palais des Nations, Geneva, on Tuesday, 16 April 1959, at 3.10 p.m.", UN Doc. A/CONF.9/SR.11, 10, 24 Apr. 1961.

[41] UNHCR, Expert Meeting: Interpreting the 1961 Statelessness Convention and Avoiding Statelessness resulting from Loss and Deprivation of Nationality, 2014, para. 43, available at: http://www.refworld.org/pdfid/533a754b4.pdf (last visited 25 May 2019).

nationality.[42] Similarly, others also expressed during the discussion of Article 7 that "refugees should be given the opportunity to free themselves from the nationality of their country of origin in order to avoid enforced repatriation"[43] and that "[t]here were many reasons why people preferred statelessness; e.g., some people wished to become stateless in order to avoid deportation".[44]

It could be an argument that development of refugee law underpinned by the 1951 Convention has made Article 7(1)(b) of the 1961 Convention needless because of the expectation that asylum states do not force repatriation of refugees. When Article 7(1)(b) was discussed during the drafting process of the 1961 Convention, a delegate raised doubts about the utility of the provision and stated that "it was inconceivable that the country offering asylum would consent to the enforced repatriation of refugees".[45] However, it is not only conceivable but also an issue of real concern, as the Rwandan case shows.

Because of the absence of state practice in applying Article 7(1)(b) of the 1961 Convention, an interpretation of the principles concerning the right of asylum in terms of UDHR Article 14 has not been elaborated. Also, in general discussions of international law, the scope and legal nature of the right of asylum are not yet settled. However, there are clues to interpreting the right of asylum in a resolution of the UN General Assembly, a decision of a regional human rights court and a UNHCR document. It is a common understanding that the right of asylum is consistent with the right of states to grant asylum as part of the exercise of their sovereignty, without giving rise to complaints by other states, as the Declaration on Territorial Asylum at the UN General Assembly indicates.[46] However, the right of asylum has gradually evolved to also embed in itself the application of the principle of *non-refoulement*, out of which the obligation of states to grant asylum partially originated. For instance, the principle of *non-refoulement* constitutes a part of the meaning of the right of asylum in American regional instruments and practice. The American Convention on Human Rights follows the "right to seek and be granted asylum" in Article 22(7) with the principle of *non-refoulement* in Article 22(8). And the Inter-American Court of Human Rights, in the case of *Pacheco Tineo*, "analysed the evolution of the right to

---

[42]UN General Assembly, "United Nations Conference on the Elimination or Reduction of Future Statelessness Committee of the Whole Summary Record of the First Meeting Held at the Palais des Nations, Geneva, on Wednesday, 1 April 1959, at 4.30 p.m.", UN Doc. A/CONF.9/C.1/SR.1, 4, 24 Apr. 1961.

[43]UN General Assembly, "United Nations Conference on the Elimination or Reduction of Future Statelessness Committee of the Whole Summary Record of the Seventh Meeting Held at the Palais des Nations, Geneva, on Monday, 6 April 1959, at 3 p.m.", UN Doc. A/CONF.9/C.1/SR.7, 3. Statement of Herment, Belgium.

[44]*Ibid*, 8.

[45]*Ibid*, 4.

[46]For example, see UN General Assembly, "Declaration on Territorial Asylum", 14 Dec. 1967, UN Doc. A/RES/2312(XXII), Article 1(1).

seek and be granted asylum and of the principle of non-refoulement"[47] and concluded that "[w]hen certain rights such as life or physical integrity of non-nationals are at risk, [such persons] must be protected against removal to the State where the risk exists, as a specific modality of asylum under article 22.8 of the Convention".[48] Similarly, in its defining of the content of the right of asylum,[49] UNHCR's Executive Committee placed the principle of *non-refoulement* at the first of the list of aspects to pay attention to.[50] Thus, when Article 7(1)(b) of the 1961 Convention is interpreted in the modern context, the development of the right of asylum, for which the principle of *non-refoulement* is an essential part, needs to be analysed.

5 Challenges in Application to the Rwandan Case

Previous part of this chapter has articulated that the 1961 Convention allows statelessness as an exception from an interpretative and normative perspective. This part elaborates on challenges in applying this interpretation for the Rwandan case from an empirical perspective, considering respectively Rwanda, UNHCR and host states.

Rwanda joined the 1961 Convention in 2006; therefore, it is bound as a contracting party to the treaty.[51] One obstacle in applying Article 7(1)(b) is the Rwandan nationality law which explicitly prohibits Rwandan nationals from renouncing their nationality in the following circumstance[52]:

> Renouncing Rwandan nationality should not compromise the laws of Rwanda, and renouncing it with the intention of seeking refugee status or being stateless in Rwanda shall not be permitted.

Suppose that an individual attempting to avoid repatriation claims to renounce Rwandan nationality under circumstances in which the evidence objectively demonstrates a conflict with the principles in the UDHR concerning the right of asylum. In such a scenario, the aforementioned article in the Rwandan nationality law would not be compatible with the requirement of Article 7(1)(b) of the 1961 Convention. The intent of Article 7(1)(b) is indeed to serve as an exception permitting a person to be

---

[47] Caso *Familia Pacheco Tineo vs Estado Plurinacional de Bolivia, Sentencia de 25 de noviembre de 2013*, 3. Translated and quoted in M-T. Gil-Bazo, "Asylum as a General Principle of International Law", *International Journal of Refugee Law*, 27(1), 2015, 13.

[48] *Ibid.*

[49] G.S. Goodwin-gill and J. McAdam, *The Refugees in International Law*, 3rd ed., Oxford, Oxford University Press, 2007, 365.

[50] UNHCR Executive Committee, "Safeguarding Asylum", No. 82 (XLVIII), 48th session, 1997.

[51] UN Treaty Collection, "Convention on the Reduction of Statelessness", available at: https://treaties.un.org/Pages/ViewDetails.aspx?src=TREATY&mtdsg_no=V-4&chapter=5&clang=_en (last visited 13 May 2019).

[52] Article 18 of the Rwandan nationality law. The English translation of the Rwandan Nationality Law is available from the following website of the Citizenship Rights in Africa Initiative. http://citizenshiprightsafrica.org/wp-content/uploads/2016/07/Rwanda-Organic-Law-Nationality-No30-2008.pdf (last visited 13 May 2019).

stateless. The Rwandan law does not allow renunciation of a nationality even when an inconsistency with the principle of the right of asylum is established. This would be problematic from the viewpoint of compatibility between the 1961 Convention and the Rwandan law if one submits a claim to invoke renouncement of nationality for the purpose to avoid illegitimate repatriation.

The difficulty in applying Article 7(1)(b) to actual cases was predicted during the drafting process of the 1961 Convention by the Belgian delegate. The delegate noted that "[s]ince it was unlikely that [states of origins of refugees] would be parties to the [1961 Convention] or would be willing to recognize the right to unilateral renunciation of their nationality if they considered it to be contrary to their interests to do so, the argument [of Article 7(1)(b)] seemed to be purely hypothetical".[53]

However, at the present time, UNHCR is equipped with the legitimacy and capacity to influence the factors concerning nationality law. UNHCR may be in a position to negotiate with Rwanda and have an impact on their decision to amend it. It is unrealistic to expect that UNHCR, the highly politicised institution, which actively commends the withdrawal of refugee status for Rwandan refugees regionally,[54] and the end of statelessness globally,[55] would try to persuade the government of Rwanda to apply Article 7(1)(b) to the Rwandan case. Nonetheless, it is worth remembering that, since 1976, UNHCR has been designated by the UN General Assembly as a body within the meaning of Article 11 of the 1961 Convention "to which a person claiming the benefit of this Convention may apply for the examination of his claim

[53]UN General Assembly, "United Nations Conference on the Elimination or Reduction of Future Statelessness, Committee of the Whole, Summary Record of the Seventh Meeting Held at the Palais des Nations, Geneva, on Monday, 6 April 1959, at 3 p.m.", UN Doc. A/CONF.9/C.1/SR.7, 3.

[54]See a chapter titled "'Voluntary' Repatriation of Rwandan Refugees in Uganda: An Analysis of Law and Practice" and section 4 "Forced repatriation under the UN-sponsored cessation clause" of a chapter titled "Where is Rwanda's Peace" of this book. See also The Fahamu Refugee Programme, "Rwanda: Cessation of Refugee Status is Unwarranted" (Memorandum of Fact and Law), 2011, 2, available at: http://www.refugeelegalaidinformation.org/sites/srlan/files/fileuploads/Memo%20of%20Fact%20and%20Law.pdf (last visited 9 June 2019); Ahimbisibwe, "The Politics of Repatriation: Rwandan Refugees in Uganda, 2003–2017", 13–14.

[55]In 2014, UNHCR launched the "#IBelong" campaign to end statelessness globally by 2024. For more details on the campaign, see UNHCR, #IBelong, https://www.unhcr.org/ibelong/ (accessed on 20 May). For the effects and challenges of the #IBelong campaign, see H. Akiyama, UNHCR niyoru Mukokuseki no Yobou to Sakugenni Muketa Torikumi: Sono Kouka to Kadai [UNHCR's Role in Preventing and Reducing Statelessness: Its Effects and Challenges], *The United Nations Studies*, 19, 2018, 191–219. UN General Assembly, "Declaration on Territorial Asylum", UN Doc. A/RES/2312(XXII), Art. 1(1). UN General Assembly, "Question of the Establishment, in Accordance with the Convention on the Reduction of Statelessness, of a Body to which Persons Claiming the Benefit of the Convention may Apply", UN Doc. A/RES/3274 (XXIX), 10 Dec. 1974; UN General Assembly, "Question of the Establishment, in Accordance with the Convention on the Reduction of Statelessness, of a Body to which Persons Claiming the Benefit of the Convention may Apply", UN Doc. A/RES/31/36, 30 Nov. 1976. In 1996, UNHCR was requested to "provide relevant technical and advisory services pertaining to the preparation and implementation of nationality legislation". UN General Assembly, "Resolution Adopted by the General Assembly [on the Report of the Third Committee (A/50/632)] 50/152 Office of the United Nations High Commissioner for Refugees", UN Doc. A/RES/50/152, 9 Feb. 1996, para. 15, available at: http://www.un.org/documents/ga/res/50/ares50-152.htm (last visited 1 Nov. 2017).

and for assistance in presenting it to the appropriate authority".[56] The activities of UNHCR under this article include "[r]eaching out to individuals who Field Offices believe may have valid claims under the terms of the Convention" and "[a]ssessing the compatibility of the State's legislation with its obligations under the 1961 Convention with relevance to the case".[57] Suppose that someone expresses her or his will to renounce Rwandan nationality and submits reliable evidence which warrants the conclusion that the adverse human rights situation in Rwanda conflicts with the principles of Article 14 of the UDHR.[58] In such a case, UNHCR would need to open a dialogue with the state party so that it may consider complying with Article 7(1)(b) of the 1961 Convention.

The second obstacle is that the actual application of Article 7(1)(b) of the 1961 Convention to Rwandans would make them stateless persons exposed to a legal vacuum in host states after the severance of their ties to Rwanda. However, in states where the 1954 Convention is invoked, stateless persons are not thrown away into a state of legal limbo. Two major destinations for Rwandan refugees, that is to say, Uganda and Zambia, are contracting parties to the 1954 Convention.[59] The practice of these states should correspond to the obligations enshrined in the 1954 Convention. The 1954 Convention guarantees a minimum set of rights for stateless persons concerning education, employment, housing and so on.[60] Pursuant to Article 31 of the 1954 Convention, if stateless persons are lawfully in the territory, they must

---

[56]UN General Assembly, "Declaration on Territorial Asylum", UN Doc. A/RES/2312(XXII), Article 1(1). UN General Assembly, "Question of the Establishment, in Accordance with the Convention on the Reduction of Statelessness, of a Body to which Persons Claiming the Benefit of the Convention may Apply", UN Doc. A/RES/3274 (XXIX); UN General Assembly, "Question of the Establishment, in Accordance with the Convention on the Reduction of Statelessness, of a Body to which Persons Claiming the Benefit of the Convention may Apply", UN Doc. A/RES/31/36. In 1996, UNHCR was requested to "provide relevant technical and advisory services pertaining to the preparation and implementation of nationality legislation". UN General Assembly, "Resolution Adopted by the General Assembly [on the Report of the Third Committee (A/50/632)] 50/152 Office of the United Nations High Commissioner for Refugees", UN Doc. A/RES/50/152, available at: http://www.un.org/documents/ga/res/50/ares50-152.htm (last visited 1 Nov. 2017).

[57]UNHCR, "UNHCR Action to Address Statelessness: A Strategy Note", March 2010, para. 69, available at: https://www.unhcr.org/protection/statelessness/4b960ae99/unhcr-action-address-statelessness-strategy-note.html (last visited 25 March 2019).

[58]As to information relevant to the claim of possible incompatibility between the human rights situation in Rwanda and the principles in Article 14 of the UDHR, see 2018 Country Reports on Human Rights Practices published by the US Department of State noting that torture took place in Rwanda, referring to a report by Human Rights Watch. US Department of State, 2018 Country Reports on Human Rights Practices: Rwanda, 2019, available at: https://www.state.gov/reports/2018-country-reports-on-human-rights-practices/rwanda/ (last visited 20 May 2019).

[59]Uganda became a contracting party in 1965 and Zambia in 1974. UN Treaty Collection, "Convention relating to the Status of Stateless Persons", available at: https://treaties.un.org/Pages/ViewDetailsII.aspx?src=TREATY&mtdsg_no=V-3&chapter=5&Temp=mtdsg2&clang=_en (last visited 20 May 2019).

[60]For the rights to be protected as stateless persons pursuant to the 1954 Convention, see UNHCR *Handbook on Protection of Stateless Person under the 1954 Convention relating to the Status of Stateless Persons, Geneva,* UNHCR, 2014.

not be expelled.[61] It should also be stressed that Article 32 of the 1954 Convention encourages states to facilitate the naturalisation of stateless persons, so they should have easier access to acquire a nationality in Uganda and Zambia. Even on the policy level, naturalisation is a vital strategy to avoid their statelessness being lengthened and causing friction and instability inside the host societies and to promote the socio-economic and legal integration of the former Rwandans with the locals. It is highlighted that UNHCR stated that those who voluntary renounced a nationality and became stateless should enjoy the right enshrined in the 1954 Convention.[62]

6 Conclusion

This chapter has described the Rwandan case in which nationality operates to rebuild the "Rwandan" nation, causing a risk of illegitimate repatriation and, consequently, human rights violations upon refugees' return. Following a brief review of the increasing attention paid to the progress of international norms to prevent statelessness, the chapter has highlighted the fact that the 1961 Convention—which aims at the prevention, not complete elimination, of statelessness—allows for someone to become stateless if being stateless prevents her or his illegitimate repatriation under circumstances incompatible with the principles in Articles 13 and 14 of the UDHR as expressed in Article 7(1)(b) of the 1961 Convention. It has also pointed out the challenges of applying this provision to the Rwandan case from empirical perspectives.

Although this chapter has focused on a normative understanding of Article 7(1)(b) of the 1961 Convention, the general value of its feasibility in practice is circumscribed by the following conditions and circumstances of the host state, state of nationality and UNHCR. With respect to the host state, the need for applying Article 7(1)(b) can be considered when certain factors are pressing such as that the 1951 Convention is dysfunctional in the state, the state has status as a non-state party to the 1951 Convention and so on. In addition, the host state must be a party to the 1954 Convention so as not to cause any gap in international protection when Article 7(1)(b) is applied. Concerning the state of nationality, the situation needs to exist whereby the state is a party to the 1961 Convention and it allows its nationals to renounce nationality even if they would become stateless. However, it is unlikely that the government of the state of nationality would permit the renunciation of its own nationality on the basis of a human rights concern within its own territory. Thus, unless renunciation is permitted, UNHCR must be ready to engage in dialogue with state parties to secure their compliance with Article 7(1)(b) of the 1961 Convention through individual

[61] However, it must be noted that unlike the 1951 Convention, the 1954 Convention does not possess a clause on *non-refoulement*.

[62] UNHCR, *Handbook on Protection of Stateless Person under the 1954 Convention relating to the Status of Stateless Persons,* para. 51.

claims. To do this, UNHCR would need to look into its responsibility seriously to examine the compatibility between the 1961 Convention and national law.

Recently, the international commitment to prevent and end statelessness has been strengthened by the efforts of UNHCR and like-minded states.[63] However, it should be emphasised that the effect of nationality is not limited to human rights protection. It may also have the opposite effect of functioning as an instrument to promote illegitimate repatriation and causing human rights violations upon refugees' return to the state of nationality. The findings of this chapter suggest the need for further critical research on the various effects of nationality and on the norm to prevent statelessness.

Acknowledgements The authors of this chapter express gratitude towards Associate Professor Herman Salton, International Christian University, and Associate Professor Yue Fu, Ibaraki University, who reviewed draft and provided valuable comments. This work was partially supported by JSPS KAKENHI Grant Number 18K01479.

References

F. Ahimbisibwe, The politics of repatriation: Rwandan refugees in Uganda, 2003–2017, Working Paper/2017.09, ISSN 2294-8643, IOB, University of Antwerp, 2017. https://www.uantwerpen.be/images/uantwerpen/container2673/files/Publications/WP/2017/wp-201709.pdf (last visited 9 June 2019)

H. Akiyama, Enforcement of Nationality and Human Insecurity: A Case Study on the Securitised Japanese Nationality of Koreans During the Colonial Era. *J. Hum. Secur. Stud.* **7**(2) (2018)

H. Akiyama, UNHCR niyoru mukokuseki no yobou to sakugen ni muketa torikumi: sono kouka to kadai [UNHCR's Role in Preventing and Reducing Statelessness: Its Effects and Challenges]. *The United Nations Stud.* **19** (2018b)

O. Arakaki, Mukokusekisha no Nanminsei: Nyujirando no jissen no kentou wo chuushinni [Stateless Refugees: Practice of New Zealand as a Case Study of the Refugee Status Determination]. *Yearbook of World Law* **31** (2012)

O. Arakaki, Mukokuseki toha nanika? Mukokuseki sakugen johyaku no gendaiteki kadai niokeru sayo [What is statelessness? Function of the 1961 Convention in Modern Issues], in *Nanmin wo do toraeruka?* [How Do We Conceive of "Refugees"?], K. Koizumi (ed.) (Tokyo, Keio University Press, 2019)

S. Buckley-Zistel, Dividing and Uniting: The Use of Citizenship Discourses in Conflict and Reconciliation in Rwanda. *Glob. Soc.* **20**(1) (2006)

R. Donner, *The Regulation of Nationality in International Law*, 2nd edn (New York, Transnational Publishers, 1994)

A. Edwards, The Meaning of Nationality in International Law in an Era of Human Rights: Procedural and Substantive Aspects, in *Nationality and Statelessness under International Law*, A. Edwards, L. van Waas (eds.) (Cambridge University Press, 2014)

A. Eide et. al. (eds.), *The Universal Declaration of Human Rights: A Commentary* (Drammen, Scandinavian University Press, 1992)

M.-T. Gil-Bazo, Asylum as a General Principle of International Law. *Int. J. Refug. Law* **27**(1) (2015)

[63]For the role of likeminded-states in preventing and ending statelessness, see Akiyama, UNHCR niyoru Mukokuseki no Yobou to Sakugenni Muketa Torikumi: Sono Kouka to Kadai, 199–202.

G.S. Goodwin-gill, J. McAdam, *The Refugees in International Law*, 3rd edn (Oxford University Press, 2007)
J. Hathaway, M. Foster, *The Law of Refugee Status*, 2nd edn (Cambridge University Press, 2014)
Human Rights First, "A Decade of Unrest: Unrecognized Rwandan Refugees in Uganda and the Future of Refugee Protection in the Great Lakes", (2004), available at: https://www.humanrightsfirst.org/wp-content/uploads/pdf/Decade-of-Unrest.pdf (last visited 10 May 2019)
J.P. Humphrey, The Universal Declaration of Human Rights: Its History, Impact and Juridical Character, in *Human Rights: Thirty Years after the Universal Declaration*, B.G. Ramcharan (ed.) (The Hague, Boston and London, Martinus Nijhoff, 1979)
H. Hintjens, Post-genocide Identity Politics in Rwanda. *Ethnicities* **8**(1), HAL Id: hal-00571890 (2008)
L.N. Kingston, Bringing Rwandan Refugees 'Home': The Cessation Clause, Statelessness, and Forced Repatriation. *Int. J. Refug. Law* **29**(3) (2017)
K. O'Connor, Repatriation: The Politics of (Re)-constructing and Contesting Rwandan Citizenship, Working Paper Series No. 92 (Refugee Studies Centre, University of Oxford, 2013)
G.G. Schram, Article 15, in *The Universal Declaration of Human Rights: A Commentary*, A. Eide, G. Alfredsson, G. Melander, L.A. Rehof, A. Rosas (eds.) (Drammen, Scandinavian University Press, 1992)
UNHCR, *Handbook on Protection of Stateless Person under the 1954 Convention relating to the Status of Stateless Persons* (Geneva, UNHCR, 2014)
D. Weissbrodt, C. Collins, The Human Rights of Stateless Persons. *Hum. Rights Q.* **28** (2006)
P. Weis, The United Nations Convention on the Reduction of Statelessness, 1961. *Int. Comparative Law Q.* **11**(4) (1962)
D. Weissbrodt, *The Human Rights of Non-citizens* (Oxford University Press, 2008)
M. Yonekawa, *Ayatsurareru Nanmin: seifu, kokuren, NGO no hazama de* [Manipulated refugees: in between governments, UN and NGOs] (Tokyo, Chikuma Shobo, 2017)

The Legacy of RPF Violence and Why Rwandan Refugees Refuse to Return

Judi Rever

1 Introduction

The construction of history is crucial to understanding Rwanda and its refugee crisis. There's a familiar adage that says that the history of the world is the history of violence. This aphorism can be taken to mean that the construction of history—assembling the pieces of historical events together and telling them—is done as a consequence of, or in the aftermath of violence. If we believe this notion, then it is also true that the suppression of history is carried out using violence. The use of violence to silence victims and control historical narrative is integral to the powerful rise of the Rwandan Patriotic Front. This political-military movement used violence to seize power, hold onto that power, flourish on the international stage, and change history. With the support of the West, the RPF has effectively used violence to tell the world an official narrative, which is only one side of the story.

2 The RPF's Impunity and The Danger of a Single Story

"I left Rwanda in 1994 because I was afraid", said a Rwandan Hutu who fled to Zaire when his homeland descended into genocide. "There was a war and everyone ran. People were dying. My family was killed in 1994 in Gitarama where there was no Hutu militia. The Interahamwe had already moved on. My wife and five children

[1] In 1997 I went to Congo after the ousting of Mobutu Sese Seko to cover the humanitarian crisis, and interviewed Rwandan Hutu refugees in the forests south of Kisangani and in transit camps throughout the country. I also conducted interviews with Congolese civilians displaced by the invasion of Rwandan troops in Zaire. I later went to Rwanda to speak to Hutu returnees as they were arriving home.

J. Rever
Montreal, Canada

M. Yonekawa and A. Sugiki (eds.), *Repatriation, Insecurity, and Peace*,
https://doi.org/10.1007/978-981-15-2850-7_3

were slaughtered. My youngest child was three weeks old. It was sheer horror. Only God knew what my life would become next. There are some things I cannot tell you", he whispered, shaking his head, his hands trembling. He asked me, as a journalist for Radio France Internationale at the time, to shut off my microphone.[1] We were at a transit camp in Runda, a sector in Rwanda, in late June 1997. The middle-aged man had just returned home, after losing a second family—his wife and 10-month old daughter—in eastern Zaire. He said the soldiers he saw kill and beat refugees in Congo were now in this transit camp. He nodded in their direction. "I am a survivor", he said in a low voice. "People talk as though only one ethnic group in Rwanda was victim of war. And the other was an executioner. But that's not true".

The man was trying to tell me that Rwandan Tutsi soldiers killed his first family during the genocide, and his second family in Congo.

Over the years I've spoken to hundreds of Rwandan refugees, both Hutu and Tutsi. More recently one of them said to me: "I am a Hutu survivor. I survived Paul Kagame's[2] war of invasion from 1990; I survived his death squads in 1994 and later in the Congo, and then I managed to flee the country to avoid getting killed afterward".

Yet the story of why Rwandan Hutu refugees fled their homeland in the first place, why they stayed in camps in eastern Congo and refused to go home after the genocide is still very poorly understood.

In the forests of the Congo in 1997, Rwandan Hutu refugees told me they'd fled Rwanda in 1994 because the Rwandan Patriotic Front (RPF) had killed their families during the genocide[3] and even before. They said they were afraid of the RPF. They said they stayed in the camps because they were afraid they'd be slaughtered if they returned. These refugees also told me that other refugees who were pushed or encouraged to go home, by the United Nations (UN) or the new Rwandan government, were disappearing.

The dearth of knowledge about why Rwandan Hutus fled in the first place and why they have since been reluctant to go home has had a significant impact on stability in Central Africa. The lacuna in empirical studies underscores the colossal failure to fully document one of the gravest events of the twentieth century. It also underscores a failure of empathetic imagination. The lack of rigorous, independently conducted interviews with Rwandan Hutu refugees in Africa and beyond—and with

[2]Paul Kagame was the commander of the Rwandan Patriotic Front whose military wing, the Rwandan Patriotic Army (RPA), invaded Rwanda in October 1990. In July 1994, his army seized power and he became de-facto leader before officially becoming Rwandan president in 2000. Kagame had grown up in Uganda and helped former rebel leader turned president, Yoweri Museveni, topple the regimes of Idi Amin and Milton Obote, in 1979 and 1986. Kagame became President Museveni's spy chief and was known for torturing enemies of the Ugandan state. Kagame became Rwanda's de facto leader when his troops seized power in July 1994, and has received considerable international support to rebuild the country since the genocide. In 2000, he was declared president and has since won three presidential elections. Kagame and his ruling RPF have been accused of silencing and jailing critics, and assassinating opponents at home and abroad.

[3]There is a general consensus among UN agencies, scholars and journalists that an estimated 800,000 Rwandans, the majority of them from the Tutsi ethnic group, were killed during the genocide. The perpetrators were most often members of a Hutu militia, civil defense forces, and in some cases the Hutu military. Hard-line elements of the state apparatus helped steer the campaign.

Tutsis who have broken with the regime in the intervening years—has impeded our understanding of the dynamics of violence in 1994. It has clouded our decision-making and invited well-substantiated accusations from victims of a collective bias on the part of international agencies, governments, human rights experts and journalists in the West.

An examination of the RPF's record on an evidence basis—understanding what its forces actually did before, during and after the genocide—should inevitably lead policy makers to a paradigm shift in how we view repatriation and UN policy regarding Rwandan refugees.

The ruling RPF has benefitted in astonishing ways from our ignorance about its record. The RPF was able to create an official narrative that cast the conflict in a binary way, of good versus evil, of victims at the hands of executioners. The regime was particularly adept at cultivating close contacts with researchers, western governments, and journalists[4] and has been skilled at infiltrating international institutions, in particular the UN, at the Department of Peacekeeping, the UN Human Rights Council of the UN High Commission for Human Rights, the UN Development Programme and the UN Habitat Department.[5] The post-genocide government also benefited from the cover of powerful insiders in the US security, military and political establishment. The RPF's official narrative helped bestow moral credibility to the post-genocide regime. It also served to justify and appease its campaign of violence in the Congo in the decades thereafter. The narrative amounted to gaslighting an entire ethnic group, and provided fertile ground for increasing levels of RPF propaganda about the nature, composition and activities of refugees in the camps along the border of the Congo. The ignorance and bias, especially among prominent

---

[4]Former US President Bill Clinton and former British Prime Minister Tony Blair have been among the most staunch supporters of Kagame and his regime. Other westerners who have consistently framed Kagame and the RPF in a positive light include Philip Gourevitch, a writer for the *New Yorker*; Bernard Kouchner, France's former Foreign Minister; Rick Warren, a US evangelical pastor; Phil Clark, a London-based academic who has written on transitional justice; William Schabas, a Canadian professor and president of the International Association of Genocide Scholar; and Linda Melvern, a British journalist.

[5]Prominent RPF officials who have been appointed to powerful positions at the UN DPKO include Emmanuel Karenzi Karake, who served from 2007 to 2008 as Deputy Commander of UNAMID in Darfur, despite being indicted by Spain on genocide charges in 2008; Patrick Nyamvumba, who commanded UNAMID in Darfur from 2009 to 2013; Jean Bosco Kazura was commander of the UN's stabilization force in Mali from 2013 to 2014; Francis Mutiganda became deputy chief of military planning services at DPKO in 2011, and Joseph Mutaboba who has held a deputy position at UNAMID and was the UN Secretary General's Representative in Guinea-Bissau. Other prominent appointments have included Francois Xavier Ngarambe as Vice President position at the UN's Human Rights Council, whose secretariat is the UN Office of the High Commission for Human Rights in Geneva; Christine Umutoni, who was UNDP's Representative in Eritrea, and is now the UNDP's Representative in Mauritius and the Seychelles; and Kirabo Aisa Kacyira has long served as deputy executive director and assistant secretary general of the UN Habitat Department and is the wife of Brigadier General Rwakabi Kacyira, who served as the head of the RPF's DMI and was head of the RPF military police in Congo.

members of the media and academic community,[6] led to a significant amount of fear mongering by the RPF and misinformation in the public domain.

Thousands of Rwandan and Congolese people have tried to alert the international community to these crimes but these individuals have been intimidated, jailed, silenced or killed. At the same time, powerful interests at the UN and within Western governments have buried crucial evidence and dismissed the experiences of people who fled, thereby contributing to an environment in which suspicion of an entire ethnic group has flourished and overshadowed the very foundation of enquiry. The misrepresentation of historical events has enabled a feedback loop of human rights violations that exists to this day.

Among the first, most high profile people who tried to draw international attention to RPF crimes were Theoneste Lizinde and Seth Sendashonga. Both men were Hutu members of the Tutsi-led RPF but broke ranks and fled in the aftermath of the genocide as they came to understand the full criminal nature of the Rwandan regime, led by Paul Kagame. They were guided by the notion that all victims deserved justice, regardless of ethnicity. With other colleagues, Lizinde and Sendashonga began assembling in Nairobi, Kenya a considerable body evidence of RPF crimes against Hutu peasants and community leaders committed during and after the genocide. The material they collected included carefully compiled lists[7] of an estimated 18,000 victims in the prefecture of Gitarama, in addition to witness accounts of mass killings elsewhere, including executions at detention camps such as Kami in Kigali and operations that rounded up Hutu civilians on trucks, transporting them to Akagera Park (in particular to Gabiro, a military barracks where the Rwandan Patriotic Army trained recruits) where they were slaughtered, burned and in most cases incinerated.

Some of the evidence was in the form of letters written to Sendashonga, who became Interior Minister in Rwanda's post genocide government in July 1994. Sendashonga and Lizinde painstakingly transcribed the names of the Gitarama victims on a computer disk, and gave it to their colleague Faustin Twagiramungu, Rwanda's former prime minister who also fled in 1995 and began residing in Belgium. The disk, along with three packages of documents, was handed over to the International Criminal Tribunal for Rwanda (ICTR), with the hopes that the RPF would be prosecuted for these heinous crimes.

The court never acted on the evidence and never bothered to explain why. Sendashonga held a press conference in 1996, brandishing the evidence before media and human rights organisations, but his efforts got scant coverage. In October 1996, RPF agents kidnapped and killed Lizinde, dumping his body on the outskirts of Nairobi. Two years later, RPF agents gunned down Sendashonga and his driver in the Kenyan capital. Before his assassination, Sendashonga had been due to testify at

[6] A. de Waal, "No Bloodless Miracle", *Guardian*, 15 Nov. 1996; P. Gourevitch, "The Return", *New Yorker*, Jan. 1997; P. Gourevitch, "Continental Shift", *New Yorker*, Aug. 1997.

[7] The Gitarama lists, chronicled in Chap. 12 in my book *In Praise of Blood*, were compiled by André Sibomana, a highly regarded Rwandan human rights activist and journalist. Sibomana suffered from ill health, was unable to get access to medicine because of RPF restrictions on his movements. He died in 1998.

the ICTR, against the RPF, according to his widow, who fled to Montreal with their three children.[8]

Investigators from the ICTR's Special Investigations Unit probing RPF crimes eventually came to Canada to copy most if not all of Sendashonga's evidence that his wife Cyrie held in her apartment in Montreal. The work of the Special Investigations Unit continued until 2008 but never led to any prosecutions against the RPF, despite significant prima-facie evidence collected by well experienced investigators, among them senior police and crime analysts.

Incredulously, the ICTR instead struck a deal with the RPF; at the recommendation of the United States government, the ICTR decided to allow Rwanda to prosecute its own army and officials. The deal, which was negotiated between Rwanda and the United States Ambassador for War Crimes at the time, Pierre Prosper, recommended that the ICTR share evidence collected by the Special Investigations Unit with Rwandan authorities, even though senior members of the government were alleged to have committed these crimes. It was tantamount to letting the killers investigate themselves.

The US political and defense establishments backed Kagame after the genocide and green-lit his invasion of Congo, even when there was clear evidence were murdering Hutu refugees in the jungle of Congo.[9]

It's not the first time politically powerful insiders have protected the RPF regime. The following are just a few of the alarming reports the West chose to deliberately conceal[10]:

- At the height of the genocide in 1994, a UN cable revealed that Kagame's forces were shooting, stabbing and burning refugees and dumping bodies of victims in the Kagera River. Others were hauled off in trucks, according to survivors fleeing to neighbouring Tanzania.
- In 1994, an international consultant with extensive experience in African war zones named Robert Gersony concluded, in a report tabled to the UN, that 40,000 Hutu civilians were slaughtered in less than one third of the country's communes he visited, and he believed the operations were systematic. The UN buried his report to protect Kagame's regime. A whistleblower released it online in 2010.[11]
- Early evidence from RPF informants indicated that on 6 April, 1994, Kagame's commandos had shot down the plane carrying Hutu President Juvenal Habyarimana and his Burundian counterpart, Cyprien Ntaryamira. Their assassinations

[8] Author's interview with Cyrie Sendashonga in 2013.

[9] J. Rever, *In Praise of Blood, The Crimes of the Rwandan Patriotic Front* (Random House Canada, 2018), 160–165.

[10] J. Rever, "Why We Must Listen to Those Who Have Fled Kagame's Rwanda", Open Canada, 9 April 2018, available at https://www.opencanada.org/features/why-we-must-listen-those-who-have-fled-kagames-rwanda/ (last visited 1 June 2020).

[11] R. Gersony, "Summary of UNHCR Presentation, Before Commission of Experts, Prospects for Early Repatriation of Rwandan refugees currently in Burundi, Tanzania and Zaire", 10 Oct. 1994, available at: https://graphics8.nytimes.com/packages/pdf/world/gersony_report.PDF#page=17&zoom=auto (last visited 1 June 2020).

triggered the Rwandan genocide, which claimed the lives of several hundred thousand Tutsis. Louise Arbour, the Canadian prosecutor of the UN's International Criminal Tribunal for Rwanda (ICTR), shut down that probe in 1997. She argued that the tribunal did not have jurisdiction to investigate the plane attack. Yet Article 4 of the ICTR Statute specifically called for the body to investigate acts of terrorism.

- A political group comprised of Rwandan Hutu refugees known as the Rassemblement pour le retour des Réfugiés et la Démocratie (RDR) conducted a partial investigation in camps in Congo and Tanzania. That investigation listed the names of 20,000 victims, most from northern Rwanda, who had been killed in RPF zones by Kagame's army. In many cases the names of witnesses to the killings were listed, and occasionally the names of the alleged killers, who were members of the RPF, were identified. The investigation, which I got access to, was submitted to the ICTR in 2000, but the court buried the findings.[12]

Congo was the prism through which I first began the question the RPF narrative that arose after Kagame's troops seized power in July 1994. In 1997, I interviewed scores of Rwandan Hutu refugees in the Congolese jungle during search and rescue missions with local staff from the UN refugee agency (UNHCR), Doctors Without Borders and the Red Cross. The refugees had been hunted down across a brutal terrain by Kagame's Tutsi-led troops. An estimated 200,000 Hutu refugees went missing under Congo's triple layer canopy and were presumed murdered by the Rwandan Patriotic Army. Many of the survivors, orphans and women, were ravaged by disease and hunger, and were hollowed out with grief. Some were suffering from infections due to gunshot wounds; a countless number were severely malnourished and had contracted a host of waterborne and parasitic diseases. Stripped of all dignity and strength, their trauma was laid bare and their stories were harrowing. And yet many were willing to talk about their experiences. Their testimony contained crucial clues to why Hutus, en masse, fled Rwanda in 1994, and why they continued to live in difficult conditions in camps in Congo after the genocide, as Kagame was touted by the international community as reconstructing Rwanda and fostering an era of renaissance in Central Africa. Many refugees told me—anecdotally yet emphatically—that their families and neighbors had been targeted and killed by Kagame's rebels during the genocide. Their stories shocked me, and I struggled to overcome my own bias and ignorance about the Rwandan conflict in 1994, having absorbed a significant level of propaganda from books, mainstream media reports and academic research.

Their stories do not amount to an empirical study of the Rwandan genocide or why Hutus fled the violence, but offer a narrative synthesis of decades of crimes committed by Rwandan President Paul Kagame and his RPF. The accounts from victims and Tutsi soldiers and officers who broke with the regime because they disagreed with RPF violence cannot be underestimated. The historicity of their narratives ultimately

[12]RDR, "Résultats des Enquêtes Partielles sur les crimes du FPR réalisées par le RDR dans les camps de réfugiées dans l'est de l'ex Zaïre et en Tanzanie". An employee at the ICTR leaked the documents to me.

establishes a pattern of crimes that Hutu victims first spoke of many years ago. I have interviewed an estimated 200 direct and contextual witnesses to crimes committed by the RPF and have accessed confidential documents from the ICTR.

3 The Planning and Pattern of RPF Crimes

In April 1994, two weeks after President Habyarimana was assassinated, the RPF used mortar and gunfire to target the camp of Nyacyonga, one of the largest settlements in the northern prefecture of Byumba that housed Hutus displaced by the invasion war that began in 1990. Kagame's troops surrounded the camp and pushed thousands of these Hutus further north toward Byumba town. On Radio Muhabura, RPF officials announced that the war was over and internally displaced persons (IDPs) could return to their homes and reclaim their belongings. The RPF herded thousands of these internally displaced Hutus into the courtyard of the town hall. The IDPs, surrounded by troops, were famished by force to wait a few days before being sent into the town's soccer stadium. They were promised food, drink and cooking supplies. Once the IDPs got inside, under escort, they began to relax and cook food for their children.

A number of RPF's military figures showed up at the stadium, including members from military intelligence, an RPA ground commander in Byumba, and a chief political commissar. Théogène Murwanashyaka, a soldier from Kagame's High Command battalion, was stationed to guard outside the stadium. He saw the IDPs file in and the RPF officers arrive. Another young recruit named Patrick, from the RPF's military police, whose troops were stationed inside, gave me his account of what happened inside the stadium. At nightfall, amid the faint light of cooking fires, military police and high command soldiers began to select robust men and led them to the stadium dugout where they proceeded to shoot them dead. As the IDPs began to scream and scramble, the soldiers threw grenades and unleashed gunfire. Those who did not die immediately were finished off with the RPF's signature instrument, agafuni or sharp hoe.

Théogène Murwanashyaka said the killing went on for hours, and the agony could be heard outside the stadium. The soldiers spent hours clearing the bodies out of the stadium and putting them on trucks, and cleaning up the blood on the premises. Some of the bodies were buried in Byumba and others were taken to a location called Rukomo, at the edge of the prefecture. When Kagame found out the bodies had been buried there, according to Patrick, he ordered the remains to be dug up and brought to a more remote park where they could be burned. The witness said Kagame was worried about satellites providing evidence in the future of mass graves in RPF-controlled territory.

The Byumba stadium butchery displayed the operating tactics of the RPF, according to former military members and an investigator who worked at the Special Investigations Unit of the ICTR. RPF troops and intelligence would control access to an area, lure Hutus to a designated site with promises of food and safety, and proceed to murder them often at night before hauling the corpses to a park where they were burned. As the weeks wore on, it became too risky to kill refugees in villages so the Hutus were put on trucks and hauled away to Gabiro or other isolated locations in Akagera Park. Concealing the evidence was central to the RPF's impunity and strategy of propaganda and ambitions to seize power and keep it. The ICTR investigator said he and his colleagues collected testimony from soldiers who took part in the killings, those who transported the bodies and those who burned the bodies. "In my life I've never seen a situation where so much evidence was collected and no indictment was issued", he said.

"This was the politics of the UN", he said, adding that the proof was there and tribunal lawyers agreed that indictments should be prepared. But the prosecutions were not allowed to proceed. An ICTR document, dated 2003, leaked to me identified the Byumba stadium as a massacre site. "During meetings with the population that had taken refuge in the stadium, the military had gained their confidence", the investigators noted. The document said that Lieutenant-Colonel James Kabarebe, head of High Command, arrived at the stadium, where he talked with his military colleagues. After Kabarebe left, a Lieutenant Masumbuko gave the order to "open fire on the IDPs". Kabarebe and Masumbuko, along with senior RPA officials, were named as potential targets for indictment. Of course no indictments were ever issued.

Murwanashyaka and other former members of the RPF said Hutu civilians were killed as part of an ethnic cleansing operation to free up land for Tutsi returnees who had grown up in neighboring Uganda, Burundi and Congo. RPF founder Alphonse Furuma has publicly stated that when the Arusha peace talks started in 1993, Kagame launched a deliberate policy to create a Tutsiland through Hutu massacres, massive population displacement and land grabbing in the northeast, southeast and central Rwanda.

4 Deep Structure of RPF Violence: DMI

How, logistically speaking, did the RPF manage to get away with this mass ethnic killing? How was it that they were able to hide massive crimes against humanity in plain sight and escape censure for their actions? Part of the answer lies in the deep structure of RPF violence, which at its core is wielded by the directorate of military intelligence (DMI). It is the principal organ through which criminal ideas and propaganda are concocted. UN investigators wrote: "The DMI is hated and feared by most of the Rwandan population, inside and outside of Rwanda, due to its reputation for cruelty and killing. Most of the massacres attributed to the RPA were committed by the DMI".

The DMI oversees the departments of Counterintelligence, Criminal Investigations and Prosecutions and Research, Records and Registry. Crucially, it also has officers and lower ranking staff at every level in every battalion, from the company, platoon down to the smallest section, and in every other military unit: from the

Republican Guard, the Gendarmerie, the Military Police, and its Training Wing.[13] The RPF's military intelligence is the main instrument through which crimes were inflicted on Rwandans during the genocide, and it is the continuing source of RPF violence against Rwandan and Congolese. Even before the genocide, it used Tutsi civilians as a support network to carry out crimes, creating civilian militia and guerilla-type DMI units in the same manner as China's Mao Zedong and Vietnam's Vo Nguyen Giap. Its DMI representatives have infiltrated international organisations to steer policy and have used Rwandan embassies to attack, kidnap and intimidate people outside Rwanda's borders.

The genocide against Tutsis by Hutus was sparked in part by fear of a Tutsi army encroaching from the north, but also its secret allies on the ground, the so-called fifth column. A growing body of evidence shows that Tutsi civilians killed their Hutu neighbours in the same way that Hutus turned on Tutsis. Most of Tutsi civilians who engaged in crimes for the RPF were *abakada*, or civilian cadres—Tutsis who had been recruited by the RPF before, during and after the genocide. Many abakada delivered Hutus over to RPF death squads; they helped located Hutus and lock them in dungeons; they dug mass graves and helped conceal crimes; and in some cases they picked up hoes and guns and joined in the killing. These abakada also became the interface between the RPF and UN agencies, NGOs, human rights investigators and international journalists, playing a crucial role in Rwanda's statecraft, stagecraft and propaganda system.[14]

Thousands of RPF cadres, both Tutsi and Hutu, wield significant power in today's Rwanda. They are no longer called *abakada*. They are now known as *intore*, a word meaning "chosen one" in Kinyarwanda, and they work in every profession, at home and abroad. They spy on Rwandans in all walks of life, in particular through a neighbourhood surveillance system called *nyumbakumi* that uses agents from military,

[13]Former DMI have separately explained to me the pervasive nature of DMI within the RPF. DMI has officers and lower ranking staff in the RPF's Republican Guard—a military unit formerly known as the High Command that provides bodyguards for Kagame and his top aides—in addition to the Gendarmerie, Military Police and the Training Wing. DMI is highly concentrated in the regular army; its agents have representatives at every level of the battalion, from the company and platoon to the smallest section. The result is a kind of a military Matryoshka structure, recalling the Russian dolls one opens, only to find another one inside. For example, every RPA battalion has an intelligence officer (IO) from DMI, so there were 11 IOs during the genocide at the battalion level, and each IO had six to a dozen lower-ranking intelligence staff (IS) from DMI, at his side. Each company in every battalion had a IS. There were on average 10 companies in each battalion, depending on the size of the battalion. That created an estimated 110 IS at the company level. Each company consisted of at least three platoons, each having an IS, allowing for about 330 IS at the platoon level. In each platoon there were three sections, each of these sections having two or three IS. That created between 1980 ($2 \times 3 \times 3 \times 10 \times 11$) and 2970 IS at the section level. The CND (RPF headquarters at the parliamentary buildings in Kigali), had a small battalion of 600, with about six companies, 18 platoons and 36 sections, which allowed for an estimated 100–140 IS. At the Training Wing, there were several IOs and an estimated 50 IS working for DMI. DMI headquarters and special platoon intelligence staff numbered about 75 IS. The total number of IS representatives working for DMI, therefore, in the battalions down through to sections during the genocide was estimated to be between 2740 IS at a minimum, and 3800 IS at a maximum, not including intelligence officers.

[14]Rever, *In Praise of Blood*, Chaps. 8 and 9.

political and civilian spheres to exert control. There are often as many as four intore members monitoring every ten houses. The intore report to DMI agents and representatives of the RPF Secretariat (political bureau), and they work jointly with members of a separate military reserve forces known as the *inkeragutabara*. The objective is to instill fear in order to keep civilians in their place, to intimidate and to force obedience.

The bidirectional nature of ethnic violence during the Rwandan genocide—Hutu-on-Tutsi, and Tutsi-on-Hutu—is not spoken of in Rwanda and barely so abroad. Hutu victims and former members of Kagame's army nevertheless have shared their stories in explicit detail. One Hutu, a man named Daniel recounted to me his experience in Gituza, Byumba. On 9 April 1994, less than two days after the plane attack, RPF troops entered the area and began killing Hutu civil servants, teachers, businessmen and community leaders. Those who could get away ran east in a wild panic toward the commune of Rukara. After 10 days of running, he, his wife and three children, along with three thousand other people settled at Karambi Training Centre. They were famished and exhausted. By 20 April, RPF troops invaded the area and had them surrounded. Brandishing machine guns and rifles, a group of 60 of the soldiers herded the Hutus into a garden, ordered them to sit down and listen to what they had planned for them. Within minutes the soldiers began to spray the crowd with machine gun fire and throw grenades. Victims who tried to run were shot. Daniel survived and managed to flee, but his wife and their three sons died in the attack.

Joseph Matata, a Belgium-based Rwandan human rights activist who undertook a partial investigation of crimes in RPF zones, said Kagame's soldiers "hunted people down like rabbit and other prey. The soldiers did *clean-up operations* in the hills. They went from house to house, shooting people". Some people hid in banana groves or escaped to the Akagera park. "Quite a few victims would see the soldiers coming and throw themselves into the lake and drown", he told me. In 1994, before he fled Rwanda, Matata also documented the entrapment methods used by the RPA to kill larger groups of people. "They asked people to gather in certain areas, in schools and markets. Those who showed up at these meetings were given cooking equipment, clothes and food. These people were told to spread the word about other meetings. When larger groups of people showed up, the RPA used grenades or guns to kill them". Matata described the way the RPF tried to instill trust before going in for the kill: "They caress their victims before they kill them. It's appalling. Not even the Nazis did this".

Dozens of other witnesses, in particular former soldiers in Kagame's High Command, DMI units, Training Wing and regular battalions, recounted the methods used to kill Hutu community leaders and peasants. The mobile death squads operated behind the military front, in areas already under RPF control—initially in the rear of the army 157th and 7th brigades—that swept from the north down the eastern flank of the country, to the south and then fanning out into Gitarama in July, before going to Butare and then onto the northeastern regions in July. Thousands of victims were put on trucks and taken to Gabiro barracks and other areas of the Akagera where they shot, burned and incinerated. "From Gabiro, Hutus could not escape; they were surrounded by soldiers. They were thrown into mass graves dug by bulldozers. Then soldiers started shooting at them", an intelligence officer who had received daily reports of the sweeping operations said. The officer said five to ten lorries, each carrying from 100 to 200 people, went through Gabiro and into the park nightly for months. The military base at Gabiro had bulldozers, stocks of diesel and petrol to burn corpses, and even acid to dissolve the victims' remains. The dead were then mixed with soil or dumped into the lakes in the park.

Matata and former RPF members said the commander of these operations was Patrick Nyamvumba, Rwanda's former chief of defense staff and a highly respected figure on the international military stage. In 2009, Nyamvumba was appointed commander of UNAMID, the joint UN and African Union peacekeeping mission in Darfur in western Sudan, a post he held until 2013. In October 2017, alongside General Nyamvumba, Canadian Senator Romeo Dallaire, who headed the UN peacekeeping force in Rwanda during the genocide, unveiled the Rwandan Peace Academy. The two men stood for photos and gave lectures on the importance of peacekeeping. The rhetoric and spectacle only reinforced the trauma of Hutu survivors whose families were wiped out by RPF troops during the genocide, and fed into deep-seated resentment of an international community that continues to applaud Kagame's army for its record during the genocide. "Patrick Nyamvumba's name is synonymous with terror and pain", one Hutu survivor from eastern Rwanda told me, sobbing.

The nature of the violence in Rwanda in 1994 has not been fully researched, to the degree that historians, academics and journalists believe it was. The UN tribunal became aware that the RPF trained commandos known as technicians and had infiltrated Hutu militias before the genocide. These technicians proceeded to work actively with Hutu militia at roadblocks to kill Tutsis. Testimony explaining this phenomenon was collected by the Special Investigations Unit, and has been corroborated by Tutsi officers and soldiers now in exile. "I realised that interior Tutsis were pawns in Kagame's end game. Killing Tutsis and further discrediting the Hutu regime was part of an elaborate strategy to take power with the approval of the international community", said Théogène Murwanashyaka, formerly a High Command soldier.[15]

5 The Counterinsurgency

By late 1996, Kagame had sent his troops and military intelligence teams into eastern Congo to uproot more than a million Hutu refugees living in camps inside the border. He used propaganda to sell Western governments and media on the rationale behind this campaign. The RPF claimed that Rwanda could never be safe unless it succeeded in hunting down Hutu genocidaires hiding among the refugee population in the camps. His strategy worked. Kagame's invasion of Zaire led to an endless war in Congo that cost the lives of millions of Congolese civilians, and allowed him and his senior commanders, through a variety of client militia and proxies, to profit from

[15] *Ibid*, 68–70.

the country's mineral and natural resources. The invasion also sent hundreds of thousands of Rwandan Hutus home where they faced a new round of ethnic cleansing. The heart of his campaign was in northwestern Rwanda, around Gisenyi and Ruhengeri. In the early stages of the counterinsurgency campaign, an alarming number of former soldiers who had served in Habyarimana's Hutu army were systematically eliminated. In addition, a vast number of young Hutu men who were recruited by Kagame's army in the aftermath of the 1994 were also slaughtered or disappeared.[16] The RPF screened Hutu men from all over Rwanda, and rounded up thousands of them at night or deliberately recruited them into RPF military ranks in order to eliminate them at Akagera Park and in the Nyungwe Forest in southwestern Rwanda. The RPF seized many young men coming back from Congo, mostly in Gisenyi, forcing them into airtight compartments in trucks and piping in the exhaust while the engines were running.[17]

Interviews with Hutu survivors gave harrowing accounts of the RPF conducting massacres in Rwanda during the counterinsurgency hill by hill, or in public meeting places such as markets, most often under the guise of fighting a Hutu insurgency whose rear bases were in Congo. In October 1997, thousands of civilians sought refuge from Kagame's security forces in deep, dark caves in the Rwandan commune of Kanama, which had long been a hiding place during previous waves of violence. By the end of the month the RPF moved in on the caves in a macabre operation carried out by DMI operatives and several brigades. They cordoned off the area, and threw grenades into the caves' entrances, and then followed with machine gunfire before sealing off the opening. Several thousand civilians died inside. A young Tutsi soldier who was part of the DMI operations on the caves confirmed that many raids in which the RPF killed unarmed Hutus were part of a larger scheme. "There was a plan during the counterinsurgency to eliminate the civilian population in the north. Yes, there were insurgents trying to overthrow the government. But the war against these fighters was used as a pretext to reduce the Hutu population. There was no doubt about it".

It is clear that the RPF killed massively and in most cases, did so methodically and with the intent to eliminate or reduce the numbers of Hutu civilians and establish ethnic domination. The motives for these ethnic-based killings were strategic, according to former members of the RPF. One of the principle reasons was to remove Hutus from political and military power, and replace them with Tutsis. The RPF also targeted Hutu teachers, artists, business people, lawyers and judges because once the core military, political economic and cultural leadership of the previous regime was gone, the RPF could govern with little resistance. The RPF also ordered its military to cleanse regions—exterminating as many Hutu peasants as possible—especially in the north, because it wanted to mould the population map and secure housing and belongings for Tutsis returnees who had been living for decades in Uganda, Congo and Burundi.

---

[16] *Ibid*, 133–134, 218.

[17] *Ibid*, 94.

The international community largely kept silent about the atrocities of the counterinsurgency, which led to even greater RPF impunity and more suffering among Rwandans, including refugees. Outsiders who tried to break the silence were eventually targeted as well. In the first five weeks of 1997, more than a dozen foreign nationals were killed in orchestrated operations conducted by Kagame's intelligence network. Four UN observers were killed in Rwanda on 11 January; three Spaniards working for the non-governmental organization, Doctors of the World, were slain on 18 January; a Canadian priest was shot dead as he offered communion in Ruhengeri on 2 February; and five UN human rights staffers were massacred in Karengera on 4 February. These were not random acts caused by the heightened violence in the region. A former intelligence official with direct knowledge of these assassinations said the operations that targeted foreigners in Rwanda during the counterinsurgency were planned and coordinated by the DMI and the Gendarmerie's Special Intelligence Division.[18]

For more than a quarter century, Paul Kagame's regime has systematically killed people in order to cover up its true record and stay in power. The disregard for the rule of law, the repression of the media, of free speech and political expression in Rwanda today are a tragic result of the world's failure to investigate and prosecute the initial crimes that facilitated the RPF's seizure and consolidation of power.

6 Refugee Fear and Their Loss of Faith in the UN

One of the most striking and tragic inconsistencies was the UNHCR's repatriation against their will of many Rwandan refugees in the Congo who were found in traumatised, ailing states in the forest in 1997. Expatriate staff insisted that these refugees—even Rwandan orphans who had been taken in by Congolese villagers—had to go back to Rwanda, because this was policy; it had been decreed by the UNHCR. Aid agencies argued that returning home would be safer for the refugees because it was too dangerous in Congo. Most of the refugees disagreed. As haggard and as traumatised as they were, they told me that they would face *more* danger in Rwanda. Somehow they knew what might await them.

In the end, refugees were given minimal food and sent to transit camps, before being loaded onto planes and sent back to Rwanda. Yet the same expatriate staff knew full well that it was Rwandan forces who had chased and killed Rwandan refugees across Congo. So their insistence that refugees would be safer in Rwanda—a country that had ordered the massacres—made no sense whatsoever. Herein lay one of the first, most flagrant ethical and moral contradictions on the part of the UNHCR that I came across. Sending refugees back to the people who killed their families was a serious breach of trust with regard to the UN's responsibility to protect Rwandan refugees.

[18] *Ibid*, 145–150.

Refugees and their advocates have long argued the UNHCR has blatantly disregarded Rwanda's human rights record and instead pursued political objectives at the expense of the safety and well being of refugees. Despite the findings a decade ago of the UN Mapping Report, which concluded that the RPF may have committed genocide against Hutu refugees in the Congo, the UNHCR insists that refugees would be safer living in a RPF-controlled state.

Refugee suspicion of the international community is also fuelled by the RPF's influence over and infiltration of, through a variety of means, agencies that deal with refugee applications in host countries in Africa and the West. Rwanda has been known to exert influence in how asylum cases are treated abroad. There is a growing body of evidence[19] that Rwandan agents have infiltrated UNHCR offices handling resettlement requests, particularly in Africa. Rwandan embassies have been known to use interpreters or interns to become appraised of cases and exert influence, particularly in UNHCR resettlement requests, according to asylum-seekers I've interviewed. As a result, Rwandans are often afraid to reveal the true reasons and circumstances of their flight, and they sometimes refuse to register as asylum applicants for fear they will be identified, tracked and targeted.

In some cases, Rwandans who flee to neighbouring countries prefer to keep their whereabouts hidden. They refuse to register with authorities and instead rely on friends or relatives living in host countries to protect them. In Uganda, the safety of Rwandan asylum-seekers is often influenced by whether Uganda and Rwanda are enjoying close relations or whether their ties are strained, at any given moment. The kidnapping and killing of Rwandan refugees in Central Africa and other countries is often a function of how successful Rwanda is at bribing security officials or infiltrating host countries' institutions and police.

It is particularly risky for soldiers or officers of the RPF to flee Rwanda. If they openly disagree with the RPF, they will be executed. Very few if any members of the RPF flee simply because they disagree with the regime's human rights record. If they desert the army and flee, they will be hunted down and possibly killed. And in such cases, their family members can be targeted, so fleeing is a serious risk to take. The vast majority of RPF deserters or dissidents I have interviewed decided to flee when their lives were in danger.

For many years, Rwandan refugees have argued that the systematic crimes committed by the RPF in its early years give clues to the criminality and level of impunity it enjoys today. Until the UN and other international brokers recognize the RPF's true historical record, there can be little hope that the safety, dignity and rights of Rwandan refugees can begin to be addressed.

[19]Interviews with Rwandan refugees and asylum-seekers, separatedly conducted by myself and Masako Yonekawa.

References

A. de Waal, No Bloodless Miracle. *Guardian* (1996)

R. Gersony, Summary of UNHCR presentation, before commission of experts, Prospects for Early Repatriation of Rwandan Refugees Currently in Burundi, Tanzania and Zaire (1994), avaialbe at: https://graphics8.nytimes.com/packages/pdf/world/gersony_report.PDF#page=17&zoom=auto (last visted 1 June 2020)

P. Gourevitch, The Return, in *New Yorker* (1997a)

P. Gourevitch, Continental Shift, in *New Yorker* (1997b)

J. Rever, *In Praise of Blood, The Crimes of the Rwandan Patriotic Front* (Canada, Random House, 2018a), pp. 160–165

J. Rever, Why We Must Listen to Those Who Have Fled Kagame's Rwanda, Open Canada (2018b). https://www.opencanada.org/features/why-we-must-listen-those-who-have-fled-kagames-rwanda

Aggravated Trauma and Insecurity Among Rwandan Hutu Refugees

Marcelline Nduwamungu

1 Introduction

There is a lot of literature addressing the plight of survivors of the Tutsi genocide and its psychological impact.[1] This is undoubtedly a good thing, for they deserve compassion. However, there is little research about the traumatic experiences of Hutus who were the direct victims of, or witnesses to, the atrocities committed by the ruling Rwandan Patriotic Front (RPF) prior to, during, and after the genocide in Rwanda, and in the dense forests of Democratic Republic of Congo (DRC), formerly Zaire. Although the majority of refugees who fled in 1994 and after were Hutus, there were also Tutsis who fled and faced the same fate as Hutus. Thus, it is important to understand that Hutu refugees may also include Tutsis who fled along with Hutus.

According to many refugee accounts, upon arriving to the DRC and Tanzania, there were no Non-Governmental Organisations (NGOs) ready to deal with the trauma and psychological illnesses often experienced by refugees subsequent to armed conflicts. It is important to recall that victims of trauma and other related issues can be found in both the Diaspora and Rwanda today. It is often taken for granted that the Diaspora is immune from this traumatic experience because they now live in relatively peaceful countries. However, current and former refugees live in constant fear of arrest on fabricated charges, intimidation, forced disappearance and repatriation, or various means of assassination such as poisoning.

[1]G. Platteau, «Rencontre avec des rescapés du génocide rwandais: la transmission de l'irreprésentable est-elle possible?» *Cahiers critiques de thérapie familiale et de pratiques de réseaux* 38, 2007/1, 81–98; J. Banyanga, K. Björkqvist & K. Österman, "Trauma inflicted by genocide: Experiences of the Rwandan Diaspora in Finland", *Cogent Psychology* 4(1), 2017, 12; B. Dervaux & A. Versailles, «Rwanda, la vie après» Documentaire, 2014, 72, available at http://www.andreversaille.com/?Rwanda-la-vie-apres-Paroles-de-mères (last visited 26 Nov. 2018).

M. Nduwamungu
Fleurus, Belgium

M. Yonekawa and A. Sugiki (eds.), *Repatriation, Insecurity, and Peace*,
https://doi.org/10.1007/978-981-15-2850-7_4

The trauma and insecurity of refugees has been further exacerbated by several factors, which I will further describe in this chapter, based primarily on other studies and my own observations as a former refugee in Zaire and Belgium, as well as on the testimonies of refugees who fled to Kenya, Zambia, and Cameroon. The identified factors of Rwandan refugee trauma and insecurity identified in this study are as follows:

1. Mental health and post-traumatic stress disorders (PTSD);
2. A one-sided narrative of their collective history;
3. The demonisation and dehumanisation of one ethnic group; and
4. The denial of justice and of the right to mourn Hutus; and the Rwandan government showing no empathy to refugees, whom it calls "the enemies of the country".

2 Traumatic Experiences Leading to Mental Health and PTSD

Among those who lived in Rwanda before 1994, there is not one person who has not lost a relative or experienced the horrors of war. Many Hutu experienced the trauma of observing their neighbours—both Tutsi and Hutu—being killed, as well as the murder of relatives, parents, siblings, and friends by the Rwanda Patriotic Army (RPA), both in Rwanda and the DRC. Many fleeing the bloodshed had to abandon loved ones along the way because they were too weak or sick to walk. The mental health of children born and hunted in the Congolese jungle raised grave concerns. However, in Rwanda, Hutu are not allowed to talk about their traumatic experiences in public, and they can be prosecuted for doing so under the genocide ideology law (see below).

The traumatic experiences of the people of the prefecture of Byumba, located in Northern Rwanda, began in 1990. Residents of Byumba were driven out of their homes when the RPF began their attack, fleeing to Nyacyonga, a small town on the outskirts of capital Kigali. As the United Nations High Commissioner for Refugees (UNHCR) did not have mandate to protect these internally displaced persons (IDPs), the Red Cross and other NGOs, as well as individuals help them as best they could. I personally recall seeing the "Nyacyonga" people travelling the roads in search of help. More people were displaced when the war reached other northern parts of the country. Food became scarce. Some people managed to go back to their home villages and return with food, but some others were not so lucky—they were either killed by landmines, executed by the RPA, or even dismembered and sent back to Habyarimana with the message "see what we are capable of!" This carnage, coupled with bombing that could be heard in Kigali, traumatised many of the IDPs. It worsened when more than two million people fled the country in 1994 and later. Most refugees did not have the time to prepare for their escape. Some left their homes hoping they would come back as soon as peace returned, but their wait stretched months, years, and decades. The vast majority of refugees sought refuge in neighbouring eastern Zaire, while others were scattered in neighbouring Tanzania, Burundi, and Uganda.

I myself was a refugee in former Zaire. While the Zairean population volunteered to help refugees, its military did not welcome us. The Zairean soldiers initially sympathised with us, but as more refugees continued to pour in, the soldiers began to extort the refugees for their vehicles, money, and even mattresses. The body searches were the most degrading—the soldiers believed that money could be hidden anywhere. As time went by, it became clear to many refugees that staying in Zaire was dangerous. The newly-formed Rwandan army, the RPA, launched projectiles across the border into the refugee camps and attacked refugees at night on inflatable boats. Those who had the financial means began to gradually leave the camps for Kenya, Tanzania, and Zambia, particularly between 1995 and 1996.

However, more refugees fled to Kenya between 1996 and 1997, following an attack on refugee camps and the mass murder of refugees in Zaire by the RPA, who was helping the Congolese rebel spokesperson, Laurent-Désiré Kabila, oust Zairean President Mobutu Sese Seko, as well as subsequent forced repatriation from Tanzania. Between 1996 and 1998, the RPF public relations machine went into overdrive, convincing host countries that all these refugees were "genocidaires" that had to be sent back to Rwanda to face trial. Some refugees said that Zaireans were given rewards when they captured Rwandan fugitives but the authority rewarding them is unknown—it might have been the Alliance of Democratic Forces for the Liberation of Congo-Zaire (AFDL) rebels or the pressured Zairean authorities. The Zaireans apparently used arrows to capture Rwandan refugees for return to Rwanda, and the former were paid \$5 per male and \$3 per female and/or child. Tanzania forcefully repatriated refugees who were accused of conducting political activities in refugee camps.

In Kenya, after some members of the opposition political party were invited to go to Kigali, rumours spread on their return to Kenya that Rwandan refugees were supportive of President Arap Moi and that they would vote for him in the elections scheduled at that time. The Kenyan police took advantage of this situation by extorting money from the refugees. As a result, many refugees were imprisoned in Kenya.

The Jesuit Refugee Service (JRS), an Implementing Partner of the UNHCR in Kenya, was in charge of providing assistance to refugees. The JRS was headed by a Jesuit priest who had the power of life and death over refugees. The JRS issued so-called "protection letters", but seemed to prefer to distribute them to refugee women in heels and miniskirts. Eventually, many refugees settled in the area, with or without protection letters. On 26 February 1996, an assassination attempt was made on Seth Sendashonga, former Rwandan Minister of Internal Affairs, who fled to Kenya after being dismissed from his government post in 1995. At that time, many refugees did not take the threat seriously, thinking it was a ploy by Sendashonga to gain the sympathy and trust of the refugees. The refugees did not trust him because nobody really knew that he, a former member of the RPF, had already broken ties with the RPF. While some people began fleeing Kenya to other countries, others believed the assassination attempt was staged.

There were other assassinations—Théoneste Lizinde and Augustin Bugilimfura[2] in October 1996 and Sendashonga in 1998, all in Nairobi—which pushed more Rwandan refugees into exile further away. Their preferred destinations were Cameroon, Togo, the Republic of Congo (Brazzaville), Mozambique, Zambia, and Gabon. Those who had the financial means or benefactors to lend them the required sum of money left for Europe. However, we heard that the so-called "1959 refugees", mainly Tutsi, who had settled in Europe since 1959, were mobilised to block the lines of new asylum-seekers, mainly Hutu. Some Tutsi extremists shouted at newly arrived Hutu refugees in public transportation or on the streets and accused them of being *Interahamwe* or *génocidaires*. In many developed countries, Rwandan refugees managed to get asylum but still had to navigate many obstacles, such as long interviews aimed at checking whether any asylum seeker had committed any crimes in 1994. The biggest challenge was to prove their innocence to the local authorities. Even if you obtained refugee status, looking for a house or an apartment to rent was another challenge. Some landlords refused to accommodate people if they did not have a job or were using government aid. Many refugees were forced to accept any kind of shelter as long as it had a roof.

Looking for a job was the next step–some diplomas obtained in Rwanda were not accepted because they were not equivalent to the diploma standards of the European host country. Professionals, such as physicians and holders of a university degree were required to go back to a host country university to get their foreign degrees accepted. Those who were still young did it, but older refugees did not try. Some physicians had no other choice but to downgrade to nurses. Some younger refugees who were trained as computer scientists were lucky to be hired immediately by the NGOs for whom they worked before 1994.

To make matters worse, the Rwandan regime engaged in the assassination of critics abroad. Refugees in exile, even though protected by international laws, were not out of the reach of Rwandan death squads. Human Rights Watch called the phenomenon "repression across borders.[3]" Apart from Sendashonga and Lizinde, the death of Juvenal Uwilingiyimana in Belgium in November 2005[4] remains a mystery even today. Moreover, in May 2011, the United Kingdom (U.K.) Metropolitan Police warned two British citizens of Rwandan origin that their lives were in danger from agents of the Rwandan government, as well as one British citizen of Rwandan origin in March 2018. The Swedish government also expelled a Rwandan diplomat for

[2]Théoneste Lizinde was the intelligence chief under Habyarimana. In 1981, an aborted coup d'état that he supposedly carried out with Alex Kanyarengwe resulted in his being sent to prison in Ruhengeri. When the RPA broke into Ruhengeri prison in 1991, it took Lizinde back to Uganda. When the RPF came to power, Lizinde was promoted to Colonel and Member of Parliament. Lizinde and the RPF parted ways in late 1995 and he settled in Kenya. The day he died, he was with Augustin Bugilimfura, a former businessman.

[3]Human Rights Watch, "*Rwanda, Repression Across Borders——Attacks and Threats Against Rwandan Opponents and Critics Abroad*", 28 Jan. 2014, available at www.hrw.org/news/2014/01/28/rwanda-repression-across-borders (last visited 3 Dec. 2018).

[4]Wikipedia Juvenal Uwilingiyimana, available at https://en.wikipedia.org/wiki/Juv%C3%A9nal_Uwilingiyimana (last visited 20 Jan. 2019).

attempting to assassinate a Rwandan asylum-seeker in Sweden.[5] Colonel Karegeya Patrick, former chief of external intelligence was murdered in South Africa on 1 January 2014. The Rwandan former chief of staff, Kayumba Nyamwasa, has escaped three assassination attempts in South Africa. Two other Belgians were assassinated in South Africa in June 2018. Thomas Ngeze—the son of Hassan Ngeze, a former Rwandan journalist who owned the *Kangura Journal* in the 1990s and who was imprisoned after his trial at the International Criminal Tribunal for Rwanda (ICTR), was found hanging in a hotel room on 15 June 2018. His friend, Jan-Pieter Staelens, also died mysteriously.[6] Mr Staelens was found dead, burnt in his car alongside a highway in South Africa on 29 July 2018. It is said that Mr. Staelens, a former lawyer, was investigating the death of Thomas Ngeze whose father was convicted of involvement in the 1994 genocide. Other refugees in the DRC have been pursued in the last two-and-a-half decades under the pretext of neutralising the armed rebel group Democratic Forces for the Liberation of Rwanda (FDLR). Rwandans all over the world are haunted by the idea that they might never live in peace.

Rwandans in the Diaspora are still socially and emotionally connected with people inside the country. What happens to a family member in Rwanda also affects a relative in the Diaspora. The Rwandan regime is aware of this reality and holds relatives of people in the Diaspora as hostages, in a sense, to prevent them from engaging in political activities in the country. Many people refuse to engage in opposition politics while in exile for fear of what could happen to their relatives back home. This means that the fear of the repressive regime in Rwanda is acutely felt among the refugee community. There is sufficient evidence to show that Rwandans have been arrested at home because they have family members abroad who are critical of the government, such as Messrs Franck Rusagara and Tom Byabagamba, both relatives of David Himbara, former secretary of President Paul Kagame, and Rugigana, brother of Kayumba Nyamwasa, former Secretary General of the RPF. Recent examples include parliament member Edda Mukabagwiza, who publicly announced that she did not want to be associated with her sister who is staying in the United States and is a member of the Rwanda National Congress (RNC).

The experience of witnessing a genocide, leaving your home country, gaining asylum, looking for accommodation and a job, and the fear of being pursued by the Rwandan government is accompanied by PTSD and constant fear. However, two issues stand in the way of helping Rwandans deal with this trauma. First, Rwandan culture views mental health issues differently than how the West does. In the Rwandan context, a person is considered as having a mental health problem only when they exhibit signs of madness. People will not seek health advice for themselves or for a relative until it is too late.

---

[5] A. Meldrum, "Rwanda news: Sweden expels Rwanda diplomat for spying", *Global Post*, 13 Feb. 2012, available at https://www.pri.org/stories/2012-02-13/rwanda-news-sweden-expels-rwanda-diplomat-spying (last visited 19 Jan. 2019).

[6] J. P. Stroobants, "Enquête sur la mort de deux Belges en Afrique du Sud, en lien avec le génocide rwandais", *Le Monde Afrique*, 24 Aug. 2018, available at https://www.lemonde.fr/afrique/article/2018/08/24/en-afrique-du-sud-la-mort-suspecte-de-deux-belges-en-lien-avec-le-rwanda_5345686_3212.html (last visited 19 Jan. 2019).

The second issue is that, as the Hutu have been demonised as perpetrators of genocide, they are denied victimhood and moral consideration (see below). These two considerations make it harder for the experts to provide mental health support to many Hutus who need it. Even refugees who live in affluent societies do not seek much-needed mental health treatment. Healthcare professionals are not necessarily aware of the PTSD experienced by many Rwandan people. They may not understand the complexity of Rwandan culture and history, which can be a challenge in treating refugees. The number of Rwandan psychologists is gradually increasing, but they are scattered over the planet and some patients are still not receiving care. Others are traumatised by basic questions often asked without any sensitivity by healthcare providers. Refugees run the risk of being segregated into "good" and "bad" patients when healthcare professionals ask them which ethnic group they belong to (see below).

Sometimes I tell myself that treatment was offered too late, and would have been more useful back in 1990–1998. The International Women's Network for Democracy and Peace (IwnDP)—a women's NGO established in 2010, with offices in Canada, the Netherlands, and Belgium—has reflected on this after observing the first symptoms of psychological disturbances among some refugees through a series of conferences held in 2013 and 2015 in Belgium.[7] It is true that the awareness came a bit late, but refugees were busy fulfilling their basic needs for survival. A big challenge for refugees is the lack of financial support to carry out such ambitious projects i.e. giving proper care to those people suffering from asylum-related psychological disturbances.

3 Narrative of the Rwandan Tragedy and Role of the International Community

The current Rwandan regime has constructed and imposed a narrative about Rwanda's history of genocide. It portrays the RPF as the one that stopped the genocide, brought about national reconciliation, and ushered in an economic renaissance. It further denies the RPF's responsibility in shooting down the Juvénal Habyarimana's presidential plane, and presents the ex-Rwandan government army under President Habyarimana and Interahamwe as the only ones who were responsible for the genocide in 1994. The narrative divides Rwandans into good people and survivors (Tutsi) and bad people perpetrators of the Genocide (Hutu), and ignores the Twas—an ethnic minority group rarely mentioned in recent historical writings on Rwanda—who could be categorised as good or bad depending on unknown criteria. The regime also has the sole right to propagate this narrative, and has enacted laws to prosecute anyone who strays from its official line. The categories of "victims",

[7]Dr. S. Goffinet, "Les Mémoires Traumatiques, les Résistances, la Résilience et les Générations", 14 Dec. 2013, available at http://www.rifdp-iwndp.org (last visited 19 Jan. 2019).

"survivors", and "perpetrators" fuel the sense of trauma in the Hutu population.[8] The deaths of thousands of Hutus is officially considered collateral damage in Rwanda. To make matters worse, Hutu refugees are called "Negative Diaspora", meaning "a hostile Diaspora that stands against current Rwandan politics". Moreover, the Rwandan government mainly associates the "Negative Diaspora" with Hutu communities, according to Claudine Kuradusenge.[9]

Some reports have documented the crimes committed by the RPF. The UNHCR team led by Robert Gersony reported that the RPF systematically killed between 25,000 and 45,000 Hutus as it made its way toward Kigali in 1994. Their investigation had covered one-third of the ten prefectures they visited. The report mentioned that "the RPF has used the genocide to legitimate massacres on this civilian population".[10] There is no doubt that the Hutu population was massacred and subjected to inhuman, degrading treatment, and horrible death. Referring to this cover-up, Professor Filip Reyntjens commented in the Denmark newspaper, *Information* "by not publishing the Gersony report and other information about RPF's massacres, a blank cheque was issued to continue the murders… Publication of the [Garreton] report would have prevented the RPF to commit the massacre of over 200,000 Hutu refugees in Zaire".[11]

The Mapping Report, issued by the United Nations Office of the High Commissioner for Human Rights on 1 October 2010, exposed the most serious violations of human rights and international humanitarian law committed in the DRC between 1993 and 2003. The report highlighted the crimes committed against Rwandan Hutu refugees and Congolese Hutu, including the act which "could be characterized as crimes of genocide".[12] The Mapping Report is corroborated by other reports, such as those from Human Rights Watch, which state:

> the crimes committed by RPF soldiers were so systematic and widespread and took place over so long a period of time that commanding officers must have been aware of them. RPF soldiers massacred unarmed civilians, many of them women and children, who had assembled for a meeting on their orders.[13]

---

[8]E. Zorbas, "Reconciliation in Post-Genocide Rwanda", *African Journal of Legal Studies*, 1(1), 2004, 29–52. https://doi.org/10.1163/221097312X13397499735904.

[9]C. Kuradusenge, "Denied Victimhood and Contested Narratives: The Case of Hutu Diaspora", *Genocide Studies and Prevention* 10(2), 2016, 59–75. https://doi.org/10.5038/1911-9933.10.2.1352

[10]UNHCR, "Prospects for Early Repatriation of Rwandan Refugees Currently in Burundi, Tanzania and DRC" (hereafter, Gersony report), Oct. 1994, available at http://www.whale.to/b/gersony_report.html (last visited 19 Jan. 2019).

[11]G. Willum, "Rwanda report could have saved lives", *Information* (Denmark), 28 June 1999, available at http://www.willum.com/articles/information28jun99/index.htm (last visited 19 Jan. 2019).

[12]UN Office of the High Commissioner for Human Rights, Report of the Mapping Exercise documenting the most serious violations of human rights and international humanitarian law committed within the territory of the Democratic Republic of the Congo between March 1993 and June 2003, 2010 (Mapping Report), Aug. 2010, paras. 518–522.

[13]Human Rights Watch, "The Patriotic Front", available at http://www.hrw.org/reports/1999/rwanda/Geno1-3-03.htm#P86_35545 (last visited 5 Dec. 2018).

Amnesty International also reported—

> [I]ndividuals such as local officials and other educated—mainly Hutu—have been assassinated in circumstances which lead Amnesty International to believe that they were targeted specifically because of their social or political position, or even because of their ethnic origin.[14]

Moreover, Canadian journalist Judi Rever has given ample evidence to demonstrate that the crimes committed by the Rwandan regime against the Hutu undeniably constitute genocide.[15]

What is shocking and heart-breaking is the complicity by some political personalities and governments in the cover-up of the atrocities committed by the ruling regime in Rwanda. The personalities glossed over the gross violation of human rights by the Rwandan regime include former British Prime Minister Tony Blair, former US President Bill Clinton, and Howard Buffet. For them, Rwanda's so-called economic progress somehow excuses the regime's poor human rights record in Rwanda and the DRC. Following the publication of Mapping Report, Blair said that President Kagame's economic record outweighed other concerns.[16] In 2012, he opposed the suspension of aid to Rwanda despite UN findings that Kigali had created and supported the murderous Congolese rebel group M23 in Congo.[17] Clinton called Kagame "one of the greatest leaders of our time".[18] Concerning the alleged gross violation of human rights by the Rwandan government, Clinton stated: "I don't think human rights should be violated in the Congo to protect the territorial integrity of Rwanda. But I suppose I do make more allowances for a government that produces as much progress as that one has".[19] These statements suggest that economics is more important to these world leaders than the fundamental rights of the Rwandan people. Even governments such as the DRC, Rwanda, and the United States interfered in the investigation by Robert Garreton, the UN Special Rapporteur on Human Rights in the DRC, on the RPF crimes in the DRC.[20]

---

[14]Amnesty International, *Rwanda: Ending the Silence*, 24 Sep. 1997, available at https://www.amnesty.org/en/documents/AFR47/032/1997/en/ (last visited 5 Dec. 2018).

[15]J. Rever, *In Praise of Blood—The Crimes of the Rwandan Patriotic Front*, Penguin Random House, 2018, 72–80.

[16]C. McGrill, "Tony Blair defends support for Rwandan leader Paul Kagame", *The Guardian*, 31 Dec. 2010, available at: http://www.guardian.co.uk/world/2010/dec/31/tony-blair-rwanda-paul-kagame (last visited 6 Dec. 2018).

[17]T. Murphy, "Why Blair and Buffet are wrong about giving international aid to Rwanda", *The Guardian*, 12 Apr. 2013, available at: https://www.theguardian.com/world/2013/apr/12/rwanda-kagame-blair-aid (last visited 6 Dec. 2018).

[18]D. Smith, "Paul Kagame's Rwanda: African success story or authoritarian state?" *The Guardian*, 12 Oct. 2010, available at: https://www.theguardian.com/world/2012/oct/10/paul-kagame-rwanda-success-authoritarian (last visited 6 Dec. 2018).

[19]*News of Rwanda*, "President Clinton in spirited defense of President Kagame", 16 Aug. 2013, available at: http://www.newsofrwanda.com/featured1/20022/president-clinton-in-spirited-defense-of-president-kagame/ (last visited 6 Dec. 2018).

[20]*Report on the situation of human rights in DR Congo, submitted by the Special Rapporteur, Mr. Roberto Garretón* (E/CN.4/2001/40), 1 Feb. 2001, available at https://reliefweb.int/report/burundi/report-situation-human-rights-dr-congo-submitted-special-rapporteur-mr-roberto (last visited 4 Dec. 2018).

The nicknamed Kigali spin doctors—spokespersons hired to give a favourable interpretation of events to the media or to manipulate information (*gutekinika*)—have managed to shape international opinion on the Rwandan human rights record. In particular, Rwandan officials and propagandists have assuaged criticism over the regime's political repression and massive violations of international humanitarian law, the invasion of Congo and plunder of Congolese resources, the dangerous social engineering exercise (*Ubudehe*)[21] and social exclusion, and many NGOs helping only Tutsi orphans while the Ministry of Local Government has suspended schemes designated to help other orphans.

The Hutu community has interpreted this acquiescence of the international community as a deliberate attempt to protect criminals within Rwanda's ruling class from prosecution. At worst, the international complacency is construed to mean that Hutu lives do not matter as much as Tutsi lives. This double standard in the international community has exacerbated Hutu–Tutsi tensions, and ultimately undermined national reconciliation and long-term peace and security. The international community's apparent disregard for the rights of Hutus has also left survivors feeling helpless and aggravated their trauma.

The RPF's one-sided narrative of genocide also has a bearing on the school curriculum in many host countries. There are Hutu children and adults who, when asked, hesitate to reveal their ethnic identity for fear of being harassed or identified as the "evil" ones in the conflict. Hutu children are often traumatised by what is taught in school and begin to doubt the innocence of their parents.

The Rwandan government has made efforts to exploit this feeling by organising guided tours of Rwanda, called "come and see" visits to Rwandan youth in exile in order to sell an image of the country that is different from what the youth were told by their parents. Some parents are afraid of telling their children the full story about the Rwandan tragedy to avoid exacerbating ethnic conflict, and, therefore, leave them vulnerable to the official narrative from the Rwandan regime. Due to such propaganda, such as official phrasing like the "Genocide against Tutsi", the Hutu youth are forced to live in denial of their ancestry and their identity because the latter is often associated with the genocide. Many consider themselves on the wrong side of history, as is frequently repeated by Rwandan propaganda.

4 Policy of Demonisation and Dehumanisation of the Hutu Population

The Rwandan regime's one-sided narrative of history suggests that almost every Hutu who opposed the genocide in 1994 was killed. Those who survived, who fled and those living in the country, are considered either active participants or passive onlookers, and therefore, are considered to be perpetrators, or the descendants of

[21] P. Nizeyimana, K-W. Lee & S. Sim, "A study on the classification of households in Rwanda based on factor scores", *Journal of the Korean Data & Information Science Society* 29(2) 2018, 547–555.

perpetrators.[22] Not only are the perpetrators of the killings of the Hutu immune from prosecution, but Hutu victims are systematically demonised. Hutu are dehumanised, and are characterised as being undeserving of moral consideration or empathy. As a result, they become vulnerable to inhuman and degrading treatment.

RPF uses a well-established public relations machine to persuade the international community that every Hutu, even those born outside Rwanda, is a descendant of *genocidaires* or harbour pro-genocide ideologies. Under the Rwandan laws regarding denial of genocide against Tutsi or genocide ideology, one can be prosecuted for talking about crimes committed by the ruling RPF party and its army, the RPA. Laws punishing genocide denial and genocide ideology are tailored only for the Hutus and the Twas.

A recent example could be seen in the local level elections in Belgium in 2018, where pro-RPF operatives and Belgian supporters of the Rwandan regime launched a smear campaign against Belgians of Rwandan descent who attempted to run in local elections. The targeted group were youth emerging in Jambo, a youth NGO from the African Great Lakes Region, whose members—Gustave Mbonyumutwa, Laure Uwase, and Mugabe Nizeyimana—ran for local political parties. Alain Destexhe, a Belgian senator sympathetic to the RPF, and Olivier Nduhungirehe, a former Rwandan ambassador in Belgium, started a smear campaign that resulted in the non-participation of Mbonyumutwa, whose party Démocrate Fédéraliste Indépendant (DéFI) president, Olivier Maingain, ceded to pressure. The two other political parties Centre Démocrate Humaniste (CDH) and Christen—Democratisch en Vlaams (CD&V) resisted the pressure—Laure and Mugabe participated in the election.[23] Nduhungirehe, a descendant of a Hutu, labelled these candidates as "Nazi children".[24] It is believed that the grandparents of these Belgian-Rwandan candidates were key figures in fighting and ending the feudal monarchical regime and installing a republican regime in 1959-1960.[25] Surprisingly, Olivier's father, Jean-Chrysostome Nduhungirehe, was himself Finance Minister under Habyarimana. Why then should he compare the children of his father's colleagues to Nazis just because their parents served the previous regimes, and not apply the title to himself? Did he want to impress his boss?

---

[22] M. Mamdani, *When Victims Become Killers: Colonialism, Nativism, and the Genocide in Rwanda*, Princeton, Princeton University Press, 2002, in E. Zorbas, Reconciliation in Post-Genocide Rwanda, *African Journal of Legal Studies* Vol. 1, no. 1 (2004), 47.

[23] R. Mbonyumutwa, «Non à l'ingérence du Rwanda dans les communales belges». Carte blanche, *Le Vif L'Express* 10 Sept. 2018, available at https://www.levif.be/actualite/belgique/non-a-l-ingerence-du-rwanda-dans-les-communales-belges/article-opinion-888953.html (last visited 19 Jan. 2019).

[24] G. Musabyimana, *Echos d' Afrique.com*, «Communales belges de 2018: faisons connaissance avec ces candidats rwandais qui dérangent», 9 Sep. 2018, available at http://www.echosdafrique.com/20180909-communales-belges-doctobre-2018-faisons-connaissance-avec-ces-candidats-rwandais-qui-derangent (last visited 31 Jan. 2019).

[25] Sud-info, "Gustave Mbonyumutwa, le chef de file DéFI à Saint-Georges, a été viré pour négationnisme", 4 Sep. 2018, available at https://www.sudinfo.be/id73157/article/2018-09-04/gustave-mbonyumutwa-le-chef-de-file-defi-saint-georges-ete-vire-pour (last visited 5 Dec. 2018).

Second-generation Rwandans in exile face the pressure of navigating between two cultures, one lived by their parents and another one of their host countries, and the latter often not willing to fully accept the former. The refusal of Mbonyumutwa to stand in the local elections is an example of the frustration of young people who want to integrate into European society, but still face interference from the Rwandan government.

The anti-Hutu campaign in Belgium by the Rwandan government demonstrated how far the regime can go in harassing its Diaspora, and how successful it can be in dragging Western states into the campaign of demonising Hutu exiles. After much advocacy on their behalf, only one Rwandan-Belgian candidate opted out, but the scar left by the campaign is still fresh and is a reminder that Hutu Diaspora can be targeted any time the Rwandan regime wants to tarnish their image.

Another instance of dehumanisation was seen during the Miss Rwanda contest, which started after the genocide. In January 2019, a Hutu lady, Josiane Mwiseneza, participated in the contest. The public massively voted for her in what seemed like a protest vote, resurfacing Hutu-Tutsi tensions on social media, where Hutu expressed why they thought that Josiane should win the contest—primarily because no Hutu had won before. However, some Tutsi felt that Mwiseneza was not "in her place" and argued that a Hutu should never win the contest. As her participation stirred up tension between the Hutu and Tutsi communities, Mwiseneza ended up ironically winning the provocative title of "Miss Popularity".

The United Nations, which is ostensibly expected to defend those who are vulnerable, is well aware of these injustices. The Commission of Experts' preliminary and final reports (S/1994/1125 and S/1994/1405) on which basis the Security Council Resolution 955 set up the ICTR, point out that "during the war that followed the assassination of President Habyarimana, individuals from *both* sides to the armed conflict in Rwanda during the period from 6 April 1994 to 15 July 1994 perpetrated serious breaches of international humanitarian law (emphasis added)".

Despite the mandate of the tribunal to prosecute serious crimes and foster reconciliation, including recognition that both sides committed atrocities, only one side has been tried. The international community has favoured the victor's justice and historical narrative. Even Hutus who have been cleared of the charges by the ICTR, or those who have served their sentences, have not been allowed to join their families in exile; this is because, in most cases, host countries will not offer asylum to these individuals. The isolation has created serious socio-psychological problems for Rwandan families which are denied the right to live together as a family.

By applying the policy of victor's justice, the international community has indirectly assisted in alienating more than three-quarters of the Rwandan population. In addition, it has given the RPF regime a leeway to enact an array of laws to ensure immunity from prosecution. It has helped create two social groups in Rwanda: the Tutsi victim, survivor or returnee, and the Hutu perpetrator. Through a policy of demonisation, many Hutu feel that nobody cares about their pain and anguish, and their basic right to publicly mourn the loss of their loved ones are denied.

Nevertheless, one thing must be made clear—claiming justice for crimes against Hutus—equal protection under the law is a fundamental human right, as stipulated in Article 7 of the Universal Declaration of Human Rights. It is important to insist on equal justice for permanent peace in Rwanda.

Apart from justice, exiled Hutus are denied the right to mourn and bury their loved ones in peace and amid security. In any culture, providing a proper burial to a loved one and having time to mourn are essential parts of the grieving and healing process. However, when family members die in Rwanda, those who are in exile find it difficult to attend the funeral due to political and security concerns. For example, when Violette Uwamahoro travelled to Rwanda to attend her father's funeral, she was arrested by the police and held incommunicado for 14 days. She was allegedly detained because her husband is a member of the RNC, and was released under pressure by U.K. authorities.

According to Rwandans, who believe in life after death, the spirit of a person who has not been buried properly is considered to be dangerous to the living relatives. It is believed that they can cause illness or misfortune. Even though the belief in the malevolence of ancestral spirits may have less relevance today among a section of the Rwandan population, not being able to remember loved ones who have passed away has a psychological impact.

It is in this context that the bones and skulls exhibited in genocide memorials are unnatural. All deceased are entitled to a burial. According to ancestral beliefs, any unburied remains will not stop asking for a sepulchre. Why do the Rwandan authorities continue to expose these human remains in memorials? Some people still attribute occasional misfortunes that befall the Rwandan government to the spirits who cannot yet rest. The other question raised is the ethnicity of those human remains. At the genocide commemoration ceremonies held every April, survivors come to know where their family victims are buried insensitively, often in mass graves, after what they are buried in dignity. So, who are those who are not brought to rest? Some people think that they are the Hutu victims of the whole tragedy.

5 Conclusion

While it is important to condemn in the strongest terms possible the genocide against the Tutsi and prosecute those responsible, the fact that the international community has swept other crimes against humanity and genocide against the Hutu under the carpet is heart-breaking. It makes Hutus feel rejected by an international community that claims to defend their human rights.

The official narrative that the majority of Hutu were either active participants or passive onlookers in the genocide, and that almost every Hutu who opposed the genocide was killed, implies that every Hutu is a perpetrator and dangerous. This leaves every Hutu vulnerable. This fear, and its negative consequences have deeply entered the psyche of many people. Therefore, the Rwandan regime's official narrative and its public relations machine, coupled with its social engineering program, have eroded the image that many Hutus have of themselves. They also feel excluded from public life, as they do not have access to higher posts in politics and other fields, unless they toe the official narrative or confess their guilt of being Hutu.

By denying Hutus the right of victimhood, those who have experienced PTSD are denied access to relevant medical care, particularly mental health treatment. The propaganda in Rwanda and in the Diaspora, which is largely challenged by the Hutu community and newly exiled Tutsi refugees has confused some youth's minds. The testimonies of the Hutu witnesses and the Tutsi who no longer share the same narrative as the government's are not necessarily listened to.

It is high time that those who really want Rwanda to prosper, and that are quite knowledgeable about the truth surrounding the Rwandan tragedy speak out, as they can save Rwanda from another genocide. However, this will only be possible when deep-seated grievances over injustices and social and moral exclusion have been addressed.

References

Amnesty International, *Rwanda: Ending the Silence*, 24 Sep. 1997, available at https://www.amnesty.org/en/documents/AFR47/032/1997/en/ (last visited 5 Dec. 2018)

J.A. Banyanga, K. Björkqvist, K. Österman, Trauma Inflicted by Genocide: Experiences of the Rwandan Diaspora in Finland. *Cogent. Psychol.* **4**(1), 12 (2017)

B. Dervaux, A. Versailles, Rwanda, la vie après. *Documentaire* **72** (2014). http://www.andreversaille.com/?Rwanda-la-vie-apres-Paroles-de-mères (last visited 26 Nov 2018)

S. Goffinet, *Les Mémoires Traumatiques, les Résistances, la Résilience et les Générations* (2013). www.rifdp-iwndp.org (last visited 19 Jan 2019)

Human Rights Watch, "*Rwanda, Repression Across Borders—Attacks and Threats Against Rwandan Opponents and Critics Abroad*", 28 Jan 2014, available at www.hrw.org/news/2014/01/28/rwanda-repression-across-borders (last visited 3 Dec. 2018)

Human Rights Watch, "The Patriotic Front", available at http://www.hrw.org/reports/1999/rwanda/Geno1-3-03.htm#P86_35545 (last visited 5 Dec. 2018)

C. Kuradusenge, Denied Victimhood and Contested Narratives: The Case of Hutu Diaspora. *Genocide Stud. Prev.* **10**(2), 59–75 (2016). https://doi.org/10.5038/1911-9933.10.2.1352

M. Mamdani, *When Victims Become Killers: Colonialism, Nativism, and the Genocide in Rwanda*, Princeton, Princeton University Press (2003)

R. Mbonyumutwa, Non à l'ingérence du Rwanda dans les communales belges. Carte blanche, *Le Vif L'Express* (2018). https://www.levif.be/actualite/belgique/non-a-l-ingerence-du-rwanda-dans-les-communales-belges/article-opinion-888953.html (last visited 19 Jan 2019)

C. McGrill, Tony Blair Defends Support for Rwandan Leader Paul Kagame, *The Guardian* (2010). http://www.guardian.co.uk/world/2010/dec/31/tony-blair-rwanda-paul-kagame (last visited 6 Dec. 2018)

A. Meldrum, Rwanda News: Sweden Expels Rwanda Diplomat for Spying. *Global Post* (2012). https://www.pri.org/stories/2012-02-13/rwanda-news-sweden-expels-rwanda-diplomat-spying (last visited 19 Jan 2019)

G. Musabyimana, Communales belges de 2018: faisons connaissance avec ces candidats rwandais qui dérangent (2018). http://www.echosdafrique.com/20180909-communales-belges-doctobre-2018-faisons-connaissance-avec-ces-candidats-rwandais-qui-derangent (last visited 31 Jan. 2019)

T. Murphy, Why Blair and Buffet are Wrong about Giving International Aid to Rwanda. *The Guardian* (2013). https://www.theguardian.com/world/2013/apr/12/rwanda-kagame-blair-aid (last visited 6 Dec 2018)

News of Rwanda, "President Clinton in spirited defense of President Kagame", 16 Aug. 2013, available at: http://www.newsofrwanda.com/featured1/20022/president-clinton-in-spirited-defense-of-president-kagame/ (last visited 6 Dec. 2018)

P. Nizeyimana, K.-W. Lee, S. Sim, A Study on the Classification of Households in Rwanda Based on Factor Scores. *J. Korean Data Inf. Sci. Soc.* **29**(2), 547–555 (2018)

G. Platteau, Rencontre avec des rescapés du génocide rwandais: la transmission de l'irreprésentable est-elle possible?*Cahiers critiques de thérapie familiale et de pratiques de réseaux* **38**(1), 81–98 (2007)

Report on the situation of human rights in DR Congo, submitted by the Special Rapporteur, Mr. Roberto Garretón (E/CN.4/2001/40), 1 Feb. 2001, available at https://reliefweb.int/report/burundi/report-situation-human-rights-dr-congo-submitted-special-rapporteur-mr-roberto (last visited 4 Dec. 2018)

J. Rever, *In Praise of Blood, The Crimes of the Rwandan Patriotic Front* (Penguin Random House, 2018), pp. 72–80

D. Smith, Paul Kagame's Rwanda: African Success Story or Authoritarian State? *The Guardian* (2010). https://www.theguardian.com/world/2012/oct/10/paul-kagame-rwanda-success-authoritarian (last visited 6 Dec. 2018)

J.P. Stroobants, Enquête sur la mort de deux Belges en Afrique du Sud, en lien avec le génocide rwandais. *Le Monde Afrique* (2018). https://www.lemonde.fr/afrique/article/2018/08/24/en-afrique-du-sud-la-mort-suspecte-de-deux-belges-en-lien-avec-le-rwanda_5345686_3212.html (last visited 19 Jan. 2019)

UN Office of the High Commissioner for Human Rights, Report of the Mapping Exercise documenting the most serious violations of human rights and international humanitarian law committed within the territory of the Democratic Republic of the Congo between March 1993 and June 2003, 2010 (Mapping Report), Aug. 2010, paras. 518–522

UNHCR, "Prospects for Early Repatriation of Rwandan Refugees Currently in Burundi, Tanzania and DRC" (hereafter, Gersony report), Oct. 1994, available at http://www.whale.to/b/gersony_report.html (last visited 19 Jan. 2019)

Wikipedia Juvenal Uwilingiyimana, available at https://en.wikipedia.org/wiki/Juv%C3%A9nal_Uwilingiyimana (last visited 20 Jan. 2019)

G. Willum, Rwanda Report Could Have Saved Lives. *Information* (Denmark) (1999). http://www.willum.com/articles/information28jun99/index.htm (last visited 19 Jan 2019)

E. Zorbas, Reconciliation in Post-genocide Rwanda. *Afr. J. Leg. Stud.* **1**(1), 29–52 (2004). https://doi.org/10.1163/221097312X13397499735904

Refugee Repatriation and Peace Process: Motive and Nature of Repatriation of Rwandan Refugees (1990–2017)

Masako Yonekawa

1 Introduction

Returning to one's homeland following the end of a conflict is an optimal solution for individual refugees. It is also the most desirable durable solution from the perspective of the United Nations High Commissioner for Refugees (UNHCR). Further, the return of refugees has begun to be recognised as a central pillar of peace processes[1] as they have evolved since the end of the Cold War.[2] In other words, the end of a conflict is associated with "a return to normality, peace and stability".[3] As such, it has been recognised that repatriation is part of post-conflict peacebuilding, and refugee repatriation is a sign that peace is actually in process.[4]

On the other hand, two main arguments by two prominent refugee scholars challenge this connection between repatriation and the peace process. First, Howard

[1]Peace processes, which do not have any universal agreed definition, are perceived in this chapter not only as two main phrases of peace negotiations leading to a political/constitutional agreement, and post-conflict peace building, but also a transition from negative peace—merely absence of war— to positive peace—absence of the structural violence, institutionalized discrimination, and poverty. J. Darby and R.M. Ginty, "Introduction: Comparing Peace Processes", J. Darby and R.M. Ginty, "Conclusion: The Management of Peace", J. Darby and R.M. Ginty eds., *The Management of Peace Processes*, New York, Palgrave Macmillan, 2000, 6–7, 228; J. Galtung, "Violence, Peace, and Peace Research", *Journal of Peace Research*, 6 (3), 1969, 190.

[2]R. Black and S. Gent, "Sustainable Return in Post-Conflict Contexts", *International Migration*, 44 (3), 2006, 17.

[3]B.S. Chimni, "Refugees and Post-Conflict Reconstruction: A Critical Perspective", *International Peacekeeping*, 9 (2), 2002, 163.

[4]UN Secretary-General, "Secretary-General's address to UNHCR Executive Committee", 6 Oct. 2005. UNHCR also stipulates that "(i)n post-conflict situations, UNHCR should situate its repatriation and reintegration work within a broader context of transition from conflict to peace and try to build peace". UNHCR, *Handbook for Repatriation and Reintegration Activities*, Geneva, May 2004, One-2, available at: https://www.unhcr.org/411786694.pdf (last visited 1 June 2020).

M. Yonekawa
Tsukuba Ibaraki, Japan

M. Yonekawa and A. Sugiki (eds.), *Repatriation, Insecurity, and Peace*,
https://doi.org/10.1007/978-981-15-2850-7_5

Adelman argues that repatriation does not necessarily imply that there is peace: "refugee repatriation is neither a necessary nor a causal condition of peace", and "[p]eace may be in process without refugee repatriation, and refugee repatriation need not even be a manifestation of peace".[5] This argument can be justified for several reasons: returnee movements often spontaneously start when refugees think that it is safe to return. Refugees may not wait for peace agreements to come into existence or for organisations to sponsor movement for voluntary repatriation to and eventual reintegration in the country of origin.[6] Some repatriation takes place, not necessarily because of the signing of peace agreement, but because of which side won.[7] Premature repatriation may lead to counterproductive results by putting returnees at risk, jeopardising a successful transition from war to peace.[8] Finally, some refugees who were permanently settled in countries of asylum may assist in reintegration initiatives through the transfer of remittances to relatives.[9] Most importantly, Adelman argues that "the connection between peace and repatriation meant that the refugee problem had to be addressed, not that the refugees had to be repatriated".[10]

Second, the motivations behind the decision to repatriate need to be analysed. Regarding the principal reason for the UNHCR becoming involved in peacebuilding activities since the 1990s, B.S. Chimni argues that the organisation aims to promote voluntary repatriation even in conflict situations.[11] To explain this *voluntary* repatriation, which is one of the three durable solutions of refugees, it implies in theory that a refugee's decision to return home must always be voluntary, and refugees are the main decision-makers in voluntary repatriation.[12] The UNHCR's promotion of repatriation is associated with the change of refugees' characteristics, which gradually became less convenient for donor and host countries. Before the 1970s, resettlement of refugees was promoted instead of repatriation, mainly due to the ideological and geopolitical value of refugees in the Cold-War context, and labour requirements in Europe after World War II.[13] The reason behind that preferred solution was that "normal" refugees were perceived as being "male, white, Christian, and anti-communist" and were beneficial for Western countries.[14]

---

[5] H. Adelman, "Refugee Repatriation", S.J. Stedman, D. Rothchild and E.M. Cousens (eds.), *Ending Civil Wars: The Implementation of Peace Agreements*, Boulder, Lynne Rienner, 2002, 273.

[6] UNHCR, *Handbook for Repatriation and Reintegration Activities*, Four-1.

[7] Adelman, "Refugee Repatriation", 277.

[8] S. Ogata, "Opening Statement at the eighth meeting of the Standing Committee of the Executive Committee of the High Commissioner's Programme (ExCom)", Geneva, 24 June 1997.

[9] Adelman, "Refugee Repatriation", 278, 293.

[10] *Ibid*, 275.

[11] B.S. Chimni, "Post-Conflict Peace-Building and the Return of Refugees: Concepts, Practices and Institutions", E. Newman and J. v. Selm (eds.), *Refugees and Forced Displacement: International Security, Human Vulnerability, and the State*, Tokyo, United Nations University, 2003, 198, 206.

[12] F.C. Cuny, B.N. Stein and P. Reed eds., *Repatriation During Conflict in Africa and Asia*, Texas: Centre for the Study of Societies in Crisis, 1992, 16.

[13] Chimni, "Post-Conflict Peace-Building", 195; R.F. Gorman and G. Kibreab, "Repatriation Aid and Development Assistance", *Reconceiving International Refugee Law*, The Hague, Martinus Nijhoff Publishers, 1997, 39.

[14] Chimni, "Post-Conflict Peace-Building", 195.

Since the 1970s, however, the number of asylum requests from countries in Asia and Africa to their neighbouring countries and to the Global North has increased. This growing number and changes in the East–West to South–North refugee movement imposed increased financial, political, and environmental burdens on donor and host countries.[15] Gradually, both donors and hosts became intolerant of supporting refugees.[16] In 1980, the UNHCR examined voluntary repatriation for the first time, acknowledging it as the most appropriate solution.[17] Subsequently, High Commissioner Sadako Ogata stated in 1992 that the 1990s would be the decade of repatriation for refugees.[18] In the same year, the UN Secretary-General Boutros Boutros Ghali described repatriating refugees as one of the main tasks of peacebuilding.[19]

While both Adelman and Chimni's arguments are valid, I argue that the nature and objectives of refugee repatriation also need to be examined from the perspectives of refugees, rebel groups and the government of origin, which can run counter to the peace process. This issue is not well studied except for the argument that the government of origin accelerated the return of refugees in order to obtain supporters for the upcoming election.[20] My main argument is that, using the case study of Rwandan refugees, rebel groups and governments of origin can use repatriation to attain their own political objectives, which are not necessarily related to the peace process. The Rwandan Patriotic Front (RPF), a former rebel group, was composed of refugees that seized power in 1994. It continued to use repatriation as a means to attain its political objectives since its first massive repatriation effort in the early 1990s. As this political objective was prioritised, neither sustainable repatriation nor peace has been achieved. Apart from the RPF's objectives, President J. Habyarimana prior to 1994 also had a political agenda that would be served by receiving refugees from Uganda.

Regarding the research methodology employed in this study, the author conducted individual interviews from 2014 to 2018 with 83 former and current Rwandan refugees. The interviews were conducted in five African countries, including four that invoked the cessation clause, and in five countries in Europe and North America. Some have refugee status while others have lost that status because the cessation clause was invoked at the end of 2017. A few are asylum seekers or had obtained nationality or residence permits in the countries of asylum. All of the interviewees categorically refused to return. The author conducted most of these interviews privately.

---

[15] M. Barnett and M. Finnemore, *Rules for the World: International Organizations in Global Politics*, Itacha and London, Cornell University Press, 2004, 94–95.

[16] *Ibid.*

[17] UNHCR, Executive Committee of the High Commissioner's Programme, "Voluntary Repatriation, No. 18 (XXXI)—1980", 16 Oct. 1980, (a), avaiable at:https://www.refworld.org/docid/3ae68c6e8.html (last visited 2 June 2020).

[18] UNHCR, "Statement by Mrs. Sadako Ogata, United Nations High Commissioner for Refugees, at the International Management Symposium", St. Gallen, Switzerland, 25 May 1992, available at:https://www.unhcr.org/admin/hcspeeches/3ae68faec/statement-mrs-sadako-ogata-united-nations-high-commissioner-refugees-international.html (last visited 1 June 2020).

[19] B. Boutros-Ghali, *An Agenda for Peace*, New York, United Nations, 1992, 32.

[20] Adelman, "Refugee Repatriation", 295.

Gaining access to Rwandan refugees for interviews has been extremely difficult or impossible without a referral from other refugees or foreigners, such as Barbara Harrell-Bond, who previously worked with, and advocated for, Rwandan refugees. This situation is due to the Rwandan refugees' strong mistrust which can be attributed to their experiences. Thus, except for a few cases, where the interviews took place depended mainly on referrals. Apart from Uganda, where some researchers have conducted research, in most cases these were the first interviews for research purposes these refugees had given since fleeing Rwanda.

In order to protect the refugees, their names as well as the locations and dates where interviews were conducted, are not disclosed in this paper. The author's interviews with refugees mentioned in the footnotes all refer to Rwandans. Apart from the refugees, 25 individuals were interviewed from 2011 to 2018, consisting of researchers, journalists, former International Criminal Tribunal for Rwanda (ICTR) defence lawyers, UN/NGO workers, members of church groups and Congolese refugees.

This chapter first provides an overview of the refugee repatriation and peace process from the refugees' perspective. It then examines the nature and objectives of repatriation of three Rwandan refugee groups. The first group is composed mostly of minority Tutsi, the so-called "old-caseload", who fled after 1959, and returned from 1990 onwards. The second group members are mostly majority Hutu, or "new-caseload", who fled during and in the aftermath of the 1994 genocide, and returned in 1996–1997. The third group comprises both Hutu and Tutsi, post-genocide or present-day refugees, who have fled Rwanda from 1995 until today, some of whom returned during the same period. For the old-caseload refugees, the motives for accelerating repatriation for both the Rwandan government under President Habyarimana and the RPF are examined. For the new-caseload and present-day refugees, only the motives of the Rwandan government under the RPF are analysed.

2 Repatriation and Peace Processes from Refugees' Perspective

Since the early 1990s, as explained above, repatriation has become part of the peace process package. The refugee factor, being a very strong component of the peace process may apply when forced displacement was the objective rather than a consequence.[21] There are, however, two main misconceptions and problems related to repatriation and the peace process. These misconceptions require critical review particularly from the perspective of the refugees.

First, it is generally taken for granted that returning home is the most preferable and desirable option for refugees, that they yearn to go home, and that the return is

[21] S. Ogata, "Refugee Repatriation and Peace-Building", *Refugee Survey Quarterly*, 16 (2), 1997, vii.

a "'natural' and thus a 'problem-free' process".[22] Based on this hypothesis, repatriation has been organised by the UNHCR.[23] As John R. Rogge argues, however, this assumption is "undoubtedly one of the most misleading myths surrounding the process of repatriation".[24]

Although refugees' intentions differ from case to case, their intentions are not well known in general because refugee representation is not seriously considered by the parties of the Tripartite Commission (governments of origin and asylum, and the UNHCR).[25] "Voluntariness" of repatriation initially involved "the ability to exercise one's free and unconstrained will in making a meaningful choice between returning or not returning to one's country of origin".[26] Thus, according to the UNHCR's draft Guidelines on Voluntary Repatriation (1993), the possibility of establishing a *quadripartite* commission, which could include the refugees, was indicated.[27] This idea, however, was replaced by the term *tripartite* in the UNHCR's *Handbook on Voluntary Repatriation* in 1996. The *Handbook* stated that, "[t]he refugee community should be kept informed of the progress of repatriation negotiations".[28] Refugees do not take part in the entire peace process and have no decision-making authority although they, as key actors, should be included in the peace process.[29] Most of the peace processes are represented mainly by conflict actors, such as governments and rebel groups.

This refugees' absence in the Tripartite Commission partially explains why voluntariness can be highly questionable in certain circumstances as reported by some human rights NGOs.[30] UNHCR-led voluntary repatriation does not take place in ideal circumstances,[31] and return can be often involuntary particularly in conflict situations. It is often "not easy to determine the dividing line between acceptable and unacceptable pressure, encouragement, suggestion, persuasion, and inducement".[32]

---

[22] J.R. Rogge, "Repatriation of Refugees", T. Allen and H. Morsink eds., *When Refugees Go Home*, Trenton, UNRISD, James Currey and Africa World Press, 1994, 20.

[23] B.S. Chimni, "From Resettlement to Involuntary Repatriation: Towards a Critical History of Durable Solutions to Refugee Problems", *Refugee Survey Quarterly*, 2004, 23 (3), 59; UNHCR, Executive Committee of the High Commissioner's Programme, "Voluntary Repatriation, No. 18 (XXXI) – 1980", 16 Oct. 1980, (a).

[24] Rogge, "Repatriation of Refugees", 21.

[25] Chimni, "Post-conflict peace-building", 207.

[26] UNHCR, "Protection Guidelines on Voluntary Repatriation" (draft), September 1993, 52, cited in M. Zieck, *UNHCR and Voluntary Repatriation of Refugees: Legal Analysis*, Leiden, Martinus Nijhoff Publishers, 1997, 114.

[27] UNHCR, "Protection Guidelines" in Zieck, *UNHCR and Voluntary Repatriation*, 120.

[28] UNHCR, *Handbook on Voluntary Repatriation*, 1996, para. 3.6.

[29] Darby and Ginty, "Introduction: Comparing Peace Processes", 7.

[30] See Human Rights Watch, *Ensuring that Repatriation is Voluntary*, 1997; Amnesty International, *Not Time to Go Home: Unsustainable Returns of Refugees to Somalia*, 2017.

[31] Chimni, "Post-conflict peace-building and the return of refugees", 203.

[32] B.N. Stein and F.C. Cuny, "Repatriation in a Civil War/Conflict Situation", paper presented at Roundtable Consultation on Voluntary Repatriation and UNHCR, Geneve, 2–3 June 1993, 16,

In other words, the boundary line between voluntary repatriation and *refoulement* (expulsion or forced repatriation) has become ambiguous in some cases.[33]

Second, it is said that upon refugees' return to their countries of origin, they are expected to contribute to peacebuilding efforts. The UNHCR states that "[I]t should be stressed that communities in areas of return can benefit a great deal from returnees, as they can bring new skills, resources, higher standards of education, health and gender equality, which they may have acquired during their displacement and exile".[34] As the former High Commissioner of the UNHCR, António Guterres, stated, "[R]efugees return with schooling and new skills, in itself a critical factor in any post-conflict situation. Over and over, we see that their participation is necessary for the consolidation of both peace and post-conflict economic recovery".[35]

While this situation may apply in some circumstances, the refugees' situation in general *after* their return, especially after a *long-term* period, has not been sufficiently researched. Thus, the details of that situation are not well known.[36] The situation of returnees comprises several issues including whether returnees are alive and well integrated, whether they are forced to remain at home without any social and political participation, whether they have re-fled the country, and how refugee repatriation has impacted their political and social situation. A repatriation process is not a merely a *short-term* physical movement from the country of asylum to the country of origin but is also a *long-term* process to regain their rights in the country of origin. Thus, the human rights situations of these individuals and their security *after* returning home are an important subject for examination.[37]

A repatriation process can be considered durable when sufficient protection from the government of origin is available,[38] and re-empowerment of returnees in the sense of being able to exercise control over one's life, and re-building relationships

---

cited in B. S. Chimni, "The Meaning of Words and the Role of UNHCR in Voluntary Repatriation", *International Journal of Refugee Law*, 5 (5), 1993, 449.

[33]J. F. Crisp, "Voluntary Repatriation Programmes for African Refugees: A Critical Examination", British Refugee Council/Queen Elizabeth House Working Papers on Refugees, 1 (2), Dec. 1984.

[34]UNHCR, *Handbook for Repatriation and Reintegration Activities*, 5.

[35]UNHCR, "Statement by Mr. António Guterres, United Nations High Commissioner for Refugees, to the United Nations Security Council", New York, 24 Jan. 2006.

[36]B. Harrell-Bond, "Repatriation: Under What Conditions is the Most Desirable Solution for Refugees? An Agenda for Research", *African Studies Review*, 32 (1), 1989, 58. The volume of literature on repatriation has increased since the 1990s. See R. Black and K. Koser eds., *The End of The Refugee Cycle? Refugee Repatriation & Reconstruction*, New York, Berghahn Books, 1999; M. Bradley, *Refugee Repatriation: Justice, Responsibility and Redress*, Cambridge, Cambridge University Press, 2013.

[37]S. Takahashi, "The UNHCR Handbook on Voluntary Repatriation: The Emphasis of Return over Protection", *International Journal of Refugee Law*, 9(4), 1997, 605–606.

[38]B.N. Stein, "Refugee Repatriation, Return, and Refoulement During Conflict", USAID Conference, Promotion Democracy, Human Rights, and Reintegration inf Post-conflict Societies, 30–31 Oct. 1997, 13.

at individual and communal levels under the principle of equality can be ensured.[39] Ensuring such re-empowerment can depend on land and political reforms, which are the key factors for analysing the peace process in the long term.[40] This reform is essential when home areas and the radical change of political-economic system were destroyed during the period of exile. These factors can affect refugees' willingness to return and to reintegrate.[41] For example, land previously owned by refugees could be occupied by those who remained or by new populations (including new returnees). Communal land tenure may have replaced freehold systems, or the control of all agricultural land and production may now be entirely vested in the state.[42]

Furthermore, it is important to consider that when the root causes of flight and the preconditions for sustainable return are left unaddressed, repatriations can result in future refugee movements.[43] This situation was observed with Liberian refugees in Guinea, Rohingya refugees in Bangladesh and Afghan refugees in Pakistan.[44]

Based on these misconceptions and the problems of repatriation, the case of the Rwandan refugees is examined below.

3 Old-Caseload Refugees: Motives of President Habyarimana's Change of Refugee Policy (1970s–1994)

It is generally known that since the 1970s, using the pretext of land shortage, President Habyarimana refused to receive Rwandan refugees.[45] Moreover, Habyarimana did not receive refugees when they were expelled from Uganda to Rwanda in 1982. It has been asserted that Habyarimana's refusal provided justification for the argument that Rwandan refugees in Uganda needed a policy intervention (that is, taking up arms) in order to return and secure their land rights.[46] Habyarimana, however, gradually changed his refugee policy, especially since the 1980s.

What is not well known is that in July 1974, the Rwandan government, led by its Foreign Minister met in Kampala with Ugandan government officials, including President Idi Amin, to discuss the refugee issue, and drafted a preliminary agreement

---

[39] A. G. Rodicio, "Restoration of Life: A New Theoretical Approach to Voluntary Repatriation Based on a Cambodian Experience of Return", *International Journal of Refugee Law*, 12 (1/2), 2001, 134.

[40] Adelman, "Refuge Repatriation", 276.

[41] Rogge, "Repatriation of Refugees", 36.

[42] *Ibid.*

[43] J. Milner, "Refugees and the Regional Dynamics of Peacebuilding", *Refugee Survey Quarterly*, 28 (1), UNHCR, 2009, 26.

[44] *Ibid.*

[45] J.-P. Kimonyo, *Rwanda: Popular Genocide*, Boulder, Lynne Rienner, 2008, 51.

[46] S. Takeuchi and J. Marara, "Land tenure security in post-conflict Rwanda", S. Takeuchi ed. *Confronting Land and Property Problems for Peace*, Oxon, Routledge, 2014, 99.

on the gradual repatriation of refugees.[47] The preconditions for this initiative were the "desire expressed by Rwandan refugees […] to return […] and live a […] peaceful life in respect of the Constitution and the laws of the Rwandan republic".[48] The refugees set six conditions for their repatriation, one of which was the restoration of the monarchy.[49] Despite the some ambiguities, it was argued that this specific condition was the reason why the Rwandan government rejected the refugees' return.[50] Additionally, Amin's intention to repatriate the refugees was questioned as he used and recruited refugees from Rwanda, the Democratic Republic of Congo (DRC) and south Sudan in his army and secret service.[51] In order to encourage the refugees to join his organisations, Amin even invited Rwanda's deposed *Mwami* (king) Kigeri IV to leave Kenya and move to Uganda.[52]

In August 1976, the Rwandan Minister to the Presidency sent presidential directives issued on 22 June 1976, to those ministers involved with refugee issues.[53] The content of the instruction included the following: "[t]he return of refugees must be strictly controlled and only encouraged when those applying to return are useful to the country […] since their massive return would conflict with the population explosion".[54] Subsequently, in 1982, President Habyarimana expressed his wish in the *European Economic Community Review* that refugees permanently settle out of the country due to Rwanda's high population density.[55]

The expulsion of Rwandan refugees from Uganda in October 1982, however, was a turning point for Habyarimana. He was concerned not only because of his opposition to receive his countrymen in exile, but also because those who were expelled were suspected of being members or supporters of the RANU, and the remaining refugees, including RANU supporters, would flee to Rwanda.[56] This expulsion crisis, along with international pressure, led the governments of Rwanda and Uganda to organise a meeting at the end of October 1982, soon after the expulsion, in Rwanda to address

---

[47] Kimonyo, *Rwanda: Popular Genocide*, 47–48.

[48] *Ibid*, 48.

[49] *Ibid*, 48–49.

[50] Interview with a refugee. However, as not all Rwandan refugees were monarchists, this requires verification.

[51] O. Otunnu, *Crisis of Legitimacy and Political Violence in Uganda 1979 to 2016*, Cham, Palgrave McMillan, 2016, 134.

[52] M. Mamdani, *When Victims Become Killers: Colonialism, Nativism, and the Genocide in Rwanda*, Princeton, Princeton University Press, 2003, 167.

[53] Kimonyo, *Rwanda: Popular Genocide*, 51.

[54] Republic of Rwanda, "Office of the President, Instruction présidentielles relatives aux réfugies", 12 June, 1976 cited in *Ibid*.

[55] Le Courrier ACP/CEE, Brussels, No. 72, March–April 1982, cited in A. Guichaoua, *The Problem of the Rwandese Refugees*, UNHCR, May 1992, 27.

[56] Otunnu, *Crisis of Legitimacy and Political Violence in Uganda*, 142–143.

the voluntary repatriation issue.[57] The UNHCR held another joint ministerial meeting in March 1983 in Uganda, at which it was agreed to begin screening refugees.[58]

Rwanda's agreement to examine voluntary repatriation became clear after the victory of the NRM in January 1986. Rwandan refugees accounted for more than 25% of that organisation's personnel.[59] One of the refugees was Fred Rwigyema, the NRM's Commander-in-Chief and Minister of Defense, an individual with a distinguished military career. The MRND declared in July 1986 that it would recognise the principle of return, considering the delivery of passports and travel documents, allowing the refugees' sporadic visit to Rwanda.[60] Several meetings between the two governments and the UNHCR took place between 1988 and 1990, that resulted in arranging refugees' visit to Rwanda in early October 1990. In January 1991, the UNHCR was to conduct survey concerning the refugees' desire to return to Rwanda or remain in Uganda.[61] On 28 September 1990, at the UN General Assembly Habyarimana announced his intention to offer citizenship and travel documents to those refugees who wished to return.[62]

Despite this change of President Habyarimana's policy, Gerald Prunier argued that he "had no intention of accepting the refugees back, except on his own personal terms".[63] It is argued that in addition to the Rwandan government's fear of the RPF's military influence which helped the NRM to seize power, it appears that three factors facilitated a shift in Rwanda's approach vis-à-vis refugees. First, there was a great possibility that the refugees would demand the right to repatriate. Second, Rwanda was aware of Museveni's favourable relations with the Rwandan refugees.[64] Third, "Habyarimana held a major trump-card—the French fear of an 'Anglo-Saxon' erosion [RPF's invasion coming from Anglophone Uganda] of their position on the African continent—which probably made him decide to embark on the risky course of not trying to deflect the invasion through serious negotiation".[65] His intention was to use the external crisis to silence the internal crisis.[66] Habyarimana rightly acknowledged that France would support him in any event even if his actions were contrary to democracy, as mentioned in President Mitterrand's speech.[67]

Similarly suspect was the democratisation movement initiated by Habyarimana. According to Prunier, it seemed that Habyarimana's personal conviction on this

[57] O. Otunnu, "Rwandese Refugees and Immigrants in Uganda", in H. Adelman and A. Suhrke eds. *The Path of a Genocide: The Rwanda Crisis from Uganda to Zaire*, New Jersey, Transaction, 2000, 22.

[58] *Ibid*, 23.

[59] J-M. Ndagijimana, M. Collins translated, *How Paul Kagame Deliberately Sacrificed the Tutsi*, La Pagaie, 2016. Kindle version.

[60] Guichaoua, *The Problem of the Rwandese Refugees*, 27, 30–31.

[61] C. Watson, *Exile from Rwanda: Background to an Invasion*, The U.S. Committee for Refugees Issue Paper, 1991, 13.

[62] Kimonyo, *Rwanda demain!*, 108.

[63] *Ibid*, 98. It is noteworthy that Prunier interviewed only the RPF officers, and not the Rwandan government officials, and depended on his sources from French government.

[64] Watson, *Exile from Rwanda*, 13.

[65] G. Prunier, *The Rwanda Crisis: History of a Genocide*, Kampala, Foundation Publishers, 1999, 99.

[66] *Ibid*

[67] *Ibid*, 99, 106.

matter was rather shallow.[68] He was obliged to accept a multiparty system to counter the RPF's argument that it was fighting against a single-party dictatorship as discussed below.[69]

4 Motives of the RPF's "Armed Repatriation"

These political and economic crises (see p. xi) implied that the Habyarimana's regime was "resting on shallow political soil", thus, the conditions and timing were suitable for the RPF's invasion.[70] Through this invasion in 1990, the RPF sought to redress two major problems. The first focused on democracy, human rights, restoration of unity and promotion of the economy.[71] The second and most important problem was the rallying cry for the return of refugees.[72]

All of these factors, however, had been already been the subject of debate within Rwanda. Thus, there was no need for the RPF to invade. This preparation for refugees' visit was, in fact, an unfavourable development for RPF officers who risked losing refugees' support if the refugees believed that they could return to Rwanda without fighting.[73] Refugees were under heavy pressure and were dissuaded from following the UNHCR's repatriation plan. The forms of dissuasion included the RPF leaders' popular slogan "We left together, we will return together",[74] obliging all refugees to obey the RPF's policy on repatriation as the RPF's influence extended into the refugee camp.[75] In addition, the RPF was not pleased to have observed a democratic development in Rwanda as they could no longer claim that their fight was against an oppressive dictatorship.[76]

Therefore, in order to block the repatriation process as well as democratisation reform, the RPF had to accelerate its preparation for invasion before the October deadline on refugees' visit, that eventually did not take place.[77] As part of the preparation, the RPF began growing and harvesting crops for the troops in April 1990, six

[68] *Ibid*, 90.

[69] *Ibid*, 91.

[70] O. Otunnu, "As Historical Analysis of the Invasion by the Rwandan Patriotic Army (RPA)", H. Adelman and A. Suhrke (eds.), *The Path of a Genocide: The Rwanda Crisis from Uganda to Zaire*, New Brunswick, Transaction, 2000, 35.

[71] F. Reyntjens, "Rwanda: Genocide and Beyond", *Journal of Refugee Studies*, 9 (3), 1996, 245.

[72] Rudasingwa, *Healing a Nation*, 76.

[73] Prunier, *The Rwanda Crisis*, 91.

[74] Guichaoua, *From War to Genocide*, 26.

[75] Interview with Rudasingwa.

[76] G. Prunier, "The Rwandan Patriotic Front", C. Clapham, *African Guerrillas*, Oxford, James Currey et al., 1998, 129.

[77] Prunier, *The Rwanda Crisis*, 91.

months prior to the invasion. It grew maize in Tanzania and organised transportation across Lake Victoria into Rwanda via the Kagera River.[78] This preparation may explain the "slow pace and extended length of the negotiations with Habyarimana [which could have] […] influenced the timing of the invasion".[79] Moreover, Kagame, acting head of the NRA's military intelligence from November 1989 to June 1990, was alleged to have used its resources to intimidate dissenters within the RPF who did not favour an armed return; some of these dissenters were imprisoned or killed.[80]

These events imply that whether Rwandan government modified its refugee policy or not, the RPF was already determined to launch an invasion since 1980 when the RANU was formed, and especially since 1987 when the RPF was established. The RANU subordinated the question of the return of refugees for those people who desired, to achieve the political and social transformation of the country "with all the possible means, whether political or military".[81] RANU's original mission changed; the RPF broadened its political agenda to include the removal of President Habyarimana so that returning refugees could seize political power.[82]

Ultimately, Rwandan Foreign Minister, Casimir Bizimungu's, accusation that the RPF invaders were seeking a reversal of pre-1959 Tutsi domination had become true.[83] The RPF argued that it had invaded Rwanda in the first place in order to liberate its people, however, this turned out to be an occupation of territory, and not liberation for the population.[84] Thus, the population "showed no enthusiasm for being 'liberated'" by the RPF, and were displaced to create a "Hutu-free territory" so that the 1959 returnees could occupy their land.[85] This displacement of a mostly Hutu population, which was caused by the Tutsi-led RPF, contributed to the rise in ethnic tensions, fuelling Hutu radicals.[86]

Subsequently, when the Arusha peace talks started in 1992, Kagame launched a deliberate policy to create a Tutsiland by massacring and displacing the Hutus.[87] This policy, which continued until 1995, enabled the old-caseload refugees to return and resettle in Rwanda.[88] Even when the RPF advanced during the civil war, these returnees started to occupy the land they had owned in the northeast before fleeing

[78] A. J. Kuperman, "Provoking genocide: A Revised History of the Rwandan Patriotic Front", *Journal of Genocide Research*, 6 (1), 2004, 82.

[79] Otunnu, "As Historical Analysis of the Invasion by the Rwandan Patriotic Army (RPA)", 36.

[80] Watson, *Exile from Rwanda*, 13.

[81] Kimonyo, *Rwanda Demain!*, 111.

[82] Kuperman, "Provoking genocide", 68.

[83] *Washington Post*, "Invasion Stirs Tribal Tension in Rwanda", 14 Oct. 1990.

[84] Mamdani, *When Victims Become Killers*, 185, 189.

[85] J. Rever, *In Praise of Blood: The Crimes of the Rwandan Patriotic Front*, Random House Canada, 2018, 217; A. J. Ruzibiza, *Rwanda l'histoire secrète*, Paris, Editions du Panama, 2005,138.

[86] J. Gasana, "Natural Resource Scarcity and Violence in Rwanda", in M. Halle, J. Mathew and J. Switzer (eds.), *Conserving the Peace: Resources, Livelihoods and Security*, Winnipeg, International Institute for Sustainable Development, 2002, 223; R. Lemarchand, *The Dynamics of Violence in Central Africa*, Philadelphia, University of Pennsylvania Press, 2009, 126.

[87] Rever, *In Praise of Blood*, 217.

[88] *Ibid*; Author's email exchange with Rudasingwa, 7 April 2018.

in 1959.[89] This situation may explain why even after signing Arusha Peace Accord in August 1993, the RPF, under the "security pretext", did not want 600,000 IDPs to return home until the Accord's full implementation.[90] The same conditions, however, were not enforced for the old-caseload returnees.

To summarise, the RPF intended to return in order to seize land and power, which they did following the civil war and genocide, and established the RPF-led government in July 1994. Subsequently, 750,000 old-case refugees returned to Rwanda from neighbouring countries.[91] At the same time more than two million people (new-caseload refugees) fled mainly to Zaire during and after the genocide. Therefore, this invasion should be recognised as "armed repatriation"[92] with a forcible nature.

5 New-Caseload Refugees: RPF's Intent for Refugee Repatriation (1994–1996/7)

The Rwandan government categorised refugees into three groups based on the background of those who fled after April 1994. The first category was "the criminals who had committed the genocide and feared being brought to justice by the new Government". Second were those "innocent people who were confused by the propaganda of the criminal clique and were actually intimidated and coerced into running away to exile [by the ex-FAR and *Interahamwe*]". The third category was "the people who genuinely ran away, because the situation in the country was highly volatile".[93] The repatriation of these refugees was the new Rwandan government's top priority, as declared by the newly appointed Prime Minister, Faustin Twagiramungu.[94]

However, very few refugees returned. According to the UNHCR and Rwandan government, upon their arrival in Zaire (present DRC) and Tanzania, these refugees were allegedly held as political hostage under the ex-FAR and *Interahamwe* to prevent their repatriation.[95] It was said that when these refugees attempted to return, they

[89] A. Des Forges "Land in Rwanda: Winnowing out the Chaff", F. Reyntjens and S. Marysse eds., *L'Afrique des Grands Lacs: Annuaire 2005–2006*, Paris, L'Hartmattan, 2006, 358.

[90] R. Dallaire, *Shake Hands with the Devil: The Failure of Humanity in Rwanda*, London, Arrow Books, 2004, 67.

[91] Prunier, *The Rwanda Crisis*, 364.

[92] Mamdani, *When Victims Become Killers*, 36; Ogata, "Refugee Repatriation and Peace-Building", vii; "The OAU [...] leadership had seen the RPF invasion of Rwanda not as aggression by a neighbouring state, but as an attempt by the children of exiled refugees to go home". L. Melvern, *A People Betrayed: The Role of the West in Rwanda's Genocide*, London, Zed Books, 2009, 59.

[93] United Nations Security Council (UNSC), S/1994/1115, "Letter dated 28 September 1994 from the Permanent Representative of Rwanda to the United Nations Addressed to the President of the Security Council", 29 Sep 1994, 2.

[94] R. Winter, "Lancing the Boil: Rwanda's Agenda in Zaire", H. Adelman and G. C. Rao eds., *War and Peace in DRC/Congo: Analyzing and Evaluating Intervention, 1996–1997*, Trenton, Africa World Press, 2004, 114.

[95] UNHCR, *The State of the World's Refugees: Fifty Years of Humanitarian Action*, Oxford, Oxford University Press, 2000, 258; Republic of Rwanda, Ministry of Foreign Affairs and Cooperation, "Rwanda's Comments on the Draft UN Mapping Report on the DRC", 30 Sep 2010,

were intimidated or killed by ex-FAR and *Interahamwe*, who "use propaganda and misinformation, alleging that there is insecurity in the country and that they will be killed on return".[96] In addition, the Rwandan government argued that the refugees in Zaire were used "as a future military recruitment pool [..., and] as human shields".[97]

The refugees, however, denied that they were held hostage or used as human shields by the ex-FAR and *Interahamwe* in the refugee camps; they had the freedom to decide whether to return.[98] They refused to return not because they were prevented from repatriating, as argued by the Rwandan government, but because of two factors.

The first factor is that this refusal to return was based simply on their strong fear of the RPF, which had systematically massacred civilians, especially Hutus, during the civil war and genocide period.[99] UNHCR consultant Robert Gersony, who assessed the prospects for the repatriation of refugees from August to September 1994, reported that the overwhelming majority of refugees stated that "their main—in most cases their only—constraint to [returning] was the fear of being killed in their home areas, either upon their return or at a later time".[100] The report concluded that conditions were not yet conducive for their safe return.[101] In fact, the refugees' fear of the RPF, which had caused them to flee, was well known at the time of their arrival in eastern DRC. Their fear, however, was rejected by the UNHCR as "largely unfounded and merely a product of extremist propaganda".[102]

The second factor is that some elite refugees, mostly educated individuals, including former politicians, former soldiers and students, were aware of the RPF's interest only in the return of peasants, who were needed to re-launch the country's agriculture sector, and not the elite.[103] The RPF shared this concern with the UNHCR and proposed a deal with the elite refugees during a meeting with NGOs in North Kivu in 1995.[104] The UNHCR asked the elite refugees to convince the peasant refugees to return; in exchange, the elites would receive assistance in resettling in other countries of asylum.[105] It was difficult for the elites to pursue this challenging objective, however, as they were aware that the peasants from rural areas, especially in northern

para. 25, available at:https://www.ohchr.org/Documents/Countries/CD/DRC_Report_Comments_Rwanda.pdf (last visited 1 June 2020).

[96] UNSC, S/1994/1115, 3.

[97] Republic of Rwanda, "Rwanda's Comments", para. 22.

[98] Interview with refugees.

[99] Interview with refugees.

[100] His team did not have mandate to conduct an inquiry into the massacres by the ex-FAR and militias. UNHCR, "Prospects for Early Repatriation of Rwandan Refugees Currently in Burundi, Tanzania and DRC" (Gersony report), Oct. 1994, 3, 14, available at: https://graphics8.nytimes.com/packages/pdf/world/gersony_report.PDF#page=17&zoom=auto (last visited 31 May 2020).

[101] *Ibid*, 1.

[102] African Rights, *Rwanda: Death, Despair and Defiance*, African Rights, 1994, 1091.

[103] G. Musabyimana, *L'APR et les Réfugiés Rwandais au Zaïre 1996–1997: Un Génocide Nié*, Paris, L'Harmattan, 2004, 17.

[104] *Ibid*.

[105] *Ibid*.

prefectures where the RPF had committed atrocities, had strong grievances against the RPF.[106]

In 1994, armed ex-FAR and *Interahamwe* fled to the refugee camps in eastern DRC, which resulted in militarisation of those camps. This development explains why the Rwandan Patriotic Army (RPA, the RPF's army) invaded and destroyed the refugee camps in October and November 1996, justifying this action as a self-defence (security) measure.[107] During this invasion, the UN accused Congolese rebels[108] and RPA soldiers of a six-hour indiscriminate killing spree. During that massacre, an unknown number of refugees were murdered with heavy weapons at one refugee camp called Mugunga and in the surrounding area in eastern DRC in November 1996.[109] The Rwandan government claimed to have "moved against the ex-FAR and *Interahamwe* forces in the camps, and in the process, rescued and repatriated 600,000 Rwandan refugees in the course of four days from the Mugunga camp only".[110] Thus, for the Rwandan government, the operation at Mugunga camp was "aimed at liberating and repatriating innocent civilian refugees".[111]

During the RPA's invasion, some refugees returned to Rwanda, not because of their strong desire to return but because it was the only solution. In Goma, the only path not blocked by the RPA/AFDL was the one that led to Rwanda.[112] While some refugees did not have the financial means or educational credentials to use in other countries of asylum, others decided to return because of fatigue and hunger after hiding in the forest in eastern DRC for several months.[113] Nevertheless, among those who returned, some once again left the country after returning.[114]

Regarding the narrative that refugees were held hostage in the refugee camps, one question remains: how and why has that narrative become dominant?

As stated above, the majority of refugees had no intention of returning. Likewise, the Rwandan government had no intention of receiving refugees. It was important for the Rwandan government to ensure that refugees were forced to remain in the camps under the ex-FAR/*Interahamwe*, a situation that could justify the RPA's invasion of eastern DRC under the pretext of security. This situation existed because, after the genocide in 1994, Kagame and his senior intelligence officers planned to invade the Congo to acquire natural resources.[115] Thus, the RPF created the story about Hutu

[106] *Ibid.*

[107] Republic of Rwanda, "Rwanda's Comments", para. 19.

[108] The RPA formed a "Congolese" rebel group to make the rebel movement as Congolese.

[109] UN Office of the High Commissioner for Human Rights, *Report of the Mapping Exercise documenting the most serious violations of human rights and international humanitarian law committed within the territory of the Democratic Republic of the Congo between March 1993 and June 2003*, 2010 (*Mapping Report*), Aug. 2010, para. 220.

[110] Republic of Rwanda, "Rwanda's Comments", para. 13.

[111] *Ibid*, para. 24.

[112] M. B. Umutesi, *Surviving the Slaughter: The Ordeal of a Rwandan Refugee in Zaire*, Wisconsin, The University of Wisconsin Press, 2004, 120.

[113] *Ibid*, 93; Interview with a refugee.

[114] Des Forges, "Land in Rwanda", 363–364.

[115] E-mail correspondent with J. Rever, 15 Sep. 2017.

refugees being held hostage, and the RPF used agents to infiltrate the camps, as well as using Congolese civilians, to gain entry through bribery or coercion.[116] Refugees were threatened by the infiltration, reconnaissance and espionage of RPF agents, including Hutu recruited by the RPF who settled inside the refugee camps falsely posing as refugees, to harass some refugees and rape others.[117] It was not true that "[r]efugees were being threatened, attacked, and killed for being 'RPF spies'"[118]; in contrast, *authentic* RPF spies threatened the refugees.[119] Moreover, the Rwandan government even launched false flag attacks in north-western Rwanda in 1996, which helped convince the international community that Hutu rebels were threatening to reignite the genocide.[120] In sum, forced and massive repatriation from the DRC in 1996 was used by the Rwandan government to establish its presence and seek wealth there.

6 Present-Day Refugees: Motives of the Rwandan Government to Repatriate Refugees

The present-day refugees comprise three categories: refugees who did not return in 1996–1997 and continue to remain outside of Rwanda, mainly in the DRC; old-caseload and new-caseload returnees who fled at least twice; and genocide survivors, both Hutu and Tutsi, who fled for the first time.

Moreover, present-day refugees have three characteristics. First, Hutu refugees are generally branded as *génocidaires* and "suspect" who are hesitant to return home.[121] This labelling of certain groups has been a useful propaganda tool employed by the RPF to boldly hunt, repatriate or target refugees. Second, these refugees are framed as being anti-Rwandan, who oppose the state process of reconciliation and national unity.[122] The ideal Rwandan citizen is considered a refugee who voluntarily returns to the motherland to contribute to the reconstruction of the state.[123] Third,

[116]Confirmed by former RPF officials. E-mail correspondent with Rever, 15 Sep. 2017; this infiltration and use of Congolese was also confirmed by refugees and a former Congolese military official.

[117]Confirmed by one former RPF officer.

[118]I. Martin, "Hard Choices after Genocide: Human Rights and Political Failures in Rwanda", J. Moore ed., *Hard Choices: Moral Dilemmas in Humanitarian Intervention*, Maryland, Rowman & Littlefield, 1998, 160.

[119]Interview with refugees.

[120]Testified by ex-RPF officer. Rever, *In Praise of Blood*, 142, 221.

[121]R. Lemarchand, "The Politics of Memory in Post-Genocide Rwanda", P. Clark and Z. D. Kaufman eds., *After Genocide: Transitional Justice, Post-Conflict Reconstruction and Reconciliation in Rwanda and Beyond*, New York, Columbia University Press, 2009, 71.

[122]L. N. Kingston, "Bringing Rwandan Refugees 'Home': The Cessation Clause, Statelessness, and Forced Repatriation", *International Journal of Refugee Law*, 29 (3), 2017, 3.

[123]K. O'Connor, "Repatriation: The Politics of Re-Constructing and Contesting Rwandan Citizenship", Refugee Studies Centre, University of Oxford, June 2013, 28.

many refugees are outspoken members of the elite, such as journalists, human rights activists, teachers and former RPF war comrades, both Hutu and Tutsi. Some refugees are politically active and have formed various political organisations that oppose the RPF regime. The fact that these refugees were considered to be the brains of the country has made them even more vulnerable, resulting in security incidents. These threats resulted in the political assassinations of ten persons as of 2017, allegedly by the RPF, while others, assassination attempts, attacks, or kidnappings.[124] Those individuals who were assassinated apparently had incriminating information concerning the RPF's crimes.[125]

The majority of these refugees have categorically refused to repatriate and some Rwandans continue to flee. This attitude and movement by refugees are associated not only with political assassination, as mentioned above, but with various factors as well. The ICTR and *Gacaca* community-based courts were established in late 1994 and 2001, respectively, to prosecute genocide leaders, which prosecuted only Hutus. New-caseload returnees cannot claim and recover their land and property, which are now occupied by old-caseload returnees. "Genocide ideology" was enacted in 2008 that outlaws "any mention of alleged RPF war crimes or human rights abuses",[126] aiming at silencing dissent.[127] Moreover, President Kagame's attitude vis-à-vis Rwandan refugees was evident in his speeches, which greatly influenced refugees' intention to return.[128]

Thus, the fear of persecution among present-day Rwandan refugees is not caused only by the RPF's *past* crimes, but also by *ongoing* crimes and human rights violations. This situation contradicts the cessation clause of refugee status of Rwandan refugees that was applied in June 2013 by some African host countries and recommended by the UNHCR. This cessation clause was applied on the basis that Rwanda "has changed significantly since the 1994 genocide, and today enjoys an essential level of peace and security".[129] Before invoking the cessation clause, the states and the UNHCR need to carefully assess the fundamental character of the changes in the country of origin, including the general human rights situation, as well as the particular causes of fear of persecution.[130] To be more precise, the states and the UNHCR must not look into *any* changes of the human rights situation, but must "assess

---

124 Rever, *In Praise of Blood*.

125 A. Guichaoua *From War to Genocide: Criminal Politics in Rwanda 1990–1994*, Wisconsin, University of Wisconsin Press, 2015, 146.

126 L. Waldorf, "Revisiting Hotel Rwanda, Genocide Ideology, Reconciliation, and Rescuers", *Journal of Genocide Research*, 11 (I), 2009, 111.

127 Amnesty International, *Safer to Stay Silent: The Chilling Effect of Rwanda's Laws on 'Genocide Ideology and 'Sectarianism'*, 26 March 2011, 20, available at: https://www.amnesty.org/en/documents/AFR47/005/2010/en/ (last visited 1 June 2020).

128 Interview with refugees.

129 UNHCR, "Implementation of the Comprehensive Strategy for the Rwandan Refugee Situation, including UNHCR's recommendations on the Applicability of the 'ceased circumstances' Cessation Clauses", 30 Dec. 2011, para. 28.

130 UNHCR, "Guidelines on International Protection: Cessation of Refugee Status under Article 1C(5) and (6) of the 1951 Convention relating to the Status of Refugees", 10 Feb. 2003, para. 8.

the impact of those changes" on the refugees.[131] This assessment, however, never took place prior to the invocation of the cessation clause of the status of Rwandan refugees.[132]

James Hathaway states that once the criteria of the cessation clause have been met, states are permitted to cease granting refugee status and repatriate former refugees to their home countries *by force*.[133] This cessation clause signifies "the *ability* to forcibly repatriate refugees—that has become particularly attractive to states with faced mass influxes".[134] State cessation of refugee status is also termed "mandated repatriation".[135] Ultimately, the invocation of the cessation of refugee status itself can be considered one means of imposed return. It is considered to be a last resort "where there has been a fundamental failure in the mechanism of international protection".[136]

In order to force refugees to return, the Rwandan government has reportedly deployed a "refugee spy" group.[137] Composed of "diplomats", "students" and even "refugees", members of this group pose as Rwandan, Congolese or Burundian refugees, they infiltrate the host government's refugee office, the UNHCR, Red Cross and refugee camps/settlements.[138] This group allegedly monitors and reports on refugee movement to the RPF, encourages or convinces refugees to return and spreads defamatory rumours to refugees.[139] All of these actions aim to divide and weaken the refugee community, as well as to threaten and kill refugees.[140] This infiltration tactic for the purpose of repatriation apparently began around 2002–2003, at the time of the UNHCR-led promotion of voluntary repatriation.[141]

Apart from the "refugee spy" group, the Rwandan government reportedly used refugee leaders to convince refugees to repatriate. To give one example, Séraphine Mukantabana, a refugee leader in Republic of the Congo, was reportedly co-opted by

[131] A. Garcia v. Canada (1993) FCJ 635 (Can. FC, June 23, 1993), J. C. Hathaway, *The Rights of Refugees under International Law*, Cambridge, Cambridge University Press, 2005, 924.

[132] Rights in Exile Programme, "Open Letter to EXCOM: The Threat of Invoking the Cessation Clause with Particular Reference to Rwanda", 1 Oct. 2012, available at: http://rightsinexile.tumblr.com/post/32664830259/open-letter-to-excom-the-threat-of-invoking-the (last visited 30 Apr. 2018).

[133] J. Hathaway, "The Meaning of Repatriation", *International Journal of Refugee Law*, 9 (4), 1997, 551–552.

[134] Y. Siddiqui, "Reviewing the application of the Cessation Clause of the 1951", Refugee Studies Centre, University of Oxford, Working Paper Series No. 76, Aug. 2011, 8 fn (emphasis added).

[135] M. E. Cwik, "Forced to Flee and Forced to Repatriate? How the Cessation Clause of Article 1c (5) and (6) of the 1951 Refugee Convention Operates in International Law and Practice", *Vanderbilt Journal of Transnational Law*, 44 (3), May 2011, 714.

[136] K. Long, "Back to where you once belonged: A historical review of UNHCR policy and practice on refugee repatriation", UNHCR, Sep. 2013, para. 165, available at: https://www.refworld.org/docid/5226d8f44.html (last visited 1 June 2020).

[137] Interview with refugees.

[138] G. Verdirame, B. Harrell-Bond, *Rights in Exile: Janus-Faced Humanitarianism*, New York, Berghahn, 2005, 165.

[139] Interview with refugees.

[140] Interview with refugees.

[141] Interview with a refugee.

the Rwandan government around 2000 to convince refugees to return.[142] However, very few refugees returned, including a vulnerable group with chronic disease whose medical aid stopped in 2010 by the UNHCR's implementing partner and others who were allegedly bribed by the Rwandan government.[143] The vast majority of refugees in Republic of Congo did not repatriate as they mistrusted Mukantabana, as being the double agent, that is both a refugee leader and coordinator with the RPF.[144] Allegedly converted by the RPF, she returned to Rwanda in 2011.[145] As the Minister of Disaster Management and Refugee Affairs from February 2013 to July 2017, she had actively promoted repatriation, to no avail.

As noted above, the Rwandan government (RPF) has a strong obsession with refugees and pursuit of repatriation not only because repatriation promotes the country's international image.[146] Roger Winter, the then Director of the US Committee for Refugees and an RPF supporter,[147] argues that Rwanda's real intentions were otherwise:

> the repatriation [of] Rwandans [...] was always a primary goal of the government. [...] for the government, the two primary reasons were politically motivated. Firstly, because the RPF leadership grew up in exile without a solution, it understood that having such a large portion of the Rwandan population outside of the country was a destabilizing factor. Secondly, having the population inside Rwanda was the only way to win its support, or, for those whose support could not be won, to *effectively control them*. Thus, repatriating was the only realistic means of winning the support of the Rwandan population, and stabilizing the region.[148]

Although Winter referred to the government's goal mainly during the period from July 1994 to 1996, the same aim and practice of containing refugees has continued until today, which explains why refugees have long refused to return. On the other hand, one RPF dissident claims that the RPF has no intention of repatriating *all* refugees due mainly to the lack of space in the country. Thus, the RPF's intention is only to destabilise and silence the outspoken refugee community by threatening

---

[142]Interview with refugees.

[143]It is unclear why medical assistance stopped, but refugees suspected that Mukantabana, who worked as refugees' translator for the UNHCR and NGOs, deliberately mistranslated as a way to force refugees to repatriate. Interview with refugees.

[144]Interview with refugees.

[145]*Jeune Afrique*, "Rwanda: avec Séraphine Mukantabana, tous les chemins mènent à Kigali", 5 July 2013, available at: http://www.jeuneafrique.com/136964/politique/rwanda-avec-s-raphine-mukantabana-tous-les-chemins-m-nent-kigali/ (last visited 28 June 2020).

[146]International Refugee Rights Initiative and Refugee Law Project, *A Dangerous Impasse: Rwandan Refugees in Uganda*, June 2010, 21, available at: http://refugee-rights.org/a-dangerous-impasse-rwandan-refugees-in-uganda/ (last visited 1 June 2020).

[147]P. Péan, *Carnages: Les Guerres Secrètes des grandes puissances en Afrique*, Paris, Fayard, 2010, 425–455.

[148]R. Winter, "Lancing the Boil: Rwanda's Agenda in Zaire", H. Adelman and G. C. Rao eds., *War and Peace in DRC/Congo: Analyzing and Evaluating Intervention, 1996–1997*, Trenton, Africa World Press, 2004, 128 (emphasis added).

refugees with repeated repatriation calls and stripping them of their refugee status by invoking the cessation clause.[149]

7 Conclusion

By using the case study of Rwandan refugees, this chapter has attempted to demonstrate that refugee repatriation is not necessarily part of the peace process due to the political motives that refugees, rebel groups or governments of origin may have. Moreover, the nature of repatriation which can oppose the implementation of the peace process needs to be examined.

As for the repatriation of the old-caseload refugees in early 1990s, the Rwandan government under President Habyarimana had no choice but to accept them due to his fear of the RPF's military influence or his wish to use the RPF invasion as a distraction from the internal crisis. The RPF, on the other hand, aimed to return by force and seize power. Regarding the massive repatriation of the new-caseload refugees from Zaire in 1996, the Rwandan government had motives to invade Zaire and acquire natural resources. In order to make that objective happen, the RPF destabilised the refugee camps in eastern Zaire by sending its agents and creating narratives using security concerns as a pretext. Finally, concerning the repatriation of the present-day refugees, the Rwandan government wanted to control the outspoken refugees, or simply to threaten and destabilise them without intending to repatriate them. As this political objective was prioritised, neither the sustainable repatriation nor peace has been achieved.

Regarding the nature of repatriation, most cases of Rwandan refugees returning examined in this chapter were not voluntary, but simply forced. The RPF, when it was a rebel group and even today as a government, has used arms, threats and the invocation of the cessation clause or "mandated repatriation" to forcefully repatriate refugees. The only time that the peace agreement was used to discuss return of refugees was during the Arusha Peace Accords in 1993. Since then, however, no peace talks were held but only the Tripartite Meetings and that without the presence of refugees. Thus, when examining the connection between repatriation and the peace process, it is important to analyse both the motives for, and the nature of, repatriation.

References

H. Adelman, Refugee Repatriation, in *Ending Civil Wars: The Implementation of Peace Agreements*, S.J. Stedman, D. Rothchild, E.M. Cousens (eds.) (Boulder, Lynne Rienner, 2002), p. 273
African Rights, *Rwanda: Death, Despair and Defiance*, African Rights, 1994, 1091

[149]Interview with a refugee.

Amnesty International, *Safer to Stay Silent: The Chilling Effect of Rwanda's Laws on 'Genocide Ideology and Sectarianism'*, 26 March 2011, 20, available at: https://www.amnesty.org/en/documents/AFR47/005/2010/en/ (last visited 1 June 2020)

Amnesty International, *Not Time to Go Home: Unsustainable Return of Refugees to Somalia*, 2017

M. Barnett, M. Finnemore, *Rules for the World: International Organizations in Global Politics* (Itacha and London, Cornell University Press, 2004), pp. 94–95

R. Black, S. Gent, Sustainable Return in Post-Conflict Contexts. *International Migration*, vol. 44, no. 3 (2006), p. 17

B. Boutros-Ghali, *An Agenda for Peace* (New York, United Nations, 1992), p. 32

B.S. Chimni, The Meaning of Words and the Role of UNHCR in Voluntary Repatriation. *Int. J. Refug. Law* **5**(5), 449 (1993)

B.S. Chimni, Refugees and Post-Conflict Reconstruction: A Critical Perspective. *Int. Peacekeeping* **9**(2), 163 (2002)

B.S. Chimni, Post-Conflict Peace-Building and the Return of Refugees: Concepts, Practices and Institutions, in *Refugees and Forced Displacement: International Security, Human Vulnerability, and the State*, E. Newman, J.v. Selm (eds.) (Tokyo, United Nations University, 2003), pp. 198–206

B.S. Chimni, From Resettlement to Involuntary Repatriation: Towards a Critical History of Durable Solutions to Refugee Problems. *Refug. Surv. Q.* **23**(3), 59 (2004)

J.F. Crisp, Voluntary Repatriation Programmes for African Refugees: A Critical Examination vol. 1, no. 2 (British Refugee Council/Queen Elizabeth House Working Papers on Refugees, 1984)

F.C. Cuny, B.N. Stein, P. Reed (eds.), *Repatriation During Conflict in Africa and Asia* (Texas, Centre for the Study of Societies in Crisis, 1992), p. 16

M.E. Cwik, Forced to Flee and Forced to Repatriate? How the Cessation Clause of Article 1c (5) and (6) of the 1951 Refugee Convention Operates in International Law and Practice. *Vanderbilt J. Transnatl. Law* **44**(3), 714 (2011)

R. Dallaire, *Shake Hands with the Devil: The Failure of Humanity in Rwanda* (London, Arrow Books, 2004), p. 67

J. Darby, R.M. Ginty, Introduction: Comparing Peace Processes. *The Management of Peace Processes* (New York, Palgrave Macmillan, 2000a), pp. 6–7

J. Darby, R.M. Ginty, Conclusion: The Management of Peace. *The Management of Peace Processes* (New York, Palgrave Macmillan, 2000b), p. 228

A. Des Forges, Land in Rwanda: Winnowing out the Chaff, in *L'Afrique des Grands Lacs: Annuaire 2005–2006*, F. Reyntjens, S. Marysse (eds.) (Paris, L'Hartmattan, 2006), p. 358

J. Galtung, Violence, Peace, and Peace Research. *J. Peace Res.* **6**(3), 190 (1969)

A. Garcia v. Canada (1993) FCJ 635 (Can. FC, June 23, 1993), J. C. Hathaway, *The Rights of Refugees under International Law* (Cambridge, Cambridge University Press, 2005), p. 924

J. Gasana, "Natural Resource Scarcity and Violence in Rwanda", in M. Halle, J. Mathew, J. Switzer (eds.), *Conserving the Peace: Resources, Livelihoods and Security* (Winnipeg, International Institute for Sustainable Development, 2002), p. 223

R.F. Gorman, G. Kibreab, Repatriation aid and development assistance, in *Reconceiving International Refugee Law* (The Hague, Martinus Nijhoff Publishers, 1997), p. 39

A. Guichaoua, *The Problem of the Rwandese Refugees and the Banyarwanda Populations in the Great Lakes Region.* UNHCR 27, 30–31 (1992)

B. Harrell-Bond, Repatriation: Under What Conditions is the Most Desirable Solution for Refugees? An Agenda for Research. *African Studies Review* **32**(1), 58 (1989)

A. Guichaoua, *From War to Genocide: Criminal Politics in Rwanda 1990–1994* (Wisconsin, University of Wisconsin Press, 2015), p. 146

J. Hathaway, The Meaning of Repatriation. *Int. J. Refug. Law* **9**(4), 551–552 (1997)

J.C. Hathaway, *The Rights of Refugees under International Law* (Cambridge, Cambridge University Press, 2005), p. 924

Human Rights Watch, *Ensuring that Repatriation is Voluntary*, 1997

International Refugee Rights Initiative and Refugee Law Project, *A Dangerous Impasse: Rwandan Refugees in Uganda*, June 2010, p. 21

Jeune Afrique, "Rwanda: avec Séraphine Mukantabana, tous les chemins mènent à Kigali", 5 July 2013

J.-P. Kimonyo, *Rwanda: Popular Genocide* (Boulder, Lynne Rienner, 2008), p. 51

L.N. Kingston, Bringing Rwandan Refugees 'Home': The Cessation Clause, Statelessness, and Forced Repatriation. *Int. J. Refug. Law* **29**(3), 3 (2017)

A.J. Kuperman, Provoking Genocide: A Revised History of the Rwandan Patriotic Front. *J. Genocide Res.* **6**(1), 82 (2004)

R. Lemarchand, *The Dynamics of Violence in Central Africa* (Philadelphia, University of Pennsylvania Press, 2009a), p. 126

R. Lemarchand, The Politics of Memory in Post-Genocide Rwanda, in *After Genocide: Transitional Justice, Post-Conflict Reconstruction and Reconciliation in Rwanda and Beyond*, P. Clark, Z.D. Kaufman (eds.) (New York, Columbia University Press, 2009b), p. 71

K. Long, "Back to Where You Once Belonged: A Historical Review of UNHCR Policy and Practice on Refugee Repatriation", UNHCR, Sept. 2013, para. 165, available at: https://www.refworld.org/docid/5226d8f44.html (last visited 1 June 2020)

M. Mamdani, *When Victims Become Killers: Colonialism, Nativism, and the Genocide in Rwanda* (Princeton, Princeton University Press, 2003), p. 167

I. Martin, Hard Choices After Genocide: Human Rights and Political Failures in Rwanda, in *Hard Choices: Moral Dilemmas in Humanitarian Intervention*, J. Moore (ed.) (Maryland, Rowman & Littlefield, 1998), p. 160

L. Melvern, *A People Betrayed: The Role of the West in Rwanda's Genocide* (London, Zed Books, 2009), p. 59

J. Milner, Refugees and the Regional Dynamics of Peacebuilding. *Refug. Surv. Q.* **28**(1), 26 (UNHCR, 2009)

G. Musabyimana, *L'APR et les Réfugiés Rwandais au Zaïre 1996–1997: Un Génocide Nié* (Paris, L'Harmattan, 2004), p. 17

M. Ndagijimana, M. Collins translated, *How Paul Kagame Deliberately Sacrificed the Tutsi*, La Pagaie, 2016. Kindle version

K. O'Connor, *Repatriation: The Politics of Re-Constructing and Contesting Rwandan Citizenship* (Oxford, Refugee Studies Centre, University of Oxford, 2013), p. 28

S. Ogata, Refugee Repatriation and Peace-Building. *Refug. Surv. Q.* **16**(2), vii (1997a)

S. Ogata, Opening Statement at the eighth meeting of the Standing Committee of the Executive Committee of the High Commissioner's Programme (ExCom) (Geneva, 24 June 1997b)

O. Otunnu, Rwandese Refugees and Immigrants in Uganda, in *The Path of a Genocide: The Rwanda Crisis from Uganda to Zaire*, H. Adelman, A. Suhrke (eds.) (New Jersey, Transaction, 2000), p. 22

O. Otunnu, As Historical Analysis of the Invasion by the Rwandan Patriotic Army (RPA), in *The Path of a Genocide: The Rwanda Crisis from Uganda to Zaire*, H. Adelman, A. Suhrke (eds.) (New Jersey, Transaction, 2000), p. 35

O. Otunnu, *Crisis of Legitimacy and Political Violence in Uganda 1979 to 2016* (Cham, Palgrave McMillan, 2016), p. 134

P. Péan, *Carnages: Les Guerres Secrètes des grandes puissances en Afrique* (Paris, Fayard, 2010), pp. 425–455

G. Prunier, The Rwandan Patriotic Front, in *African Guerrillas*, C. Clapham (ed.) (Oxford, James Currey et al., 1998), p. 129

G. Prunier, *The Rwanda Crisis: History of a Genocide* (Kampala, Foundation Publishers, 1999), p. 199

Republic of Rwanda, "Office of the President, Instruction présidentielles relatives aux réfugies", 12 June, 1976

Republic of Rwanda, Ministry of Foreign Affairs and Cooperation, "Rwanda's Comments on the Draft UN Mapping Report on the DRC", 30 Sep 2010, para. 25, available at: https://www.ohchr.org/Documents/Countries/CD/DRC_Report_Comments_Rwanda.pdf (last visited 1 June 2020)

J. Rever, *In Praise of Blood: The Crimes of the Rwandan Patriotic Front* (Random House Canada, 2018), p. 217

F. Reyntjens, Rwanda: Genocide and Beyond. *J. Refug. Stud.* **9**(3), 245 (1996)
Rights in Exile Programme, "Open Letter to EXCOM: The Threat of Invoking the Cessation Clause with Particular Reference to Rwanda", 1 Oct. 2012
A.G. Rodicio, Restoration of Life: A New Theoretical Approach to Voluntary Repatriation Based on a Cambodian Experience of Return. *Int. J. Refug. Law* **12**(1/2), 134 (2001)
J.R. Rogge, Repatriation of Refugees, in *When Refugees Go Home*, T. Allen, H. Morsink (eds.) (Trenton, UNRISD, James Currey and Africa World Press, 1994), p. 20
T. Rudasingwa, *Healing a Nation, a Testimony: Waging and Winning a Peaceful Revolution to Unite and Heal a Broken Rwanda* (South Carolina, CreateSpace Independent Publishing Platform, 2013), p. 76
A.J. Ruzibiza, *Rwanda l'histoire secrète* (Paris, Editions du Panama, 2005), p. 138
Y. Siddiqui, "Reviewing the Application of the Cessation Clause of the 1951", Refugee Studies Centre, University of Oxford, Working Paper Series No. 76, Aug 2011, 8 fn
B.N. Stein, F.C. Cuny, Repatriation in a Civil War/Conflict Situation, paper presented at Roundtable Consultation on Voluntary Repatriation and UNHCR (Geneva, 2–3 Jun 1993), p. 16
B.N. Stein, Refugee Repatriation, Return, and Refoulement During Conflict, USAID Conference, 30–31 Oct. 1997, p. 13
S. Takahashi, The UNHCR Handbook on Voluntary Repatriation: The Emphasis of Return Over Protection. *Int. J. Refug. Law* **9**(4), 605–606 (1997)
S. Takeuchi, J. Marara, Land Tenure Security in Post-Conflict Rwanda, *Confronting Land and Property Problems for Peace*, S. Takeuchi (ed.)(Oxon, Routledge, 2014), p. 99
M.B. Umutesi, *Surviving the Slaughter: The Ordeal of a Rwandan Refugee in Zaire* (Wisconsin, The University of Wisconsin Press, 2004), p. 120
UN Office of the High Commissioner for Human Rights, *Report of the Mapping Exercise documenting the most serious violations of human rights and international humanitarian law committed within the territory of the Democratic Republic of the Congo between March 1993 and June 2003, 2010 (Mapping Report)*, Aug. 2010, para. 220
UNHCR, Executive Committee of the High Commissioner's Programme, Voluntary Repatriation, No. 18 (XXXI)—1980, 16 Oct. 1980, (a), avaiable at: https://www.refworld.org/docid/3ae68c6e8.html (last visited 2 June 2020)
UNHCR, Statement by Mrs. Sadako Ogata, United Nations High Commissioner for Refugees, in *International Management Symposium* (Switzerland, St. Gallen, 25 May 1992), available at: https://www.unhcr.org/admin/hcspeeches/3ae68faec/statement-mrs-sadako-ogata-united-nations-high-commissioner-refugees-international.html (last visited 1 June 2020)
UNHCR, Protection Guidelines on Voluntary Repatriation (draft), Sept. 1993, p. 52
UNHCR, Prospects for Early Repatriation of Rwandan Refugees Currently in Burundi, Tanzania and DRC (Gersony report), Oct 1994, p. 3, 14, available at: https://graphics8.nytimes.com/packages/pdf/world/gersony_report.PDF#page=17&zoom=auto (last visted 31 May 2020)
UNHCR, *Handbook on Voluntary Repatriation*, 1996, para. 3.6
UNHCR, *The State of the World's Refugees: Fifty Years of Humanitarian Action* (Oxford, Oxford University Press, 2000), p. 258
UNHCR, "Guidelines on International Protection: Cessation of Refugee Status under Article 1C(5) and (6) of the 1951 Convention relating to the Status of Refugees", 10 Feb. 2003, para. 8
UNHCR, *Handbook for Repatriation and Reintegration Activities* (Geneva, May 2004), One-2, Four-1, available at: https://www.unhcr.org/411786694.pdf (last visited 1 June 2020)
UNHCR, Statement by Mr. António Guterres, United Nations High Commissioner for Refugees, to the United Nations Security Council, New York, 24 Jan. 2006
UNHCR, "Implementation of the Comprehensive Strategy for the Rwandan Refugee Situation, including UNHCR's recommendations on the Applicability of the 'ceased circumstances' Cessation Clauses", 30 Dec. 2011, para. 28
UNSC, S/1994/1115, Letter dated 28 September 1994 from the Permanent Representative of Rwanda to the United Nations Addressed to the President of the Security Council, 29 Sept. 1994, p. 2

UN Secretary-General, "Secretary-General's Address to UNHCR Executive Committee", 6 Oct. 2005

G. Verdirame, B. Harrell-Bond, *Rights in Exile: Janus-Faced Humanitarianism* (New York, Berghahn, 2005), p. 165

Washington Post, "Invasion Stirs Tribal Tension in Rwanda", 14 Oct. 1990

C. Watson, *Exile from Rwanda: Background to an Invasion* (The U.S. Committee for Refugees Issue Paper, 1991), p. 13

L. Waldorf, Revisiting *Hotel Rwanda*, Genocide Ideology, Reconciliation, and Rescuers. *J. Genocide Res.* **11**(I), 111 (2009)

R. Winter, Lancing the Boil: Rwanda's Agenda in Zaire, in *War and Peace in DRC/Congo: Analyzing and Evaluating Intervention, 1996–1997*, H. Adelman, G.C. Rao (eds.) (Trenton, Africa World Press, 2004), p. 114

M. Zieck, *UNHCR and Voluntary Repatriation of Refugees: Legal Analysis* (Leiden, Martinus Nijhoff Publishers, 1997), p. 114

Where is Rwanda's Peace?

Ilyayo

1 Introduction

It has been 30 years since the civil war in Rwanda started in 1990. Since then, I have been looking for peace. Amid the death and destruction of 1994, Rwandans fled from violence in desperate need of safety. They understood then, as they do today, that without peace, there can be no hope for the future.

Rwandan refugees remain homeless, rejected, and hopeless. They feel hated, hunted, and humiliated. Being a victim of the crimes committed by the regime in power, I acutely know that the Rwandan Patriotic Front (RPF) continues to conceal the crimes it has committed in Rwanda, the Democratic Republic of Congo (DRC), and elsewhere. The United Nations (UN) refuses to recognise this fact. Our voices have been silenced, and our plight is not understood.

As a result, there is neither forgiveness nor reconciliation among our people—the Tutsi, Hutu, and Twa—since the RPF seized power in 1994. Rwandans are unable to tell the truth about what fully happened in 1994. In my native prefecture of Gikongoro, peasants were killed or kidnapped by the RPF after its army entered the zone. Others recount similar stories in areas to the south of the capital Kigali, in Bugesera, Gashora. Many of my cousins in the commune of Ngenda who refused to run away were killed on the spot or kidnapped and never seen again. Like many other Rwandan Hutus, I was scared and fled to Bukavu in Zaire.

Today, the Hutus are discriminated against, intimidated, and denied equal rights to education, justice, and freedom of expression in Rwanda. Many Hutus are arbitrarily behind bars, and countless others have been killed or were made to disappear because of their political affiliations or ties to those who had parted their ways with the RPF.

The original version of this chapter was revised: The author's affiliation and belated correction have been updated. The correction to this chapter is available at https://doi.org/10.1007/978-981-15-2850-7_7

Ilyayo
Zambia

M. Yonekawa and A. Sugiki (eds.), *Repatriation, Insecurity, and Peace*,
https://doi.org/10.1007/978-981-15-2850-7_6

Without acknowledging another truth, such as the Tutsi massacring the Hutu, apart from the generally-known truth that the Hutu massacring the Tutsi, there is no genuine justice and everlasting peace. Rwandans continue to flee the country, albeit in smaller numbers.

Rwandans need to tell their stories. Who were responsible for all these crimes? Why were these crimes committed? Why were innocent Rwandan refugees abandoned by the United Nations High Commissioner for Refugees (UNHCR) that asked refugees to repatriate to Rwanda or be stripped off their status? These stories need to be understood.

2 Constant Fear and Loss Since 1990

During the RPF's invasion in 1990, our loved ones were targeted in our homeland. In 1992, my young brother Anatole's godfather Silas was killed in an RPF attack in Ruhengeri. In 1993, I lost a beloved teacher, Father Joseph Rushigajiki of the Marist Brothers, who was kidnapped in the same area. I hoped that peace would soon return but it did not; things got worse. RPF attacks in the north led to the mass displacement of a million Rwandans including the family of Bernard, my former secondary school classmate in Byumba. Forced to live in wretched conditions in internally displaced persons (IDP) camps, these people scrounged for food and fought a host of diseases. This Hutu IDPs crisis, coupled with the RPF violence against the Hutu population and the killing of President Habyarimana, laid the context for the 1994 genocide.

In April 1994, I went to visit Philip Ndayi, my former secondary school friend in Cyangugu. We went to my village in Gikongoro. We were preparing to go to Butare University for our inscription. On the morning of 7 April 1994, my father called us and advised not to go to Butare as it had been announced that President Habyarimana was killed. Meanwhile, my father ordered me to accompany Philip to the bus so he could go back home. Things were not good, and life was paralysed. Gikongoro became like a refugee camp. When French and Zambian peacekeepers arrived in June 1994, we thought security would improve. People coming from Mayaga, Kigali in the RPF controlled zone, cried for their lost and killed relatives. We waited for my aunt and cousins who were living in Bugesera; one of my cousins came crying that she was the only survivor. My elder brother suggested that we leave so we would not die together. My other four brothers and I first fled to Cyangugu, then to Bukavu. Things were not good in Zaire. Zairian soldiers were stealing refugees' belongings, and sometimes beating refugees to death.

In October and November 1996, Rwandan troops invaded Zaire and attacked refugee camps along the border. Many Rwandans, including myself, trekked thousands of kilometres, wracked with hunger, thirst, and bone-breaking fatigue. We desperately wanted physical, emotional, and spiritual relief. But it was impossible; we were hunted like animals by Rwandan and Ugandan soldiers every step of the way. My four brothers and I were terrified as gunshots and mortar explosions filled the air. We left the Nyangezi refugee camp for the north of Bukavu, before moving on to the Muku and Mushweshwe refugee camps. Shortly thereafter, unable to find respite amid the mounting violence, we ran to Mulesa to the Chimanga camp. My friend Cyprian contracted a fever and suffered from diarrhea and vomiting, so he was forced to rest. Two days later, when he found me, I was trying to recover from malaria.

I remember Cyprian recounting, with fear, how the RPF had first arrived at the camp, before he managed to flee. These RPF members were, by all appearances, an advanced team of RPF soldiers or agents. These RPF soldiers asked him if he was a Hutu. He pretended he didn't understand what they were saying. He was with a Zairian man distributing food in the Nyangezi refugee camp, who spoke the Zairean Mashi dialect. "We do not understand what you are talking about. Use Mashi or French", Cyprian said, feigning ignorance. Cyprian understood, to a limited degree, some of this dialect and knew he had to hide his Hutu ethnicity. RPF soldiers said that we were "lucky" because they would have killed us if we were Rwandans. "We'll finish off these Hutu *Interahamwe*,[1]" the RPF soldiers said. Cyprian said he saw white soldiers and suspected the RPF had ways of tracking the refugees. In retrospect, I believe Rwanda and its international backers were using all means possible at the time—technology and information it collected from international NGOs which were working on the spot for Rwandan refugees—to locate where we were.

With thousands of other refugees, I fled north to Nyamirangwe before crossing Virunga Park via Chimanga. Later, we headed to Chingulube and Shabunda, as stories of mass killings of the Rwandan and Congolese Hutu abounded. Sometimes, we did not know where we were going while running away from the RPF. At times, it felt as though we were running in circles and the RPF had us surrounded. When we arrived in the township of Bunyakili, it was raining and the Mayi Mayi, a Congolese militia, told us to keep on running, because Rwandan troops had already occupied the township. We did not know where we were. We were panicked and Congolese villagers guided us. We fled to Katusi, Bubemba, Oso, and Amisi, and felt we could go no further. We finally reached a place called Tingi-Tingi and camped for three months. The conditions were atrocious; we boiled under the hot sun, my brother Cleophas got typhoid. I thought he would die but we did manage to get antibiotics for him. Many others did die of disease and exhaustion. Tingi-Tingi was ultimately attacked by RPF soldiers who wanted to finish off the Hutus there. Just before that assault, we faced a dilemma: should we go back home or run away again? My youngest brother Deo had reached a breaking point. He was emotionally and physically exhausted. He said he could not run anymore and did not see the point. It was soul-destroying to see him give up. The rest of us had to keep going. We walked to Lubutu, Ikela, Lualaba, Kisangani, Boende, Bokungu, Mobenzeni, Mbandaka. Then, we crossed to Ndjundu in the Republic of Congo in May 1997. Others continued on to Angola where they

[1]The *Interahamwe* were a mainly Hutu militia whose members was largely drawn from the youth wing of the former ruling National Revolutionary Movement for Development (MRND) party, although some members were also Tutsi and the RPF is known to have infiltrated this militia. Many of these militia killed Tutsis and moderate Hutus during the genocide. RPF soldiers and officials have variously used the *Interahamwe* as a catch-all term to signify the Hutus in general, in a bid to demonise them as a group and justify violence against them.

met Angolan soldiers who traumatised them. Women and girls were raped; men and boys were beaten, insulted, and physically abused there.

We shed tears and blood during those nine months running for our lives in the rainforest of the DRC, and many of us still suffer from the traumas, remembering our relatives and loved ones who died including my cousins Phocas and Silas, my uncle Celestin and his family, and my childhood friend Stephania and her children. The rain pounded us, and we were constantly stung by mosquitoes and bush ants. We were hungry and angry as UNHCR did not even advocate for the vulnerable Hutus. We were forced to eat strange fruits and the roots of wild trees in the rainforest. Many were poisonous; my fellow refugees died after ingesting such things. Mothers sometimes left their babies who were shot. Fiancées left their beloved ones who were killed. Wives lost their husbands. Brothers lost their sisters and sisters their brothers. There were no burials for many of us, because we had to keep running away from the Rwandan armies.

In the south of Kisangani, we poured onto the Lubutu Bridge and were shot at from behind by the Congolese soldiers loyal to Laurent Désire Kabila, a spokesperson of Congolese rebels assisting Rwandan troops. The bridge was about fifteen meters above the river. We had no choice but to jump, and many refugees did not know how to swim. Many were injured or drowned. Amid the gunfire, pregnant women jumped off the bridge, too. I'll never forget the sight. Airplanes flew above us, not to bring food and relief but to locate us, as far as we understood.

In Kisangani, I lost my siblings Tharsisse, Deo, and Creophace and my cousins Phocas and Silas. I could not breathe when I learned what happened to them. My brother Deo, who refused to run anymore after Tingi-Tingi, was caught by the RPF, taken to Kisangani, and killed and dumped in a mass grave. In Kisangani, I was separated from my other brothers Tharcisse and Creophace when we scattered during another RPF attack on our group. Tharcisse went in another direction and ended up, weeks later, in Bangui, the capital of the Central African Republic, only to be killed by Ugandan soldiers there. Creophace was hit directly by mortar fire and mortally wounded while he was traveling with our cousin Phocas, who survived but was later seized and killed by the RPF. Our friend Anastase was travelling with them but survived the attacks and managed to escape. And my cousin Silas died after our ordeal in Congo, after arriving in Zambia in 1999.

Many Hutus were kidnapped or made to disappear; others died from food poisoning during 1994 and 1995 in refugee camps in Zaire, such as Leonard Yambabaliye and Jean de Dieu, the nephew of Sylvestre Nsanzimana, the former Rwandan prime minister. Jean de Dieu was kidnapped on his way to a Congolese tea plantation in Muku near Bukavu, and his body was found a few days later. I wish he were still alive, just like so many thousands of others who have been targeted, abused, slaughtered, but never forgotten. He had a lot of information from his uncle on how the 1990 war started, which I wanted to know.

As we fled across Congo, I saw pregnant mothers going into labour and giving birth under heavy rains in the bush, bleeding continuously. No one could help them. I saw a mother giving birth to a child and her placenta falling out of her body while she ran away from her hunters. Many people died before my eyes. I witnessed things that should never have been seen. I saw people dying from chronic hunger, fatigue, and depression. I saw children give up on life, having lost their parents and other family members. I saw parents carrying their dead children, seemingly unaware that they were not living anymore, walking day and night without rest. I saw babies sucking the breast of their already dead mothers. I saw people choosing to jump into rivers and devoured by crocodiles instead of being killed by human beings. I saw refugees who were bitten by snakes and would slowly die from infection. We abandoned these people along the roads and in the forests, because we had no possibility to bury their bodies. I saw parents selling their children, especially their young girls, to Congolese villagers, instead of dying from hunger. This happened particularly in Butembo and Kisangani.

I was among those who arrived in Mbandaka and surrounding areas, which became its own kind of nightmare. It was there that RPF and Ugandan soldiers lured refugees out into the open and slaughtered them in broad daylight, before dumping them in mass graves or in the river. Others were forced into big containers—the kind used to transport goods on trucks and ships—and set on fire. Those who tried to escape were killed and thrown in the Congo River. I encountered volunteers from the Red Cross in Mbandaka on my second day. During the following night, we left Mbandaka proper, because Congolese soldiers started shooting in air to scare us, and we ran away along the river. Many of us who hid in the forest around Mbandaka were bitten by ants. My brother Anatole, who was seven years old, began to scream, and so did Pascalina, the three-year old daughter of my friend named Joseph Kayishema. We were scared when the children screamed, as the RPF could discover where we were. In the morning, we could see crocodiles jumping on the bodies of the dead, devouring skulls; the water was mixed with blood. We were scared and horrified. Many Congolese peasants warned us to run away, otherwise, we'd be killed by RPF and Ugandans soldiers steadily arriving in the town. We gave cloves and domestic utensils to Congolese civilians who transported us in their big canoes for four days from Mbandaka village to Mobenzano, the other side of Ndjondo in the Republic of Congo.

I lost my three brothers and two cousins. I experienced so much loss during my flight that I thought I would be the next one to be killed.

Apart from refugees, the clergy has never been spared by the RPF. I recall the killings of bishops, including Phocas Nikwigize of Ruhengeli, Thaddée Nsengiyumva and others in Gakurazo in June 1994. Similarly, in Bukavu and Kalima, after Rwandan troops invaded Zaire, many Hutu priests including Father Antoine Hategekimana, Milimo, and Father Simon and many Catholic sisters were traumatised and killed by RPF soldiers. Archbishop Christophe Munzihirwa of Bukavu condemned the attacks and assassinations of Rwandan refugees and catholic clergy in Bukavu in 1996. He was later assassinated by the RPF.

Other refugees are still being hunted and chased to this day in Uganda, Kenya, the DRC, and Zambia. Why does the RPF want to kill all Hutus, and even Tutsis? We are innocent. And why do powerful nations who claim to respect human rights watch in silence as this is happening?

Map of author's flight across Central Africa from 1996 to 1999

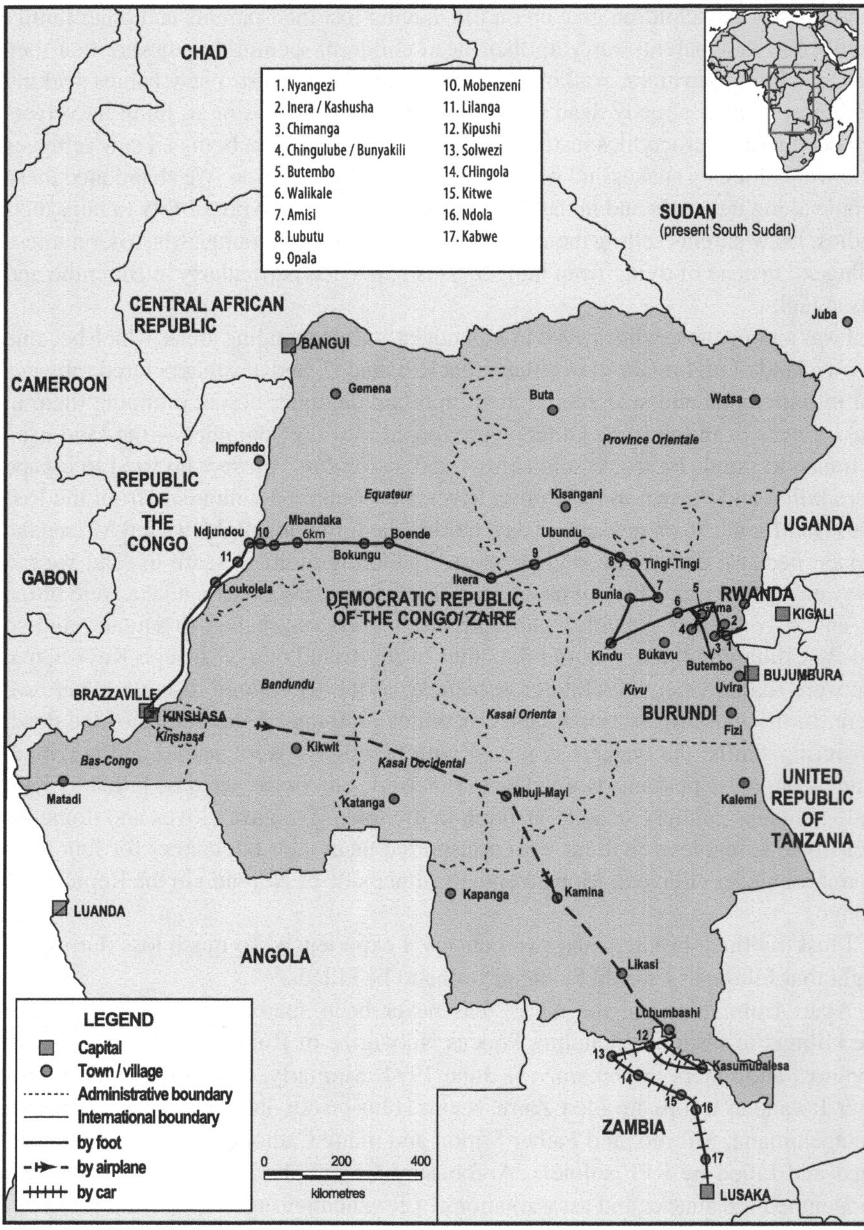

3 Those Who Promoted Our Peace

Since 1990, I have never found peace, neither physically nor in my heart. I am a powerless and traumatised Rwandan refugee. It is hard to find people who promote peace. I pray every day that Rwandans who are locked in prisons in my homeland might be set free one day. I pray for those who lost loved ones, that their hearts might somehow heal.

We, the Rwandan refugees, have largely been abandoned by the UN where justice is concerned. Yet courageous individuals from all walks of life have indeed advocated on our behalf. They have been true caregivers. Their show of international solidarity lifts us up in immeasurable ways. Father Carlos, who worked for Caritas in Inera refugee camp in Bukavu, helped refugees pursue their education. In later years, he walked a thousand kilometers from his Spanish village to Geneva in support of our plight. He trekked from Spain to Switzerland to demonstrate how hard it is to endure a long journey such as the one we had from Rwanda to the Republic of Congo, Angola, Zambia, and Tanzania.

Let me also recognise the Catholic White Sisters who saved some refugees at Mbandaka and elsewhere. May the Lord be with them. Archbishop Mazombwe visited us in Zaire in 1995, when we were at our lowest. He saw people who had been completely abandoned, and he told me in person that he was irretrievably affected by the scale of suffering and the number of the dead, especially among children and women in Goma and Bukavu. He is also known to have gone to Rwanda to pay last respects to the bishops killed in Gakurazo, slaughtered in cold blood by the RPF in a highly organised operation in June 1994. Sadly, he has passed on.

I remember Dr. Milton and his colleagues from the medical NGO, Doctors Without Borders (MSF), who provided care for refugees arriving in the Republic of Congo, as well as medical and food aid to refugees in the Ndjondu, Lilanga, and Lukolela camps. In the Ndjondo refugee camp, Anne Sophie, a nutritionist from MSF, provided refugees with food aid at the supplementary nutritional centre, and Jean Francois helped us with hygiene and building activities. I also acknowledge Dr. Sigsbert, Dr. Vincent, and Dr. Camille for their voluntary work trying to save refugee lives and helping those in need.

I remember some Rwandan refugees helping fellow refugees, such as Francois, Martin Ngayaboshya, Kayishema Joseph, Vincent, Gukuni, Laurence, Boniface, Theogene, Ephrem, Benoit, Jacqueline, Protogene, Mado, Bobo and Nshimiyimana Jean de Dieu, Benjamin, Iradukunda Cedric, Jean Damascene and his family. I still remember them today. We had some good memories, sharing meals and a journey during hard times in the camp which strengthened our relations despite our suffering, in Ndjondo.

Upon arriving in Brazzaville via Ndjundu in 1997, I managed to communicate with Bernard, my former secondary school classmate who was in Zambia at that time. He had been internally displaced from Byumba since 1991, and he insisted me to join him in Zambia, because Brazzaville was insecure due to the war between President Lisuba and Sassou Ngweso.

I am thankful to the Catholic sisters of charity who helped me to leave Brazzaville. They arranged for a Congolese passport which helped me to cross the Zaire River to Kinshasa in 1997; I took a plane with other catholic nuns to Lubumbashi. In Lubumbashi, I was connected to a Zairian woman, Sifa. Even if she was given some money to help me to cross to Kasumbalesa, she was good-hearted. After staying in Lubumbashi for four months, I crossed to Zambia in 1998. Then, I was sent to the Meheba refugee camp where I met Sister Anne Crowley, a sister of charity from Australia. In Meheba, she was like my mother. She taught me English, she fed me, and I will remember her by the blanket she gave me when I had nothing to cover me in the night. In 2003, Sister Anne arranged for me to resettle in Australia, Sydney. With other sisters of charity, she paid for my accommodation for 12 months, but the UNHCR rejected my submission to resettle to Australia. Life goes on.

In Zambia, Anglican Bishop of Lusaka, Reverend John Osmers and Archbishop Mpundu extended their hearts to refugees, assisting in education and peace efforts in camps in Zambia. They fought against the wrongfulness of the UNHCR-backed cessation clause of refugee status of Rwandan refugees (see below). Bishop Emeritus John Osmers lost his sight amid the stressful campaign he waged against forced repatriation, the cessation clause, and other draconian measures. The late Cardinal Medardo Mazombwe, Zambia's archbishop emeritus of Lusaka touched the hearts of Rwandan refugees in Zambia in his pastoral letter "I was a stranger" in 1998, and advocated for our integration into the Zambian community. The letter urged Zambia to draw on the lessons we learned from Jesus and to assist the most vulnerable, the hungry and sick. These individuals from Africa and Europe, among others, have made refugees smile, and helped restore some of our faith in humanity. Archbishop Emeritus Theresphore Mpundu has used his moral and spiritual authority to urge Zambians to accept Rwandan refugees as their brothers and sisters, and he is getting on in years. Dr. Barbara Harrell-Bond is no longer here with us—she passed away in July 2018—yet she will always be remembered and respected for her scholarship of refugee issues and her dedication to the cause of protecting refugees in the Great Lakes region and beyond. All these individuals deserve our trust and respect; they have been peacemakers in the fullest sense.

We need more churches and courageous voices to speak out on behalf of vulnerable refugees who face arbitrary arrest and deportation. Journalists need to more clearly expose the killings and human rights abuses in Rwanda. These reporters and activists need protection in spreading the word. Rwandan refugees need a stronger voice and condemnation of these violations. We are seeking help from the Human Rights Watch, Amnesty International and the United Nations to review and follow the recommendations of the UN Mapping Report (2010). It is now time to inform the world that Hutus were also killed and that the Hutus survivors should be recognised.

4 Insecurity of Rwandan Refugees

A massive number of Rwandans have either been silenced or exterminated by the RPF regime. Witnesses who tried to expose their crimes prior to, during, and after the genocide in Rwanda have been particularly targeted. The prisons in Rwanda are full, mostly with Hutus who were convicted in the traditional Gacaca courts, in trials that were widely considered to be unfair. For those refugees who ended up in Zambia, such as me, security conditions are precarious. After more than fifteen years, we still do not have the right to own a home or land, or enjoy permanent resident status.

Our very existence is threatened on a daily basis. Rwandans who try to survive by selling food or other agricultural products can face arrest by immigration authorities as they do not have work permits or rights for movement, and there is not enough assistance or advocacy by the UNHCR. Refugees can be thrown in jail or deported. Detained refugees have been beaten, sometimes to death, by prisoners who have committed serious criminal offenses. Refugees stay alive or avoid being beaten if they barter cigarettes, small fish, or cooking oil. Why are refugees who are sent to jail for small offences that should not even be considered crimes lumped in with hardened criminals? Why is being a refugee a crime?

Many security incidents took place in Zambia. In 2001, many Rwandan families in Zambia were attacked in the Kanyama refugee compound in Lusaka. In January 2004, I was attacked by a gang of five people brandishing knives and metal bars, near the Kanyama clinic. I cried for help and my hand was fractured during the assault. Before the five assailants ran, I heard them speaking Kinyarwanda and Swahili. In another case, a week before his wedding in 2007, a refugee named Ukulikiyeyezu was attacked by a group of individuals speaking Kinyarwanda and broken Nyanja, a Zambian dialect. They hit him on the head with a metal bar, and he lost an eye. He was taken to the hospital in an unconscious state by onlookers at the scene. Later the same year, another refugee Bosco Ntahontuye was shot in both arms by an unknown assailant in Kalingalinga, Lusaka, while an elderly man named Bimenyi and his colleague were shot in Kabwata, Lusaka; the latter died on the spot. The victim had tried to avoid an attack by offering money (11 million kwachas which is equivalent to 2,000 US dollars), but the assailants refused. The assailants had come with a mission to injure or kill Rwandan refugees. Upon return in Kigali, the assailants sent a message to Bimenyi asking for forgiveness. Moreover, apologising that he was given a mission to target and kill refugees.

Another Rwandan refugee family in Lusaka was attacked at night by assailants who gave their two daughters a mobile phone to inform their aunt in Belgium that their parents were going to be killed. The mother of the small girls was killed on the spot, and their father Kabera survived a gunshot wound. Many other refugees who've been assaulted say that the assailants spoke Kinyarwanda, and a bit of French and English. Zambian authorities and local UNHCR staff are aware of these attacks on and killings of Rwandan refugees, yet they do very little, if anything, to prevent them. There has also been a series of kidnappings, which began in 1996 when Agnes Ntamabyaliro,

Rwanda's former Rwandan justice minister was seized from the Zambian town of Mufurila.

The refugee community was alarmed in May 2014, when Clement Nshimyukiza, a former Rwandan refugee and successful businessman, was killed in the Lusaka compound in suspicious circumstances. His shop, which was run by his widow, was ransacked two weeks later. In October of the same year, plans were revealed to allegedly kidnap five Rwandan former refugee leaders, but they failed to materialise. The opening of a Rwandan Government High Commission office in Lusaka naturally gave cause for concern as it sponsors activities opposing the local integration of former refugees and conducts conferences on genocide that fuel hatred of refugees by citizens.

Despite most improvements in local integration, refugees in Zambia struggle to make ends meet. Refugees who want to run a small business must pay 50,000 US dollars for a permit. It is an unfathomable amount for any refugee and is evidence that refugees in Zambia are not treated according to the refugee conventions. We are being treated as foreigners who come to Zambia to invest, and we can't afford to. It is striking that refugees desperately want to integrate into Zambian society. Some immigration and UNHCR officials create obstacles. For instance, if a refugee can afford to buy a permit to run a business, his or her family members are not legally allowed any benefits or to work for him or her. And many refugees who work as labourers in other fields, independent of family members, are paid a fraction of Zambian wages and their gratuities are hardly (or not) paid. Some refugees are required to pay special fees for receiving health care, which Zambians are not subjected to.

Many pregnant mothers and children (former Rwandan refugees) hardly access health care and education, because they have no identification cards. Refugees have witnessed how the RPF has succeeded in spreading propaganda in Zambian schools, stating that only Hutus committed violence against Tutsis during the 1994 genocide, when the truth is that members of both ethnic groups were guilty of crimes and the vast majority of Rwandans are innocent.

5 Forced Repatriation Under the UN-Sponsored Cessation Clause

The UNHCR-sponsored cessation clause of refugee status for Rwandan refugees, which Zambia began implementing in June 2013 meant the official loss of refugee status for thousands of people, eroding what little protection under humanitarian law they may have hoped for. The tripartite agreement—negotiated among Rwanda, Zambia and the UNHCR without the involvement of Rwandan refugees—invoked this policy that indirectly urged the forced repatriation or deportation and heightened discrimination against Rwandan refugees. This has also led to increased levels of insecurity and violence against the refugee population. Since 2002, Rwandan refugees have balked at going home as Kigali authorities sent in agents to scare, attack, and sometimes kill refugees in their host countries. Many countries are aware of these criminal activities—which are often organised by Rwandan embassies abroad—yet the enforced local policies aimed at stripping refugees of their protection.

The UNHCR began voluntary repatriation programs in 2002, yet in 2013, only one percent of refugees voluntarily returned to Rwanda. Some of them disappeared or jailed, and others returned into exile which is significant evidence that many Rwandans do not feel safe in their own country as Rwanda is politically unstable. In 2014, the Zambian government finally accepted to locally integrate Rwandan refugees—after years of campaigning by refugee organisations and local churches. However, the condition for local integration was to issue refugees Rwandan passports. Refugees quickly understood that accepting Rwandan passports would mean that refugees no longer had a "well-founded fear of persecution", and therefore did not need international protection, which is obviously not the case. Accepting these passports would also put refugees under the control and surveillance of the Rwandan government. It would also mean that Rwandan in Zambia and other countries would become ordinary migrants and would be legally required to return to Rwanda, since they already have necessary passports for their return. Thus, we refused, and the church and other refugee rights activists such as the late Dr. Barbara Harrell-Bond supported us on these grounds.

Dr. Barbara, an old woman in her eighties, an academician in refugee law, had a passion for helping vulnerable Rwandan refugees. She started the fight against a premature cessation clause of Rwandan refugees way back in 2008 and tried to advocate for the plight of Rwandan refugees wherever they were. Despite her old age, she managed to come to Zambia where we met in 2014. She met many high authorities in Zambia trying to explain refugee rights and how we were victimised by the cessation while Rwanda was still producing refugees. She tried to educate us on how we should win the cessation clause in regard to international laws. She also tried to inform concerned staff members at UNHCR Headquarter not to violate refugees law and not to go against refugees' wish. But she realised that it was a well predetermined program to make all Hutu refugees fail exceptions interviews. She passed away but remains in our minds as one of the pillars of local integration of former Rwandan refugees not only in Zambia but in many other countries.

At the end of 2017, the Zambian government decided to locally integrate Rwandan refugees without the condition to apply for Rwandan passports, and we finally felt relieved and at peace. Many thanks to Zambian government and the church.

We fear that the UNHCR in complicity with the Rwandan government, spread misinformation and undermined refugee security in Zambia in many negotiations on the cessation clause of refugee status. UNHCR staff said those who refuse to repatriate were in fact threatening or needlessly scaring the refugee population (engaging in intimidation campaigns) or may have committed genocide in 1994. The blanket accusation that all Hutu refugees were genocidaires if they did not want to return is absurd, considering that the majority of refugees in Zambia were children during the genocide,[2] and a good number were not even born yet in 1994. Many crimes have been

[2]Approximately 60% of Rwandan refugees in Zambia are younger than 35 years old.

committed against refugees by RPF agents. The commission for the refugee office in Zambia did not appear to care about the attacks against refugees and the loss of life. Instead the commission negotiated the cessation clause of Rwandan refugees, without the involvement of refugees who were, and remain, the principle stakeholders. We discovered that a former commission officer and other known officers were in fact advisors to the Rwandan Embassy. These individuals lobbied for Rwandan passports to become a sine qua non condition for local integration. We are grateful that the Zambian government has waived the Rwandan passport requirement for the local integration of up to four thousand former Rwandan refugees. But refugees have little faith and trust in the UNHCR, not only because the UN appears to have done Rwanda's bidding, but in particular because the UN staff have refused to help refugees secure legal documents in Zambia before the cessation. We acknowledge that after 2017 the approach of UN on Rwandan former refugees ameliorated.

Lack of status and documentation has led to more arbitrary arrests by immigration authorities. For example, in April 2016, many shops in Lusaka managed by Rwandan refugees were looted, and the refugees were never compensated for it because the victims could not provide legal documents to report the crimes in court. As a result, these refugees became further impoverished and their children were forced to drop out of school because fees could not be paid. Lack of status has also meant restricted movement for the vast majority of refugees. With no travel documents, there is virtually little opportunity for refugees to earn money to feed their families. And the sense that the RPF is lurking in Zambia, through its agents, instils a permanent fear and malaise in the population.

6 Where is Peace for Rwandan Refugees?

Peace is a source of life; it is the bread of love. Those who do not know peace are without hope. If we have no love and hope, what does this mean for the future of Rwanda? So many of us live in fear and suffer psychological traumas, especially pregnant mothers, children, and the elderly.

So many Rwandan families ran away from murderers over the last two and half decades, while the international community continued to support these oppressors. And now, the same Western experts claim that Rwanda is safe for us to return. Their claims amount to a denial of our suffering. Refugees worldwide and Rwandans at home have observed the brazen impunity from which President Paul Kagame's regime has benefited. There have been no prosecutions following the findings of the 2010 Mapping Report of the UN on crimes in the DRC. The report stated that the RPF may have committed genocide against Hutus in Congo. Sadly, there were never any international consequences after the RPF killed several thousand Hutus in the Kibeho IDP camp in 1995. In spite of the broadcasting of the BBC documentary, "Rwanda's Untold Story" in October 2014, whereby the producer Jane Corbin stated "it is unfortunate that the world today believe the opposite of what happened in

Rwanda in 1994", the world at large failed to recognise the killings of Hutus by the Tutsi-led RPF.

The lack of recognition of this tragedy and the forced return of Rwandan refugees as advocated by the UNHCR, amount to policies that instil even more fear and despair for Rwandan refugees.

The UNHCR insists under the cessation clause that conditions are safe enough for refugees to return to Rwanda. The UNHCR which has a mandate to protect refugees has not been reliable; Rwandan refugees depend more on local churches. But those who have returned, for whatever reason, have been subjected to unfair treatment—if they have survived at all. Many lost their land and homes, occupied by the RPF officers and others. Others disappeared or were jailed without any legitimate reason. Some went back to Rwanda but fled again. Given these circumstances, where is the security and good governance for which the international community commends Rwanda? Where is the peace that we have long hoped for?

As an individual, I have been passionate about refugee children's education, and I was involved in teaching in refugee camps in Zaire. When we started running away in the Zaire forest, I was feeling pity for refugees and I had to seek some training from Doctors Without Borders. A Canadian doctor Milton and a Burundi doctor Audace trained me to substitute in cases there were no doctors available. I started treating tropical wounds commonly observed in refugee populations. These motivated my career in medicine, and many refugees, especially children, benefited from my services. When cessation clause campaign started, I realised that advocacy was needed. A few of us refugees worked with church leaders who tirelessly helped us fight against inequality, offered sponsorships to some Rwandan refugees, and later provided support on discrimination and cessation clauses. With church, we advocated for our local integration without Rwandan passports.

I often asked Dr. Barbara and my friend Dr. Bernard how I can study refugee law as I found a gap in my ability to advocate. Maybe one day I will study refugee law.

I don't need economic development with its tall and shiny buildings for which Rwanda is being praised. I prefer to remain poor as long as I feel peaceful where I am, and hope that Hutus and Tutsis reconcile and fully live a trustful life, in love and peace.

Correction to: Repatriation, Insecurity, and Peace

Masako Yonekawa and Akiko Sugiki

Correction to:
M. Yonekawa and A. Sugiki (eds.), *Repatriation, Insecurity, and Peace*, https://doi.org/10.1007/978-981-15-2850-7

In the original version of the book, the following corrections have been made:

The title of First Chapter has been corrected to "Voluntary" Repatriation of Rwandan Refugees in Uganda: An Analysis of Law and Practice".

In the chapter "Where is Rwanda's Peace?", the author's location details have been corrected.

In page 102, opening and closing quotes for "Rwanda's Untold Story" have been added.

The erratum chapters and book have been updated with the changes.

The updated versions of these chapters can be found at
https://doi.org/10.1007/978-981-15-2850-7_1
https://doi.org/10.1007/978-981-15-2850-7_6

M. Yonekawa and A. Sugiki (eds.), *Repatriation, Insecurity, and Peace*,
https://doi.org/10.1007/978-981-15-2850-7_7

Conclusion: Rethinking Repatriation as a Durable Solution for Refugees

Akiko Sugiki

Repatriation of refugees entails an enduring myth. A myth could be described as a common belief or notion that may not be accurate or precise but is nevertheless believed and shared by many people. The myth of refugee repatriation operates in the same way.[1] Regardless of whether it is true or not, repatriation has been widely believed to be the most desirable solution for a refugee problem. Indeed, some repatriation operations have resulted in the return of nearly all refugees and their reintegration into their home areas has been successful. However, refugee repatriation has been far more problematic in other cases.

It is often argued that the subject of repatriation has been under-researched or under-theorised in refugee or forced migration studies.[2] This is partly because it is almost impossible to collect data on all of the repatriations around the world for a comprehensive analysis. However, empirical research on repatriation has been gradually increasing and the scope of analysis expanding. Five main themes of such research can be identified: (1) conceptual and normative standards of repatriation, (2) economic, social and political reintegration of returnees, (3) confrontation between returnees and those who stayed, (4) psycho-social health and mental issues and (5) new influx of displacement.[3] This body of research demonstrates that repatriation is not a simple reversal of displacement and does not necessarily bring the refugee cycle to an end for the refugees themselves nor for the refugees' home or host countries.

Even though repatriation programmes in various countries reveal numerous problems and issues in their policy formulation, practices and consequences, the myth of

A. Sugiki
Tokyo, Japan

[1] M.-E. Desrosiers and H. J. Swedlund, "Rwanda's Post-Genocide Foreign Aid Relations: Revisiting Notions of Exceptionalism", *African Affairs*, 118(472), 2018, 437.

[2] N. Omata, *The Myth of Self-Reliance: Economic Lives Inside a Liberian Refugee Camp*, New York, Berghahn, 2017, 10.

[3] See, J. Tegenbos & K. Vlassenroot, "Going Home? A Systematic Review of the Literature on Displacement, Return and Cycles of Violence", *Politics of Return Working Paper* (1), May 2018, available at: https://biblio.ugent.be/publication/8569124/file/8569125.pdf (last visited 3 May 2019).

M. Yonekawa and A. Sugiki (eds.), *Repatriation, Insecurity, and Peace*,
https://doi.org/10.1007/978-981-15-2850-7

repatriation still survives. In the case of Rwandan refugees in particular, the myth of repatriation is perpetuated by official or government-sponsored narratives: Rwanda is sufficiently peaceful and stable for return, and refugees who refuse to go back to Rwanda are criminals or perpetrators of genocide.[4]

The Pattern of Repatriation and The Types of Governments

This book has considered why Rwandan refugees have refused to go home despite strong pressure and persuasion from the RPF government, UNHCR and countries in the region hosting refugees. It also examined under which conditions refugee repatriation should be organised and enforced. The Rwandan case offered us the opportunity to rethink the real value of repatriation in its relation to enduring solutions for refugees. Before concluding our analysis, it will be helpful to categorise the patterns of repatriation and types of governments or regimes. At the risk of oversimplification, the patterns of refugee repatriation can be divided into six types: (1) return after a fundamental political change, (2) return after a political settlement or major political change, (3) return after a political settlement that does not end the conflict and that leaves the contending parties with substantial political and military power, (4) return to an area not controlled by the government that originally caused the refugees' flight, (5) return caused by the deterioration of political security conditions in the host country and (6) return to a conflict zone.[5]

The type of government or regime in the home country is also an important variable affecting refugees' livelihood and sustainable reintegration. At the conceptual level, four types of regimes can be identified: (1) a democratic regime with a functional government which maintains political order and stability, (2) a democratic regime without a functional government, (3) an undemocratic or authoritarian regime with excessive state authority and (4) a collapsed or failed state (e.g. an undemocratic regime and a government that fails to provide security and political order).

It can be assumed that ideal conditions for repatriation are the return after a fundamental political change or political settlement under a democratic regime with a functional government. However, many repatriations have been enforced under premature conditions, such as under the last three regime types specified above. Subsequently, repatriation does not resolve the refugee crisis. In particular, repatriations such as those that involve the return after a political settlement that does not end the conflict and that leaves the contending parties with substantial political and military power or the return to a conflict zone are quite controversial, because the sudden, large flow of returnees can cause further violence and political instability. Kora Ross

---

[4] K. O'Connor, *Repatriation: The Politics of(re)-Constructing and Contesting Rwandan Citizenship*, Refugee Studies Centre, University of Oxford, Working Paper Series, No. 92, 2013, 25.

[5] B. N. Stein, "Ad Hoc Assistance to Return Movement and Long-Term Development Programmes", in T. Allen & H. Morsink (eds.) *When Refugees Go Home*, London and Trenton, UNRISD, James Currey and Africa World Press, 1994, 56.

Camarena, for instance, suggests a causal relationship between refugee return and violence. She identifies two main factors that stimulate this flow and subsequent violence: (1) violence may be instigated by rebels or armed groups moving with returnees and (2) returning refugees create additional economic, political or security burdens on the state that lead to greater instability because weak institutions and systems of governance cannot sustain both returnees and local populations.[6] Recent research produced by the International Refugee Rights Initiative and other agencies also emphasizes the need for a functioning state.[7] This explains why repatriation programmes in Somalia, DRC and South Sudan have failed.

Among various cases of refugee repatriations, there is little study of the countries under undemocratic or authoritarian regimes with excessive power. In these countries, extrajudicial killing, arbitrary arrest and detention, and gross human rights violations are quite common. The case of Rwanda can be categorised as repatriation under an undemocratic or authoritarian regime. Whether a state has no functional government over its territory or whether its control has been excessively sustained, the repatriation results are nearly identical.[8] However, much less explored is the question of how and why repatriation has been planned and enforced even in premature or non-ideal conditions where repatriation is presumed to fail.

Rwandan Refugees' Repatriation and Its Outcomes

Laura Hammond explains the reasons why the myth of repatriation has been sustained and supported by various actors:

> For hosting counties, when refugees return they are relieved of the financial, security, social, and political costs of proving safe haven for refugees. Donor countries prefer repatriation to expensive care and maintenance programme for refugees as well as to accepting them for resettlement. Countries of origin see refugees as highly politicized symbols; their return sends a strong public message that the fear of prosecution that kept people outside their country is no longer present; repatriation can be a major vote of confidence for a new government in particular.[9]

---

[6] K. R. Camarena, "Returning Home and Worsening the War: The Causal Effect of Refugee Return on Civil Conflict Intensity," Draft, Jan. 2016, available at: https://scholar.harvard.edu/files/kara_ross_camarena/files/ww_201609.pdf (last visited 19 Nov. 2019).

[7] International Refugee Rights Initiative, The Conflict Research Group, Actions pour la promotion Rurale, and Goupe D'Etudes sur les Conflits et la Sécurité, "Returning to Stability? Refugees Returns in the Great Lakes Region", Oct. 2019, available at: http://refugee-rights.org/wp-content/uploads/2019/10/Returning_to_Stability_2019-10-15-1.pdf (last visited 10 Nov. 2019).

[8] K. Long, *The Point of No Return: Refugees, Rights and Repatriation*, Oxford, Oxford University Press, 2013, 146.

[9] L. Hammond, "Voluntary Repatriation and Reintegration," in E. Fiddian-Quamiyeh and etc. (eds.), *The Oxford Handbook of refugee and Forced Migration Studies*, Oxford University Press, 2014, 508.

She also argues that repatriation is often an ideal for refugees themselves because returning can help bind together refugee communities living in exile.[10]

However, by closely examining the impact of repatriation on Rwandan refugees, it is highly doubtful that repatriation is an ideal durable solution for refugees. Measuring the success of refugee repatriation is a matter of debate. Here we regard repatriation as a process involving the remaking of citizenship and the consequent re-accessing of rights and livelihood through refugees availing themselves of national protection in their country of origin.[11] In addition, sustainable reintegration stands for a set of processes that provides refugees with sufficient means of livelihood and conditions of safety in order to prevent their further displacement within or outside country.[12] By applying these standards to evaluate Rwandan refugees' repatriation since the RPF seized power, repatriation in this case has not been successful. It is estimated that between 700,000 and 800,000 "old caseload refugees" went back to Rwanda after armed conflict and genocide ended in 1994.[13] However, the number of "new caseload refugees" (those who left Rwanda in 1994) who returned to Rwanda was fewer than the UNHCR had expected, and the latter half of 1996 brought mass repatriation of Rwandan refugees from neighbouring countries such as Tanzania, Burundi and Zaire (DRC).[14] For example, after the Tanzanian government's announcement in December 1996, around 30,000 Rwandan refugees escaped from refugee camps in the Ngara region in order to avoid forced repatriation. The Tanzanian military chased those who fled from the camps and expelled them to the border. International monitoring agencies were not allowed to visit the militarised refugee containment camps for several days. Long suggests that the whole range of repatriation exercises in Tanzania was not voluntary, safe or dignified, and represented the culmination of the failure of international refugee protection in the mid-1990s (Figs. 1 and 2).[15] According to UNHCR's statistics, about three million Rwandan refugees in total returned to Rwanda between 1994 and 1997.[16] However, those who returned to Rwanda confronted new challenges and predicaments, as Chapters "Aggravated Trauma and Insecurity Among Rwandan Hutu Refugees" and "Where is Rwanda's Peace?" illustrate. In particular, systematic violence, intimidation and gross human rights violations committed by the Rwandan authorities made it difficult for returned refugees to reintegrate Rwandan society. It was extremely rare that RPF members who had committed crimes were arrested or prosecuted. Contrary to official narratives and images, post-genocide Rwanda has been far from an ideal environment

---

[10] *Ibid.*

[11] K. Long, *Home Alone? Review of Relationship between Repatriation, Mobility and Durable Solutions for Refugees*, UNHCR Policy Development and Evaluation Service, March 2010, 1.

[12] *Ibid*, 41.

[13] Amnesty International, "Rwanda Protecting Their Rights: Rwandese Refugees in the Great Lakes Region", AFR47/016/2004, 2004, 2.

[14] *Ibid*, 9–11.

[15] K. Long, *The Point of No Return*, 130–131.

[16] UNHCR, Population Statistics, available at: http://popstats.unhcr.org/en/time_series (last visited 10 Nov. 2019).

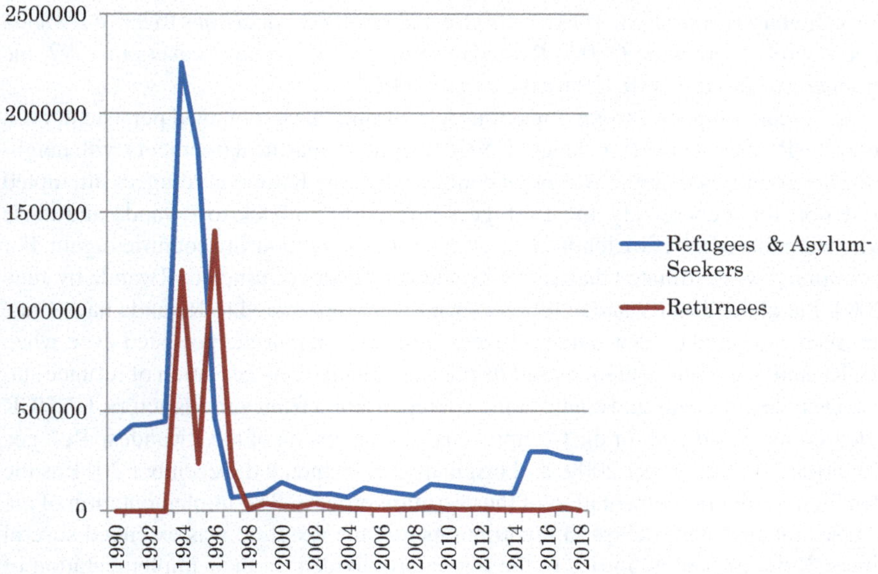

Fig. 1 Rwandan refugees, asylum-seekers and returnees since 1990. *Source* UNHCR population statistics

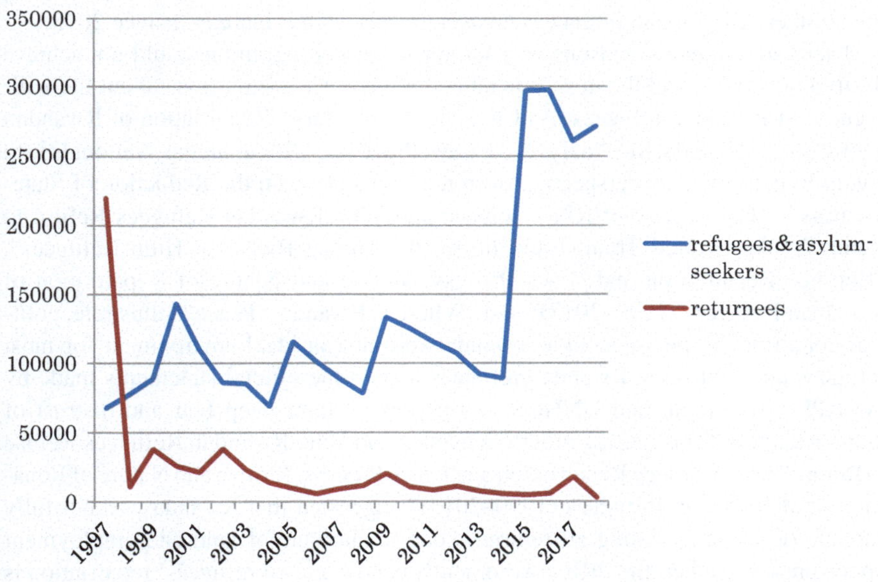

Fig. 2 Rwandan refugees, asylum-seekers and returnees since 1997. *Source* UNHCR population statistics

for voluntary repatriation. These facts affected returnees' decisions to leave Rwanda again; while there were 68,003 Rwandan refugees and asylum seekers in 1997, the number increased to 110,429 by the end of 2001.[17]

Rwandan refugees' strong objections to returning have remained persistent, even after the Rwandan government and UNHCR signed tripartite agreements with neighbouring countries in 2003. Although countries hosting Rwandan refugees attempted to deport them coercively, most refugees refused to go back to Rwanda and those who were forced to return tended to seek asylum in neighbouring countries again. For example, it was estimated that 1,945 Rwandan refugees returned to Rwanda by June 2004, but about 300 Rwandan refugees who were repatriated to Rwanda have since returned to Uganda.[18] Rwandan refugees' refusal to repatriate persisted even when the Rwandan government increased its pressure by invoking cessation of refugee status. Despite criticisms and contestations of repatriation from various actors, UNHCR released its "Roadmap for the Comprehensive Conclusion of the Rwandese Refugee Situations" in December 2009, and originally recommended December 2011 as the deadline for the implementation of the cessation process. The implementation of the clause was met with delays in repatriations and the deadline was extended several times. Refugee host countries in the region are divided on their implementation of the clause.[19] Many Rwandan refugees expressed their deep fear and disappointment, as several countries in the region initiated the proceedings of the cessation clause and forced them to go back to Rwanda. Despite this strong pressure for repatriation, the number of Rwandan refugees and asylum seekers has increased since 2015.

There are numerous reasons why the repatriation programme could not achieve desired outcomes, and the most crucial is the incorrect assumptions about the willingness of Rwandan refugees. As Chapters ""Voluntary" Repatriation of Rwandan Refugees in Uganda:An Analysis of Law Practice", "Renouncing Nationality to Avoid Repatriation: A Perspective from the Convention on the Reduction of Statelessness", "The Legacy of RPF Violence and Why Rwandan Refugees Refuse to Return", "Aggravated Trauma and Insecurity Among Rwandan Hutu Refugees", "Refugee Repatriation and Peace Process: Motive and Nature of Repatriation of Rwandan Refugees (1990–2017)" and "Where is Rwanda's Peace?" illustrate, political conditions in post-genocide Rwanda were not an ideal environment for most refugees and returnees. Rwandan refugees denied the official statements made by the RPF government and UNHCR and expressed their deep fear and distrust of them. Chapters "The Legacy of RPF Violence and Why Rwandan Refugees Refuse to Return" and "Refugee Repatriation and Peace Process: Motive and Nature of Repatriation of Rwandan Refugees (1990–2017)" suggested that Rwanda was not fully capable of accommodating all returnees due to shortage of land and employment opportunities. Rather, the PRF government's persistence of refugees' repatriation is

---

[17] *Ibid.*

[18] Amnesty International, *Rwanda Protecting Their Rights*, 19.

[19] J. Kanamugire, "African Countries in a fix as Rwandan refugee status ends", *The East African*, 20 Jan. 2018, available at: https://www.theeastafrican.co.ke/news/Rwanda-refugee-status-ends-/2558-4271610-w74qg5z/index.html (last visited 25 Sept. 2019).

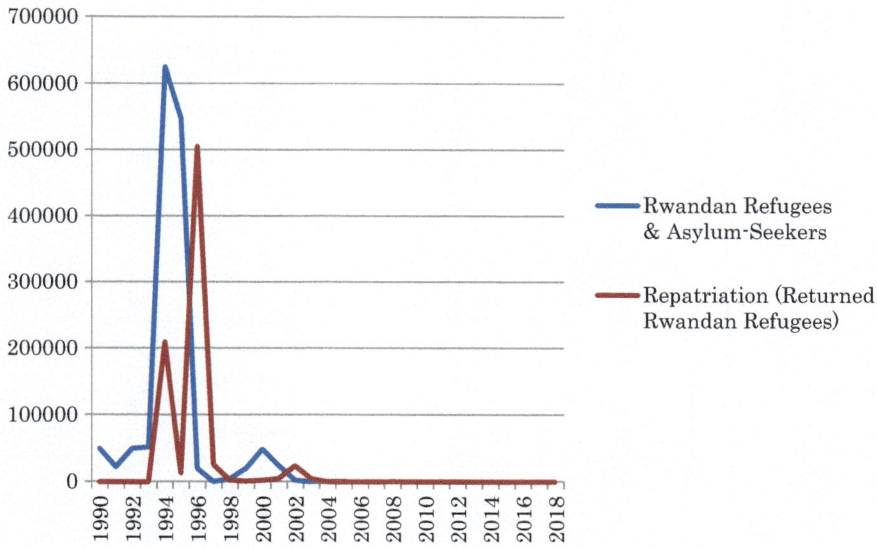

Fig. 3 Rwandan refugees, asylum-seekers in Tanzania and returned Rwandan refugees from Tanzania. *Source* UNHCR population statistics

motivated not by protecting the refugees themselves or sustaining nation-building or national integration but by consolidating their power and vested interests (Fig. 3).

The Rwandan case also casts doubt on the real value of repatriation in the context of mitigating the burden of refugees on hosting countries. Tanzania's repatriation policy demonstrates that repatriation of refugees does create problems of assistance in the region. Tanzania had been the second largest Rwandan refugee-hosting country between 1994 and 1996. However, the Tanzanian government ordered Rwandan refugees to go home by the end of 1996 and launched Operesheni Rudisha Wakimbizi (Operation Return Refugees). The massive repatriation exercise of Rwandan refugees can hardly be described as voluntary; hundreds of thousands of Rwandan refugees were expelled. As a result of forced repatriation, some Rwanda refugees chose instead to move to other neighbouring countries in the region. Even those who had returned to Rwanda left again for a variety of reasons, including insecurity, intimidation, threats, discrimination, gross human rights violations by authorities, community members or relatives, confiscation of land and property, and lack of employment or education opportunities. By 2000, 48,580 Rwandan refugees lived in Tanzania; that means that more than half of Rwandan refugees returned to Tanzania following the 1996 mass deportation. The Tanzanian government signed a tripartite agreement with UNHCR and Rwanda in 2002, and Tanzania repatriated more than 28,500 Rwandan refugees between 2002 and 2003. However, similar to the previous attempts of repatriation in 1996, many Rwandan refugees who had been forced to leave Tanzania did not return to Rwanda but moved to other countries in the region (Figs. 4 and 5).[20]

[20]UNHCR, Population Statistics.

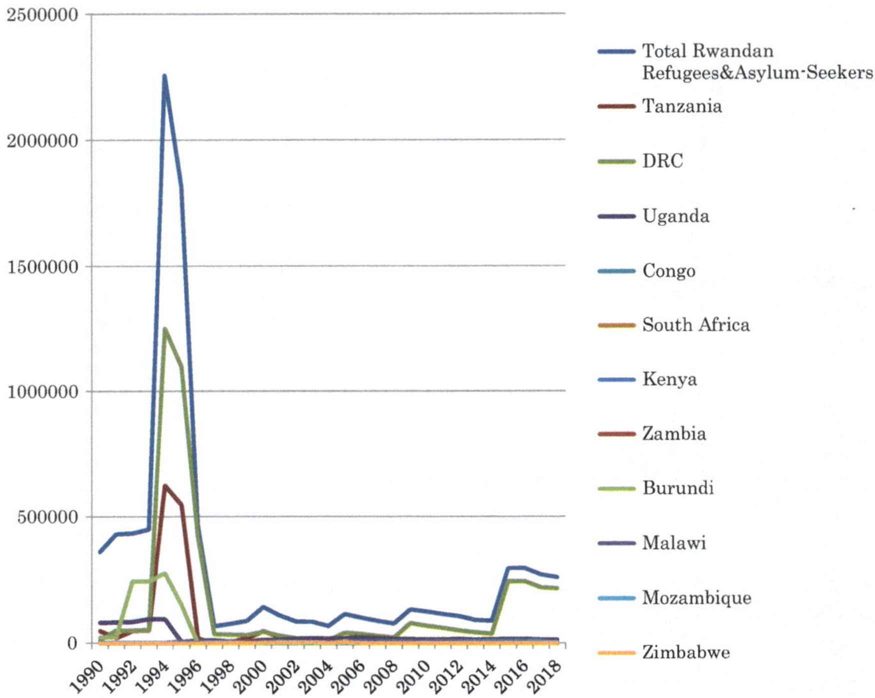

Fig. 4 Rwandan refugees in the region. *Source* UNHCR population statistics

As of 2018, no Rwandan refugees remained in Tanzania, but more than 80% still remain in the region. As a consequence, the number of Rwandan refugees has increased significantly in Republic of the Congo, South Africa, Malawi and Zambia, in addition to the DRC and Uganda, since the 2000s. Replacing Tanzania, Uganda has become host to the second largest Rwandan refugee population since 2002. These patterns of movement among Rwandan refugees clearly indicate that premature or coercive repatriation causes new situations of exile or irregular migration.[21]

Many refugee-hosting countries in the region are aware that unilateral repatriation or elimination of refugee status by implementing a cessation clause would further complicate the refugee crisis in the region. This situation has played out in different ways, as regional countries took different approaches to impose cessation clauses on Rwandan refugees. Some countries showed more enthusiasm to invoke the clause, while other countries have been more reluctant to expel Rwandan refugees to their countries of origin. Further, even a country like Zimbabwe, which took a tough stance on its implementation of the clause initially, could not avoid considering the impact of revoking refugee status on Rwandan refugees. Although Zimbabwe initiated cessation proceedings, as of May 2014, it had postponed enforce final decisions several times and had not deported any Rwandan refugees. Andrew Sniderman argues that

[21] *Ibid.*

	Total Rwandan Refugees & Asylum- Seekers	Tanzania	DRC	Uganda	Congo	South Africa	Kenya	Zambia	Burundi	Malawi	Mozambique	Zimbabwe
1990	361322	50000	12596	82156	100	0	1968	0	24200	0	0	0
1991	431246	22297	50930	84010	160	0	2191	0	24394	0	0	0
1992	434736	50012	50929	85806	160	0	2200	0	245612	0	0	0
1993	450462	51924	53490	97000	145	0	2174	0	245548	2	0	4
1994	2257573	626196	1252837	97000	117	79	2076	0	278090	0	30	15
1995	1819366	547976	1100642	6450	0	206	5861	1724	153000	258	32	138
1996	469136	20020	423561	11236	0	492	5487	1858	719	523	66	154
1997	68003	410	37000	12200	13	356	5762	2094	2000	15	33	189
1998	77743	4760	35000	7497	5200	455	8665	4048	2000	681	33	248
1999	88944	20098	33000	7983	6530	446	2858	4155	1324	603	106	299
2000	143867	48580	46329	14008	6725	834	3273	4898	1282	1939	299	1437
2001	110429	24241	30449	14378	6719	1023	4123	5283	1241	3761	738	3004
2002	86301	2717	20628	19009	5985	1439	2763	5389	789	7613	920	3063
2003	85415	185	19938	19786	5921	1695	2792	5801	425	6658	1184	3667
2004	69171	349	11906	19189	5852	1880	1811	5794	406	2783	1007	857
2005	116144	209	42438	20500	6478	2001	2561	5678	8960	4285	892	4493
2006	101597	14	37348	24914	6564	1278	2473	4078	581	4468	938	595
2007	89210	34	29847	20914	7941	1853	2577	4053	604	4495	1079	657
2008	78638	204	22645	17261	7897	1837	2634	4909	345	4352	1104	651
2009	133921	31	80559	16960	7172	1282	2630	5145	380	4004	1080	720
2010	125843	22	69988	16020	7889	1374	1946	5814	872	6482	1217	725
2011	116089	3	61737	15794	8577	1516	1867	5676	992	5265	1434	766
2012	107676	10	51484	17928	8675	1675	1545	6089	845	4962	1556	756
2013	92447	4	44071	14613	8734	1660	1430	2119	669	4464	1643	833
2014	89430	0	38348	16601	9419	2052	1443	1904	680	4910	1812	495
2015	297315	0	245409	17155	8962	2184	1609	1577	878	4813	2267	777
2016	297714	0	245448	17754	9671	1450	1630	1532	1228	5234	2237	721
2017	271803	0	220558	15260	9791	2197	1642	762	1215	5250	3404	513
2018	261181	0	217157	14613	1520	2224	1740	879	1280	5614	3935	615

Fig. 5 Rwandan refugees and asylum-seekers in the region. *Source* UNHCR Population Statistics

the delay in implementing the cessation clause stems from regional political concerns with irregular migration. He analyses the lack of voluntary return as refugees' own assessment of their best interests in staying in the countries of asylum. For this reason, if a government applies a cessation clause and forces them to leave, refugees will not go back to Rwanda but instead move irregularly to other countries to avoid repatriation. In addition, Rwandan refugees who flee from countries that remove their refugee status will renew their claims as asylum seekers or change their identities. Thus, many African countries that host Rwandan refugees have reached an agreement to suspend enforcing the cessation clause.[22] It is a matter of debate

[22] A. S. Sniderman, "Explaining Delayed Cessation: A Case Study of Rwandan Refugees in Zimbabwe", *International Journal of Refugee Law*, 27(4), 2015, 621–624.

to what extent countries in the region took burden sharing of refugees seriously, but it is clear that unilateral enforcement of a cessation clause does not end Rwandan refugee problems.

To sum up, concerning the issues of Rwandan refugees' repatriation, this book has demonstrated that coercive repatriation was far from an ideal or sustainable solution for refugees and refugee hosting countries. Repatriation provides little benefit to most Rwandan refugees, and it is highly doubtful that repatriation of Rwandan refugees helps to mitigate the burden of countries hosting refugees in the region, at least in the long run. Since 1994, Rwandan refugees' repatriation has been planned not merely for refugees' protection or enhancing nation-building and national integration but to benefit the political interests of the RPF government. There are four main problems that prevent refugees from returning to Rwanda: the lack of political space for different views and beliefs, the absence of fairness in the administration and justice system, the confiscation of land and property, and the lack of genuine reconciliation and retributive justice. Until the fundamental causes of displacement are resolved, most Rwandan refugees will be unwilling to return, and forced repatriation will merely create a new influx of displacement. Therefore, it is hard to comprehend why international organisations and donors collaborated with the Rwandan government to enforce repatriation, which has not achieved positive results. If the international community, including donors, refugee-hosting countries, UN organisations and other stakeholders, commits to resolving the refugee problem, it is important to include the voices and opinions of the refugees themselves. It is extremely rare that refugees or refugee communities are recognised as legitimate representatives and involved in the political negotiations of repatriations. There is also little opportunity for refugees to directly engage in the shaping of the repatriation processes.

The problems of repatriation are not confined to Rwandan refugees but are present in other controversial repatriation cases as well. Different outcomes of repatriation urge us to consider the conditions under which refugee return is likely to result in political instability or a new influx of refugees. The patterns and forms of repatriation are diverse in terms of degree of voluntariness in returning and levels of formal assistance provided to the returnees. Among various cases of repatriation around the world, this book provides a modest contribution to the research on repatriation; the Rwandan case has demonstrated that coercive repatriation to undemocratic or authoritarian regimes with excessive power is not successful. What is clear is that the current practices in refugee operations needs a fundamental reconfiguration of the framework of repatriation and new policy guidelines. For this purpose, all stakeholders must renounce the myth of repatriation and start from the position that repatriation is not a panacea nor is it always a sustainable solution for refugee problems.

References

Amnesty International, *Rwanda Protecting Their Rights: Rwandese Refugees in the Great Lakes Region*, AFR47/016/2004, 2004, 12.

K.R. Camarena, Returning home and worsening the war: the causal effect of refugee return on civil conflict intensity, Draft (Jan. 2016), https://scholar.harvard.edu/files/kara_ross_camarena/files/ww_201609.pdf

M.-E. Desrosiers, H.J. Swedlund, Rwanda's post-genocide foreign aid relations: revisiting notions of exceptionalism. *Afr. Aff.* **118**(472), 437 (2018)

L. Hammond, 'Voluntary' Repatriation and reintegration, in *The Oxford Handbook of Refugee and Forced Migration Studies* (Oxford University Press, 2014), p. 508

International Refugee Rights Initiative, The Conflict Research Group, Actions pour la promotion Rurale, Goupe D'Etudes sur les Conflits et la Sécurité, Returning to Stability? Refugees Returns in the Great Lakes Region, Oct. (2019), https://refugee-rights.org/wp-content/uploads/2019/10/Returning_to_Stability_2019-10-15-1.pdf (last visited 10 Nov. 2019)

J. Kanamugire, African Countries in A Fix As Rwandan Refugee Status Ends, *The East African*, 20 Jan. 2018, https://www.theeastafrican.co.ke/news/Rwanda-refugee-status-ends-/2558-4271610-w74qg5z/index.html (last visited 25 Sep. 2019)

K. Long, "Home Alone? Review of Relationship between Repatriation, Mobility and Durable Solutions for Refugees", UNHCR Policy Development and Evaluation Service, March 2010, p. 1

K. Long, *The Point of No Return: Refugees, Rights and Repatriation* (Oxford University Press, 2013), pp. 130–131, p. 146

K. O'Connor, Repatriation: the politics of (re)-constructing and contesting Rwandan citizenship, *Working Paper Series*, no. 92 (Refugee Studies Centre, University of Oxford, 2013), p. 25

N. Omata, *The Myth of Self-Reliance: Economic Lives Inside a Liberian Refugee Camp* (Berghahn, 2017), p. 10

A.S. Sniderman, Explaining delayed cessation: a case study of Rwandan refugees in Zimbabwe. *Int. J. Refug. Law* **27**(4), 621–624 (2015)

B.N. Stein, Ad Hoc Assistance to return movement and long-term development programmes, in *When Refugees Go Home*, T. Allen, H. Morsink (eds.) (UNRISD, Africa World Press, and James Currey, 1994), p. 56

J. Tegenbos, K. Vlassenroot, *Going Home? A Systematic Review of the Literature on Displacement, Return and Cycles of Violence*, Politics of Return, Working Paper1, May (2018)

The manufacturer's authorised representative in the EU is Springer
Nature Customer Service Centre GmbH, Europaplatz 3, 69115 Heidelberg,
Germany. If you have any concerns regarding our products, please
contact ProductSafety@springernature.com

Printed and bound by CPI Group (UK) Ltd, Croydon, CR0 4YY
30/09/2026
02225574-0010